AFFECT AND THE RISE OF RIGHT-WING POPULISM

This book uses affect theory to analyze the rise of right-wing populism in recent years and discusses the pedagogical implications for democratic education. It provides examples of how affect and emotion play a crucial role in the rise and reproduction of current right-wing populism. The author suggests ideas about affective pedagogies for educators to use (along with recognizing the risks involved) to renew democratic education. The chapters lay out the importance of harnessing the power of affective experiences and adopting strategic pedagogical approaches to provide affirmative practices that move beyond simply criticizing right-wing populism. The book consequently undermines the power of fascist and right-wing tendencies in public life and educational settings without stooping to methods of indoctrination. This volume is a valuable resource for researchers and policymakers in education, political science and other related fields, who can utilize the affective complexities involved in combatting right-wing populism to their advantage.

MICHALINOS ZEMBYLAS is Professor of Educational Theory and Curriculum Studies at the Open University of Cyprus as well as Honorary Professor, Chair for Critical Studies in Higher Education Transformation at Nelson Mandela University, South Africa. In 2016, he received the Distinguished Researcher Award in "Social Sciences and Humanities" from the Cyprus Research Promotion Foundation.

AFFECT AND THE RISE OF RIGHT-WING POPULISM

Pedagogies for the Renewal of Democratic Education

MICHALINOS ZEMBYLAS

Open University of Cyprus

CAMBRIDGE
UNIVERSITY PRESS

University Printing House, Cambridge CB2 8BS, United Kingdom

One Liberty Plaza, 20th Floor, New York, NY 10006, USA

477 Williamstown Road, Port Melbourne, VIC 3207, Australia

314–321, 3rd Floor, Plot 3, Splendor Forum, Jasola District Centre, New Delhi – 110025, India

79 Anson Road, #06–04/06, Singapore 079906

Cambridge University Press is part of the University of Cambridge.

It furthers the University's mission by disseminating knowledge in the pursuit of education, learning, and research at the highest international levels of excellence.

www.cambridge.org
Information on this title: www.cambridge.org/9781108838405
DOI: 10.1017/9781108974578

© Michalinos Zembylas 2021

This publication is in copyright. Subject to statutory exception and to the provisions of relevant collective licensing agreements, no reproduction of any part may take place without the written permission of Cambridge University Press.

First published 2021

A catalogue record for this publication is available from the British Library.

ISBN 978-1-108-83840-5 Hardback
ISBN 978-1-108-97889-7 Paperback

Cambridge University Press has no responsibility for the persistence or accuracy of URLs for external or third-party internet websites referred to in this publication and does not guarantee that any content on such websites is, or will remain, accurate or appropriate.

For Galatia, Orestis and Mariza

Contents

Acknowledgments	*page* ix
Permissions	x
Introduction	1

PART I SCANNING THE POLITICAL LANDSCAPE OF RIGHT-WING POPULISM

1	The Politics of Shame in the Age of Trump	19
2	Trump Pedagogy and the Affective Modes of Right-Wing Populism	37
3	The Affective Grounding of Post-truth Claims	54
4	The (Un-)Making of Microfascism in Schools and Classrooms	71

PART II RENEWING DEMOCRATIC EDUCATION

5	Affirmative Critique as a Response to Post-truth Claims	91
6	Agonistic Emotions/Affects to Counter Far Right Rhetoric	109
7	Reinvigorating the Affective Atmospheres of Democratic Education	124

PART III INVENTING AFFECTIVE PEDAGOGIES FOR DEMOCRATIC EDUCATION

8	Nurturing Political Emotions in the Classroom	141

9	Toward Shared Responsibility without Invoking Collective Guilt	158
10	Re-visioning the Sentimental in Pedagogical Discourse and Practice	176
11	For an Anti-complicity Pedagogy	192
Epilogue		209
References		215
Index		240

Acknowledgments

The idea for this book started to take form in 2015–2016, when I began noticing the increasing provocation by right-wing populist parties, movements and politicians around the world, especially after the election of Donald Trump in the United States and the refugee crisis in Europe. What preoccupied me from the beginning was the "affective atmospheres" that circulated across the rise of right-wing populist movements and its impact on democracy and education. So, this book began its life as a collection of essays – most of them already published but then reworked for the purposes of this publication – that explored various aspects of public and educational discourses on populism and interrelated phenomena (e.g., right-wing rhetoric, post-truth, fascism), and the pedagogical challenges of addressing populism in the current political climate. I cherish the intellectual opportunities that I've had over these years to discuss these ideas in formal and informal talks at several places around the world. I am grateful to my friends and colleagues for their remarkable generosity and hospitality to share their thoughts with me: Vivienne Bozalek and Tammy Shefer at the University of the Western Cape; Andre Keet at Nelson Mandela University; Zvi Bekerman at the Hebrew University of Jerusalem; Rob Hattam at the University of South Australia; Dorothee Hölscher at Griffith University; Fazal Rizvi at the University of Melbourne; Marie Brennan and Lew Zipin at the University of Victoria; Megan Boler at OISE-University of Toronto; Vanessa Andreotti and Sharon Stein at the University of British Columbia; Karin Gunnarsson at Stockholm University; Hugh Starkey at UCL Institute of Education, University College London; Yiannis Papadakis at the University of Cyprus; and Kevin Kester at Keimyung University. And, finally, a big thanks to my family – my wife, Galatia, and my two children, Orestis and Mariza, for their unconditional love and toleration, despite the numerous troubles I give them.

Permissions

Zembylas, M. (2020). Affirmative critique as a practice of responding to the impasse between post-truth and negative critique: Pedagogical implications for schools. *Critical Studies in Education*, DOI: 10.1080/17508487.2020.1723666.

Zembylas, M. (2020). Necropolitics and sentimentality in education: The ethical, political and pedagogical implications of "making live and letting die" in the current political climate. *Pedagogy, Culture & Society*, DOI: 10.1080/14681366.2020.1747108.

Zembylas, M. (2020). The affective grounding of the post-truth: Pedagogical risks and transformative possibilities in countering post-truth claims. *Pedagogy, Culture & Society*, 28(1), 77–92.

Zembylas, M. (2020). The affective modes of right-wing populism: Trump pedagogy and lessons for democratic education. *Studies in Philosophy and Education*, 39(2), 151–166.

Zembylas, M. (2020). Re-conceptualizing complicity in the social justice classroom: Affect, politics and anti-complicity pedagogy. *Pedagogy, Culture & Society*, 28(2), 317–331.

Zembylas, M. (2020). Hannah Arendt's political thinking on emotions and education: Implications for democratic education. *Discourse: Studies in the Cultural Politics of Education*, 41(4), 501–515.

Zembylas, M. (2019). Encouraging shared responsibility without invoking collective guilt: Exploring pedagogical responses to portrayals of suffering and injustice in the classroom. *Pedagogy, Culture & Society*, 27(3), 403–417.

Zembylas, M. (2019). The affective dimension of far right rhetoric in the classroom: The promise of agonistic emotions and affects in countering extremism. *Discourse: Studies in the Cultural Politics of Education*, DOI: 10.1080/01596306.2019.1613959.

Introduction

The electoral victory of Donald Trump in the United States in 2016, Brexit in the same year, and particularly the emergence of right-wing populist movements in Europe (e.g., France, Germany, Austria, Hungary) and other parts of the world (e.g., India, Turkey, the Philippines) during the last few years have revived academic and political discussions about the roots and consequences of populism, especially for the future of liberal democracy. As it was suggested by David Runciman (2018), one of the most influential political theorists in Britain today, the political trajectory that is currently followed, particularly with the rise of right-wing populism and fascism in many countries around the world, may portend the end of democracy as we know it. The rise of right-wing populism is generally associated with nationalist, racist, xenophobic and homophobic rhetoric that creates stark oppositions between "pure people" and the "corrupt elite" or "others" (social, religious, ethnic groups) who threaten the "purity" of a nation-state (Mudde, 2007). A populist leader claims to be the only genuine representative of people's will, so populism tends to be premised on the mobilization of people around an opposition to shared "enemies," aiming at establishing inclusion–exclusion binaries and identities (Laclau, 2005a). As a political project, then, populism raises serious concerns about the future of democracy, because it threatens to dismantle fundamental liberal values such as equality and human rights (Mudde & Kaltwasser, 2012).

Although the rise of right-wing populism has been linked to fundamental socioeconomic changes fueled by globalization and neoliberalism, these factors "can hardly fully explain the rise of the new right," as Salmela and von Scheve (2017, p. 567) point out. A number of scholars increasingly emphasizes that the current rise of right-wing populism and its consequences cannot be fully understood without examining the role of *affectivity* (Cossarini & Vallespin, 2019; Kemmer et al., 2019; Kinnvall, 2018; Salmela & von Scheve, 2017; Wahl-Jorgensen, 2018). The relevance of affect and emotion in social and political processes and movements, including populism, is not something new, of course. Anger – to take one example, which is central in the rhetoric of Donald Trump and other leaders in the age of populism (Davies, 2020) – has long been viewed as a major political emotion and an important resource of collective mobilization and empowerment (Gould, 2012; Lyman, 2004). The affective dynamics in political arenas have particularly characterized far-right politics by the use of fear (e.g., Wodak, 2015), rage and anger (e.g., Ebner, 2017; Mishra, 2017), and hatred (e.g., Blee, 2002; Emcke, 2019). However, as Mühlhoff argues, "what does change in the course of history is the modes of affectivity, that is, the concrete interactive forms, mediated spaces, temporal patterns of affective dynamics, as well as the way affectivity is intertwined with discourse, with power structures and with hierarchies" (in Kemmer et al., 2019, p. 26). Indeed, affective dynamics can work to reproduce power structures and hierarchies, just as much as they may galvanize resistance – which is precisely where the transformative possibilities of modes of affectivity lie.

The purpose of this book is to theorize the entanglements of affect and right-wing populism and to argue that a critical inquiry into these entanglements can provide opportunities for renewing democratic education, especially when it opens up to a more complex understanding of the affective modes of right-wing populism and its implications for democratic life. Across the world, democracy and democratic ways of life appear to be in crisis, as they are threatened by populist parties, movements and politicians. Education and schools cannot be blamed for creating this crisis, but the case can be made that educational institutions and structures contribute to crisis, merely by reproducing the social and political status quo. One might argue, for this reason, that the liberal democratic traditions in education have not been able to stop the tide of populism, given the investment that has been made in them. But why have the current approaches such as intercultural and multicultural education failed? And, more importantly, is there anything that can be done by educators to reverse these failures?

I would argue that a deeper understanding of the affective modes of right-wing populism, especially at *this* historical juncture – that is, the aftermath of a terrible pandemic that ravaged the world in so many ways – is crucial in educational efforts to address these questions for two reasons. First, paying attention to the affective modes of right-wing populism enables educators to identify the forms of affecting and being affected (and their micropolitical presuppositions and consequences) that are typical for those who engage or buy into right-wing populism that are so often dependent on conspiracy theories and "fake news" (Anderson in Kemmer et al., 2019). Hence, understanding the affective investments of youth who buy into populist ideas – e.g., fear or resentment of the "other" (Wodak, 2015) – begins to provide indications of what intercultural and multicultural education may have missed to make their message attractive intellectually, affectively and politically. Second, to move a step further, a deeper understanding of the affective modes of right-wing populism will lay out more clearly the challenge for educators in the current political climate; namely, how to create pedagogical spaces and opportunities for critical dialogue in democratic education wherein students not only identify how and why different people articulate themselves affectively in particular ways but also take action to respond critically and productively to those affective investments.

First, we must be clear on what we should expect from a project of this kind. Briefly, I would like to suggest that the best it can do is offer a comprehensive account of the affective power of right-wing populism and its consequences in various sectors of public life, especially education. Ideally, that account should also provide some new trajectories of how to deal pedagogically and educationally with the problem of right-wing populism and its affective power in schools, universities and other educational institutions, particularly in alerting us that a renewal of democratic education – both as a field of study and a practice – is more necessary than ever before. Needless to say, democratic education is not used here in lieu of intercultural and multicultural education to mark their failures in preventing the tide of populism. Although this book will shed some light to these failures, as those are intertwined with how affective dynamics work in public and education life, it would be shortsighted to leave the impression that the "problem" is our response to populism – e.g., intercultural and multicultural education – rather than populism itself. Hence, as I will argue in this book, the "response" to this problem is not more media literacy education or better "competences" for democratic education but rather how to formulate anti-fascist as well as new democratic practices that keep nationalist, racist, xenophobic and homophobic rhetoric from becoming normalized. To counteract these right-wing and fascist tendencies in public life and educational settings, educators must take into serious consideration the power of affective experiences and adopt strategic pedagogical approaches that not only avoid the risk of indoctrination but also provide affirmative practices that move beyond mere (i.e., negative) critique of right-wing populism and fascism.

My focus on democratic education in this book, rather than other education traditions or sectors, is grounded in the belief that despite the crisis of democratic education (Okoth & Anyango, 2014) or even voices against democratic education (Pennington, 2014), democracy and democratic education remain morally, politically and instrumentally appealing to many countries around the world (Sant, 2019). The crisis of democracy and democratic education though is real; there is no way one can turn a blind eye to it. It alerts us that reforms necessarily rely on renewing the faith on democratic institutions that has been lost (Asmonti, 2013) – especially after the 2008 financial crisis, the austerity measures and the strengthening of neoliberal policies in many countries. This is precisely the ground that is found by populist movements and political parties to promote their agendas, situating "the people" in opposition to "elites" who are considered both corrupt and illegitimate (Runciman, 2018). Although there is no doubt that democracy and, with it, democratic education need an urgent renewal to reconstitute democratic faith and strengthen the lost democratic participation and viability, it is equally important to not underestimate the urgency of resisting the temptations of populism. Needless to say, democratic education cannot stop populism, but it can certainly work with disaffected people who have been alienated from traditional politics to enact democracy in renewed ways (Petrie, McGregor & Crowther, 2019). As Petrie et al. point out, education can enrich democratic spaces "from below" by decoding populism and the factors that share and motivate it, and by testing out new ideas and experiences that inform democratic action.

Hence, it is crucial to examine how educators and students may invent pedagogical spaces of "affective counterpolitics" (Massumi, 2015b), namely, spaces at the micropolitical level that entail "hopeful criticism" (Anderson, 2017a) of right-wing populism – that is, criticism that is not merely negative but rather affirmative, creating spaces of hope for social transformation. This book emphasizes, then, that "negative" critique of the affective ideology of right-wing populism is not sufficient for developing a productive counterpolitics – neither in the public arena, and certainly, nor in education. An affirmative critique is also needed "to set alternative frames and agendas which endorse and disseminate alternative concepts, such as equality, diversity and solidarity" (Wodak, 2015 in Kinnvall, 2018, p. 538). This line of thinking can provide critical resources to democratic education for developing a culture and process of democracy that transcends the negativity of mere critique of either right-wing populisms or inadequate forms of democracy. In this sense, democratic education includes educational efforts where students learn, not only *about* and *for* democracy (in juxtaposition to right-wing populism) but also, critically and affirmatively, *through* democracy. Without democratic participation and practice, bodily and affectively, in educational institutions at all levels, it is hard to imagine how youth and new citizens will embrace democratic ways of living.

While the number of books focusing on populism has increased in recent years (e.g., De la Torre & Arnson, 2013; Laclau, 2005a; Mudde & Kaltwasser, 2012; Müller, 2016; Panizza, 2005), many of those publications do not look specifically on the role of education and specifically how democratic education can respond to the affective modes of populism. A principal concern of this book, therefore, is to establish the nexus among affect, populism and democratic education as all of those are evinced within educational discourses and practices. Hence, this book explores an understanding of how right-wing populism and interrelated phenomena – including extremism, post-truth and (micro)fascism – are produced and reproduced within and through educational discourses and practices, and how those might be interrogated and undone. While my analysis is primarily theoretical, I provide specific examples of populist rhetoric in Europe and the United States to situate this analysis and make the discussion of pedagogical implications explicit.

In particular, the book draws from various theories (e.g., critical, decolonial, posthumanist, feminist, political and affect theories) as well as different theorists (e.g., Hannah Arendt, Judith Butler, Rosi Braidotti, Gilles Deleuze, Michel Foucault, Achille Mbembe, Chantal Mouffe and Iris Marion Young among others). Each of these theories and theorists has something important to teach us about democracy and affect, attuning us to the centrality of these ideas for understanding right-wing populism and advancing a critical and *agonistic* democratic education. By "agonistic," I refer to Mouffe's (2000, 2005, 2013) model of democracy that reframes antagonism and disagreement into productive forms of democratic engagement – namely, democracy as a continuous struggle for renewal rather than a "fixed" political system or practice. After Mouffe, I also theorize democratic education as agonistic to emphasize the intertwining of democracy and education and their relationship as an ongoing effort for renewing democratic participation and practice in educational settings. An important, yet neglected, aspect of building agonistic relations and practices, while preserving the reality of conflict, is not to eliminate affects from the public sphere in the name of consensus but rather to mobilize affects for democratic ends. Populists know this lesson very well; only they use it to mobilize affects for other ends.

Just as democracy is in crisis, many have argued that democratic education is in a similar situation with democratic deliberation and engagement replaced by disaffection and cynicism (Biesta, 2013; Brown, 2015) as educational institutions at all levels are drowned in cultures of accountability and the pressures of neoliberal performativity (Biesta, 2010a). Although many countries around the world have introduced intercultural and multicultural education in their educational reforms during the last few decades, an increasingly crowded, yet narrow curriculum, fails to promote democratic models of participation and leadership in schools and universities (Clarke, Schostack & Hammersley-Fletcher, 2018; Fielding & Moss, 2011). These developments raise concerns not only about the status of democratic education and whether it really produces the qualities and dispositions of the democratic citizen or whether education in general creates democratic cultures and practices in schools and universities; they also raise questions whether education is complicit to the rise of populism by contributing to the general culture of disaffection and cynicism in public life. Hence, an analysis of affect, populism and education in this book contributes to the renewal of democratic education by specifically paying attention to the politicization of affects in education initiatives and their implications for pedagogical discourses and practices. Given the enormity of this task and its multiple complexities, my aim in this book is not to mount a comprehensive list of potential pedagogical actions for countering right-wing populism and promoting democratic education. Rather, my goal is much more modest and focuses on outlining some ideas that might inspire a more in-depth inquiry into concrete pedagogies and education initiatives that could respond to the current political crisis in effective ways.

In what follows, I begin by briefly outlining how I understand "affect," and present the theoretical assumptions underlying the use of this concept throughout this book. This analysis is important for two reasons. First, it provides the reader with a general presentation of how and why affect is understood as relational, political and embodied, rather than as an individualized or a psychologized entity. As will be clear in the chapters that follow, this theoretical and methodological understanding of affect is central in this book and enables the examination of forms of engagement that exist both at the individual and the sociopolitical levels. Second, this analysis of affect provides a crucial way of theoretically and pragmatically linking the micropolitics and macropolitics of right-wing populism, and showing how democratic education is inevitably intertwined with "structures of feeling" (Williams, 1961) that may strengthen or weaken democratic deliberation and participation in educational institutions. I borrow Raymond Williams' famous term to describe the potential that lies for democratic education to both reproduce and resist affective relations of populism. This introduction ends with a discussion of the structure of the book.

Affect as Social, Political and Embodied

What has been called the affective turn in the social sciences and humanities in recent years marks "critical theory's turn to affect [...] at a time when critical theory is facing the analytic challenges of ongoing war, trauma, torture, massacre, and counter/terrorism" (Clough, 2007, p. 1). As Clough further explains, this turn signals a movement from a psychoanalytically and psychologically informed lens of identity, representation and trauma to engagement with affect that focuses on the economic circulation of bodily capacities. Affect, then, can be understood as that which encompasses and exceeds the more individualized conceptions of emotion, as the "body's *capacity* to affect and to be affected," that is, as interactive and embodied intensities that circulate as "forces of encounter" (Seigworth & Gregg, 2010, p. 2). Ahmed's (2010) response to debates whether there are any clear boundaries between affect and emotion is that

> while you can separate an affective response from an emotion that is attributed as such (the bodily sensations from the feeling of being afraid), this does not mean that in practice, or in everyday life, they are separate. In fact, they are contiguous; they slide into each other; they stick, and cohere, even when they are separated. (p. 231)

The approach to affect and emotion adopted in this book is close to the one suggested by Ahmed (2010) as well as Cvetkovich (2012), who see affect as a category that encompasses affect, emotion and feeling, and "includes impulses, desires, and feelings that get historically constructed in a range of ways" (Cvetkovich, 2012, p. 4). While the affective turn signifies a range of different theoretical movements and articulations of affect and emotion (Pedwell & Whitehead, 2012), it is generally united in the notion that what is felt "is neither internally produced nor simply imposed on us from external ideological structures" (Rice, 2008, p. 205). In other words, affects and emotions are conceptualized as entangled with the complexities, reconfigurations and rearticulations of power, body, history and politics (Athanasiou, Hantzaroula & Yannakopoulos, 2008). To put this differently, affects and emotions are theorized as intersections of language, desire, power, bodies, social structures, subjectivity and materiality.

Importantly for my approach in this book, I somewhat depart from the conceptualization of affect as merely autonomous or completely a-social and a-cognitive – a conceptualization that has been challenged by some scholars (e.g., Fischer, 2016; Hemmings, 2005; Leys, 2011; Wetherell, 2013). For example, one of the criticisms is that the formulation of affect as visceral and pre-linguistic force that is contrasted with the discursive and the cognitive, and distinguished from "domesticated" emotion is problematic because it draws a dichotomy that is unsustainable. Although affect may be theorized as pre-linguistic, this does not imply that it is also pre-discursive, as bodies, emotions and affects "are depended on, and informed by, socially constructed boundaries and norms" (Morrow, 2019, p. 20). Also, emotion is not a fixed or predetermined entity "housed in bodies," but it is "one potential outward expression on the corporeal" (Morrow, 2019, p. 22). From this perspective, the affective turn represents a shift from "the text and discourse as key theoretical touchstones" toward the body (Seigworth & Gregg, 2010, p. 9). A reading of the material potentiality of the body emphasizes that the body has affective potential, yet it is still coded by and embedded within social, historical, cultural and political formations (Blackman & Venn, 2010; Pedwell & Whitehead, 2012; Wetherell, 2012).

As Morrow (2019) argues, the consideration of the dual capacity of bodies to affect and be affected broadens our understanding of affect/emotion, because bodies are not simply characterized as obedient or deviant, but rather they have the ability to enact varying affective experiences. As such, affective life may become *political* as a counter to forms of biopower that work through processes of normalization (Anderson, 2012). A theorization of affect as the capacity to act and an intensity that exists within the body and escapes the constraints of a socially constructed label offers theoretical resources for deepening our understanding of power and politics – hence, it is crucial in understanding the affective modes of right-wing populism. The dual capacity of bodies to produce affect and be affected suggests that we need to think of *power-affect* – that is, affects need to be understood as forces of becoming rather than governed by an overarching logic or regime (Schaefer, 2019). In this manner, suggests Morrow (2019, p. 20), "affect will always supersede attempts at control as engineered affects must always contend with bodies constantly feeding into and informing the affective landscape." Consequently, political measures and practices that function under the assumption that they can simply control affect and emotion, says Morrow, "have an inherently flawed understanding of the very registers that they are reliant on" (2019, p. 21). The theorization advanced here, then, highlights that affect is not something that can be engineered in any controlled manner, but rather it is unpredictable which trajectories affect will follow.

The emphasis on the body as affective, material and political highlights three ideas: the fundamental relationality of all matter (bodies, things and social formations); attention to actions and events as assemblages that develop a network of habitual and non-habitual connections and are always in flux; and, the political potential of this relational ontology, that is, the power of the materiality of bodies for the pursuit of social change and transformation, and to address injustices and inequalities, whether by practice, by influencing policy or through activism (Fox & Alldred, 2017). Theoretically, then, a number of novel questions for exploration and analysis of democratic education may be raised, such as how do we (researchers, educators, policymakers, students) identify and trace the ways in which bodies experience specific political processes (e.g., democracy, populism) within or beyond educational institutions? In such spaces, "how can we disentangle ourselves from the cultural and political scripts and power structures, in order to critique their reductive use, and reliance on, affect and emotion?" (Morrow, 2019, p. 22) What are the dangers when educators and students use affective management techniques to negotiate political discourses and practices? Which kind of affective intensities are allowed to be cultivated in educational settings? "And which kinds are excluded or cut off?" (Juelskjær & Staunæs, 2016a, p. 196) How do collective affects (e.g., solidarity, empathy) become part of affective responses to counter populist discourses and practices?

These questions challenge our understandings of just what manifestations political agency may take in relation to affective infrastructures in educational institutions. Furthermore, these questions open up new ways of looking at and understanding affect and emotion and their relations to the corporeal – as these relations are born out of producing counter-practices that can "disrupt and rupture attempts at governance" (Morrow, 2019, p. 23) in micro or macropolitical spaces of populism. Attending, therefore, to affective life in educational institutions may constitute a crucial political intervention, because it does not merely "describe" the organization of affective life on the basis of politicization processes as norms, but it also enables the subversion and reversal of the mechanisms and techniques of discipline and normalization (cf. Anderson, 2012). Hence, a theoretical framework that recognizes and examines the affective complexities of right-wing populism as those are entangled with biopower and biopolitics is likely to challenge the *invisible affective infrastructures* of social and political processes that erode democracy in educational institutions. Also, this theoretical framework offers opportunities that advance our understanding of how to invent renewed ways of democratic participations in educational institutions – in response to bringing the affective modes of right-wing populism to the fore.

Having outlined the theoretical framework driving my analysis in this book, I present briefly how the book is organized and structured.

Structure of the Book

Overall, the book is divided into three parts. Part I includes four chapters (Chapters 1–4) that "scan" the political landscape to describe right-wing populism and interrelated phenomena and how affectivity plays a crucial role in their circulation; this part provides some initial responses to what can be done pedagogically to address these phenomena. In particular, these chapters take three interrelated phenomena – right-wing populism, post-truth, microfascism – as points of entry to examine their affective dynamics and to explore how democratic education may be involved in attempts to instigate and help enact pedagogical processes of resisting the affective dynamics of these phenomena. So although each chapter takes a different phenomenon as a focal point, or point of entry, the analysis does not "end" with the phenomenon or its potential pedagogical "treatment," but rather it carries over to the following chapters in a spiral manner. However, the structure of each chapter is such that it can be read both in conjunction with other chapters and independently. Each chapter generally starts with situating the issue politically and theoretically, then specifies its affective connections, and finally discusses some pedagogical implications that are later picked up for further analysis in Parts II and III of the book.

Chapter 1 is the only one that begins with a focus on a particular affect – namely, shame – taking as its point of departure the politics of shame in the context of racism expressed by Donald Trump's rhetoric. This choice is purposive to set the political stage of a neglected, yet fundamental, affect that is central in driving populist movements. Shame constructs a collective affective community that unites people against all those who are considered the source of this feeling. In fact, Chapters 1 and 2 serve as illustrative of the wider phenomenon of right-wing populism. With reference to white shame in the context of Trump's politics, Chapter 1 analyzes how Trump has taken political advantage of different types of white shame to restore a lost sense of dignity for Whites, and argues that the response to politics of shame and its linkage to racism is not to retreat to shaming Trump and his supporters, regardless of the results of the November 2020 presidential election in the United States, but rather to understand the political and pedagogical limits of different types of white shame and shaming and seek strategies that address them. The chapter, then, develops the argument that different types of white shame require different pedagogical strategies to address white shame emerging from right-wing populist rhetoric and its linkage to racism. Some of these strategies, along with others that are added along the way, are occasionally revisited in upcoming chapters throughout the book – hence the spiral structure that has been discussed earlier.

Chapter 2 works to refine and develop further some of the ideas raised in Chapter 1, emphasizing that it is important for educators in democratic education to understand how the rise of right-wing populism in Europe, the United States and around the world can never be viewed apart from the affective investments of populist leaders and their supporters to essentialist ideological visions of nationalism, racism, sexism and xenophobia. Democratic education can provide the space for educators and students to think critically and productively about people's affects, as it is argued, in order to identify the implications of different affective modes through which right-wing populism is articulated – the example of "Trump Pedagogy" is, as mentioned, the primary example of analysis in this chapter. Furthermore, this chapter points out that "negative" critique of the affective ideology of right-wing populism is not sufficient for developing a productive counterpolitics in public life or in education. An affirmative critique (which is further analyzed in Chapter 5) is also needed to set alternative frames and agendas that endorse and disseminate alternative concepts and affective practices such as equality, love and solidarity. These ideas provide critical resources to democratic education for developing a culture and process of democracy that transcends the negativity of mere critique of either right-wing populisms or inadequate forms of democracy.

In Chapter 3, I pursue a line of inquiry motivated by the link between populism and post-truth, and use this theorization to think about what it could mean for the role of educators – that is, what can be done in education to respond critically to the affective infrastructures of post-truth politics? This question arises at a historical juncture of widespread views that post-truth politics – e.g., "fake news" or "alternative facts" – create an urgency for reframing post-truth discourses and experiences as productive pedagogical engagements for democratic education. The chapter shows how the affective grounding of post-truth claims works to govern our subjectivities and how affects and emotions matter in constructing certain truths that reproduce social and political evils such as racism, sexism and xenophobia. The analysis shows that this nuanced understanding of affect, governmentality and post-truth can be helpful in educational settings to respond critically to post-truth politics, while paying attention to risks emerging from moralization or indoctrination – concerns that make some being very skeptical and positioning themselves against democratic education.

Chapter 4 turns our attention to Deleuze and Guattari's notion of "microfascism," suggesting that it is of crucial importance to a multifaceted understanding of contemporary pedagogical efforts to combat populism, right-wing extremism and fascism as interrelated phenomena. My analysis here moves from the macro-level of politics to the micro-level of the classroom itself, namely, it is shown how "affect" and "biopower" are entangled in everyday processes of discipline and control in schools, universities and classrooms. If there is a fascist inside all of us, as Foucault and Deleuze and Guattari argue, then it is pivotal to gain a deeper understanding of the affective relations and capacities of microfascism. To illustrate how affect and biopower are intimately linked to microfascist practices in schools and classrooms, I discuss in details two examples – one in health education and another in citizenship education. Finally, the chapter, as usual, suggests pedagogical strategies that could unmake microfascist subjectivities, emphasizing that it is important to understand the complexities involved since fascism is easily disguised in many forms that are often aligned with (neo)liberal values.

Part II of the book includes three chapters (Chapters 5–7) that shift attention from scanning the political landscape of right-wing populism to renewing democratic education by using specific theoretical ideas and concepts – affirmative critique, agonistic emotions/affects, affective atmospheres – as a point of departure for examining how it would be possible to renew the content and pedagogical praxis of democratic education. Chapter 5 begins to explore how, why and under which conditions a move away from critique as a negative practice toward an – educationally more valuable – affirmative notion of critique is important in formulating pedagogies that might respond more productively to the challenges of the post-truth era. What is at stake here in reframing critique as affirmative practice in addressing post-truths in schools is the aspiration to create pedagogical spaces that enable educators and students to turn their attention to care for the world in ways that go beyond the post-truth/negative critique/us–them impasse. The chapter engages with Foucault's and Butler's analysis of critique to show how a combined Foucauldian–Butlerian framework reconceptualizes criticality as an affirmative practice. Then, it uses this framework to suggest that cultivating an affirmative attitude and ethos of critique in educational settings constitutes a virtuous practice of self-transformation and a passionate pedagogical goal that educators cannot afford to ignore.

Chapter 6 draws on the concept of agonistic emotions and affects to think with some of the arguments of Chantal Mouffe's political theory and discusses what this means pedagogically in handling far right rhetoric in the classroom. To show the possibilities of the concept of agonistic emotions and affects, the chapter puts in conversation Mouffe's work on agonistic pluralism with affect theory. The analysis makes the argument that this conversation enables the theorization of agonistic emotions and affects as an intersection of language, desire, power, bodies and politics that can be engaged with and channeled democratically in classroom debates. The chapter makes a political and pedagogical intervention into the terrain of countering extremism in education by offering ways of addressing productively the tensions emerging from the affective dimension of far right rhetoric in classroom spaces.

Chapter 7 situates the discussion of renewing democratic education at a broader level, namely, it draws on the concept of *affective atmospheres* that is currently circulating in a growing number of academic disciplines to theorize how democracy and democratic education take hold and circulate in classrooms, schools and educational settings more generally. The chapter asks under which circumstances affective atmospheres are experienced or even "engineered," encompassing affective and material features that (de)legitimate democracy, democratic education and right-wing populism. The aim is to render the concept of atmosphere tractable through a line of theorizing that recognizes the affective force of democracy and right-wing populism and asks how democratic education may respond by paying careful attention to democracy as affectively produced and transmitted. The chapter also examines what it would take to reinvigorate the affective atmospheres of democratic education in educational institutions in light of the rise of populist affectivity. The analysis adds to ideas discussed in earlier chapters how populist affectivity might be resisted in the context of democratic education.

Finally, Part III of the book includes four chapters (Chapters 8–11) and turns our attention to the affective pedagogies that educators might need to invent (along with recognizing the risks involved) in efforts to renew democratic education, focusing in particular on issues of shared responsibility/collective guilt, sentimentality and complicity. Although the last part of the book focuses more explicitly on pedagogies, it builds on the phenomena and concepts addressed throughout the book, as the "seeds" of these pedagogies have been planted painstakingly in previous chapters.

Chapter 8 begins with a question that has been troubling from the beginning, namely, when political emotions are invoked in the classroom, can this be done without the process of democratic education degenerating into a form of emotional and/or political indoctrination? The source of inspiration for addressing this question is Hannah Arendt's political thought on emotion and education. Interestingly, Arendt's work has been revisited in recent years, after the rise of populism around the world, with scholars and others seeking to find "answers" in her perennial political thinking. The aim of the chapter is to shed light on an aspect of Arendt's work that hasn't received much attention though, namely, her work on emotion and education. My analysis shows that despite the tensions and weaknesses that have been identified over the years about Arendt's views on both emotions and political education, she provides compelling insights against the possibilities of political education degenerating into moral-emotional rhetoric. Arendt highlights the dangers of constructing political emotions in the classroom as the foundation for political action, while acknowledging the constructive role for the emotions in the development of political agency. The chapter concludes that Arendt's insights on emotions and political education can help educators avoid potential pitfalls in their efforts to (re)consider the place of political emotions in the classroom, especially those emotions and affects that are more relevant to right-wing populism and democracy.

Chapter 9 moves on to discuss how pedagogically (un)productive is the idea of invoking in classrooms feelings of collective guilt, and attempts to explore not only the persistence of "collective guilt" in students' responses but also the new possibilities that are opened with reframing it as "shared responsibility." In particular, the analysis addresses the moral, political and pedagogical implications of viewing the phenomena of collective guilt and shared responsibility through the lenses of Hannah Arendt and Iris Marion Young. Using Arendt's and Young's accounts of shared responsibility offers opportunities to educators and students to make them aware of their responsibilities as members of certain social groups, rather than getting stuck in feelings of guilt. The proposed *pedagogy of shared responsibility* is not focused on blame, guilt or fault, but rather it has the potential to minimize denials of complicity and instead encourage students to interrogate the conditions under which they are responsive and responsible to others.

Chapter 10 uses the concepts of necropolitics and sentimentality as theoretical entry points to broaden understandings of death as a form of power against subjugated (e.g., Black, migrant, refugee) lives. This analysis – which is very much relevant and valuable in recent political movements such as Black Lives Matter – is approached through the dilemma of showing or not showing dead-body images in the classroom as an ethical, political and pedagogical intervention. This intervention entails numerous challenges such as the risk of traumatizing students; the danger of superficializing colonial histories, structural racism and contemporary geopolitical complicities producing such deaths; and the challenge of finding productive ways to respond pedagogically to the emotionally difficult spaces of learning that are created, without sentimentalizing death. The chapter makes an attempt to reclaim the entangled meanings of necropolitics and sentimentality in pedagogical discourse and practice by re-visioning the sentimental in ways that interrogate the normalization of death-making in the current political climate, especially after massive protests across the United States and other parts of the world following the deaths of Blacks and migrants.

The final chapter (Chapter 11) revisits the important role of affect in pedagogical efforts to engage students with complicity in democratic education. Recent theoretical shifts on affect and complicity enable education scholars and practitioners to move the focus away from what we do not want (i.e., more complicity) toward anti-complicity. The new openings emerging from these theoretical shifts create pedagogical spaces to inspire *anti-complicity* praxes – that is, actions that actively resist social harm in everyday life. It is argued that for this to happen, it is necessary that educators navigate students through the affective and political dynamics of complicity in both critical and strategic ways. The chapter concludes by discussing how an *anti-complicity pedagogy* may be "translated" into strategic moves in democratic education.

Finally, the Epilogue will summarize the conclusions of this book situating them within the broader theoretical, political and pedagogical landscape sketched throughout the chapters. The discussion here will aim to render the conclusions of this analysis relevant to the renewal of democratic education in various parts of the world. The attention to the affective politics of democratic education is crucial, if we – educators, policymakers, activists – want to gain a deeper understanding of the resistance to democratic (education) initiatives and the potential promise of this analysis to inspire some kind of transformation and renewal.

In conclusion, the issues dealt with in this book are clearly of increasing importance in education, especially in the contemporary political landscape in which populist/extremist/post-truth narratives enter public spaces and educational discourses and often create hegemonies that oppose democratic prospects. Understanding these demands and finding ways to address them pedagogically is extremely valuable for the renewal of democratic prospects in contemporary societies. Given that to date, there has been no attempt in education to address the pedagogical potential of affect to counter populism/extremism/post-truth, this book can contribute toward the direction of beginning to explore the risks and possibilities of such an attempt. Democratic education is in dire need for theoretical renewal, if it is going to provide in practice productive responses to the rise of populism around the world. Articulating some of the ideas, then, that could be valuable to such renewal is clearly not the final destination but rather a modest attempt to support the journey of democratic education into the turbulent political climate of our times.

PART I

Scanning the Political Landscape of Right-Wing Populism

CHAPTER 1

The Politics of Shame in the Age of Trump

> [Trump's] supporters have been in mourning for a lost way of life. Many have become discouraged, others depressed. They yearn to feel pride but instead have felt *shame*. Their land no longer feels their own. Joined together with others like themselves, they now feel hopeful, joyous, elated ... As if magically lifted, they are no longer strangers in their own land.
>
> (Hochschild, 2016, p. 225, added emphasis)

The following are the key questions that will be the subject of this book: What does affect have to do with right-wing populism, and what does this mean for democratic education? In other words, is there anything that educators can do – pedagogically – in light of the growth of right-wing populism across the world to renew democracy and democratic education? Chapters 1 and 2, which focus on Donald Trump, are used as illustrative examples of a wider phenomenon and of how educators may begin to reconsider some of their pedagogies in efforts to address the affective roots of right-wing populism. As this chapter emphasizes, the focus on affect introduces this concept into democratic education as a distinctive and important area of concern and study.

The point of departure for this chapter is a growing observation by several scholars and political commentators that understanding the rise and appeal of Trump requires a careful attention to the *politics of shame* (Gray, 2018; Kreiss, Barker & Zenner, 2017; Schaefer, 2020; Schrock et al., 2017; Watkins, 2018). The success of Trump, as it is argued, has emerged in part because he has shown to be a masterful "handler and broker of shame for Whites" (Watkins, 2018, p. 26), especially working-class and poor Whites who feel that they are "strangers in their own land," to use Hochschild's (2016) expression from her book title. Trump has "weaponized" shame (Haslett, 2016, p. 3) by inducing shame in his followers and "saving them from having to acknowledge its pain by publically shaming others" (Haslett, 2016, p. 3). At the same time, Trump gives Whites hope, dignity and pride, gaining affection and political power, while scapegoating African Americans, other minorities, immigrants and refugees. In this sense, shame is very much related with interest (Tomkins, 1995); this connection explains how Trump has given license to his supporters not to feel shame and this occurs because they no longer have an interest in the plight of African Americans, other minorities, immigrants and refugees.

I would argue, then, that the politics of shame in the age of Trump requires attention to two important aspects: First, how there are different types of white shame – e.g., the shame of poor and working-class Whites for being left behind, the shame of Whites as a result of their privilege – that circulate in culture and are linked to the anger of Whites and the expression of racist views and violence to ward off or diminish feelings of shame (Watkins, 2018); and second, how Trump's shamelessness is expressed through a compelling set of techniques for harnessing his audience's feelings of shame for political purposes (Schaefer, 2020). Unless scholars and educators in the fields of democratic and anti-racist education begin to gain a deeper understanding of these two aspects and their political and pedagogical consequences – i.e., white affects as a generative site for equity, democracy and social justice in education – it will be difficult to evaluate the potential of shame in both combating and, curiously, promoting racism and white supremacy.

What is truly remarkable, points out Gray (2018), is that attempts to shame Trump and his supporters only provoke more shamelessness by him (and his supporters) and fail to have substantial negative impact on his success. The rationale behind shaming attempts is that Trump and his supporters should feel shame because of their racist and white supremacist views. In fact, shame has become one of the most highlighted affects advocated by and for white people in anti-racist campaigns (Sullivan, 2014). However, as Milazzo (2017) argues, calls for shame that prescribe shame to white people are detrimental to the achievement of racial equality; they are detrimental, not only because there is no proven relationship between feelings of shame and anti-racist actions but also because demands for affective modification reproduce misconceptions that racism and white supremacy could be overcome, if only white people showed good will to transform their individual selves. In this manner, structural racism and the role of white supremacy are ignored or minimized in favor of advocating a moral behavior and attitude modification by white people (Sullivan, 2014).

My analysis in this chapter draws from the work of scholars in affect theory (Ahmed, 2004; Berlant, 2011; Cvetkovich, 2012; Gregg & Seigworth, 2010;

Probyn, 2005; Schaefer, 2019) to suggest that there are different types of white shame that require different pedagogical strategies to address shame critically and productively. That shaming is not inherently a useful and effective strategy in combating racism and white supremacy seems to be self-evident. What is less evident, however, is how and why one should pay attention to the feelings of Trump's supporters and, by extension, to different types of white shame, and why such a focus is worthwhile amidst the material violences that are being enacted daily on people of color as a result of Trump's policies and rhetoric? I would argue that to be able to appreciate the contribution of this project, it needs to be situated within ongoing settler colonial land dispossession, white supremacy and racial capitalism. If it is true that an important element of anti-racist, democratic and social justice projects is to address politically and pedagogically white feelings and desires tapped into for colonial production, then it becomes crucial to ask how public and classroom pedagogies in democratic and anti-racist education might organize, mobilize and form alternative affective structures. Furthermore, if there are political and pedagogical limits to white shame and shaming, then one needs to begin asking what pedagogical strategies may be deployed by anti-racist educators in their efforts to respond productively to politics of shame and its linkage to racism – especially in light of "white fragility" oftentimes making even minimum amount of race-based stress (e.g., as a result of shaming) intolerable (DiAngelo, 2011, 2015).

This chapter makes an attempt to address these issues by making an argument along two directions: First, the chapter analyzes how Trump takes political advantage of different types of white shame to restore a lost sense of dignity for Whites, while at the same time validating overt and other forms of racism and white supremacy; I would argue that it is important for educators and students in democratic and anti-racist education to be able to identify different types of white shame and their consequences. Second, the chapter argues that the response to politics of shame and its linkage to racism is not to resort to shaming Trump and his supporters but rather to understand the political and pedagogical limits of different types of white shame and shaming, and to seek strategies that address these limits productively. Although the chapter is theoretical, it offers some examples of pedagogical strategies that might be helpful along these directions; these examples are expanded upon in Part III of the book, so here they are only meant as illustrative of what educators may begin to think as a pedagogical response to various aspects of the phenomenon of right-wing populism.

It is with these ideas in mind that I, first, examine briefly how affect theory is useful in theorizing shame, particularly in the realm of politics, building on some of the ideas already discussed in the Introduction. In the next part of the chapter, I draw on these theoretical perspectives to analyze more specifically the politics of shame, especially as it is deployed by Trump, highlighting how different types of white shame are intertwined with the ways in which racism is legitimated in his rhetoric. The third part of the chapter discusses the political and pedagogical limits of white shame and shaming in anti-racist efforts. Finally, the chapter concludes with an analysis of how these insights enable educators to rethink their pedagogical strategies in their efforts to respond productively to different types of white shame embedded in Trump's politics of shame and its linkage to racism and white supremacy.

Affect As Political and Pedagogic Practice

Affect theory, according to Schaefer (2019), "is an approach to history, politics, culture, and other aspects of embodied life that emphasizes the role of nonlinguistic and non- or para-cognitive forces" (p. 1). It has emerged from queer theory, post-structuralism, feminism and anti-racist theory (Schaefer, 2020), exploring basically *what bodies do* and how they are impelled to do things (Schaefer, 2019). Building on the theoretical framework on affect outlined in the Introduction, there are three key points that are useful in this chapter.

The first point reminds the reader how I use affect. As noted in the Introduction, affect is variously described in the literature (Gregg & Seigworth, 2010), but it is generally understood as elusive, excessive and difficult to articulate through language (e.g., Blackman & Venn, 2010). It also refers to a transpersonal capacity that a body has to be affected and to affect (Anderson, 2014). While at times of heightened affect we may experience what could be termed categorical affects (i.e., shame, surprise, anger, fear, etc., as per Tomkins, 1995) or what other scholars call emotions (e.g., in the field of sociology of emotions), much of the time the affects we experience are inconsequential, yet they accumulate and have effect. Also, while affect may register at an individual level it can manifest at various scales (Watkins, 2016). The conceptualization of affect as transpersonal is useful in this book, because it enables to account for the fundamental changes occurring in the ways that shame is experienced and transmitted via media and politics.

The second key point has to do with the politics of affect, that is, how affect is politicized to promote certain agendas. As Berlant (2016) writes, "all politics is emotional because all politics is sentimental, attaching people to dreams of a better good life." Affects, then, can be understood as "political and cultural, i.e. symbolically coded and socially constructed patterns of perception and action" (Sauer, 2013, p. 264). In other words, the relationship between affect and politics "can be considered the result of a historically formed 'politics of feeling'" (Sauer, 2013, p. 264). As Gebhardt (2019) explains further,

> The relation between affective orders and political discourses is reciprocal: A political discourse produces a specific order of affects, where affects are hierarchically structured according to a specific normalization process. In turn, these normative orders are tacitly shaped by and implicitly underpin specific affects and feeling rules. (p. 3)

Ahmed's work on "affective economies" (2004, 2012) provides a useful resource to appreciate the affective ways with which individuals come together and move *toward* or *away* in relation to others. Ahmed uses the term "affective economies" to argue that affects do not reside in a subject but rather circulate in relations of difference, whereby what is moved and what moves is the effect of affective intensities and energies. Affective economies are social and material, as well as political and psychic; their effect is the constitution of particular affective attachments and meanings, that is, affects become attached to objects, bodies and signs. For example, an understanding of affect as economy shows how relations between bodies might be perpetuated, not because of any essence in these relations but because of the ways in which certain affects (e.g., fear, anger, repulsion, shame) "stick" to certain bodies or flow and traverse space. White privilege and racial stereotypes, for instance, are enacted through particular affective relations and embodied practices that classify Whites and "others" into exclusive subject categories.

In a similar vein, Cvetkovich's (2003, 2012) work provides a rich description of how particular affects travel along racial lines. For Cvetkovich, thinking through affect and attending to "public feelings" provides resources to think psychic and social life together in ways that move beyond social constructions and racialized categories. In particular, Cvetkovich (2012) analyzes depression as a "public feelings project" linked to the structural legacies of colonialism, slavery and racism. As she suggests, tracing the affective materiality of these legacies may produce new vocabularies of hope that avoid naïve optimism and its failure to address the past and its violence. For example, suggests Cvetkovich, it is important to explore the consequences for white people of living lives of privilege in the vicinity of the violence of racism. The response of Whites to their privilege is deeply affective, so there is no doubt that the affective dimension of politics should neither be dismissed nor instrumentalized through a lens that approaches affects as mere by-products of discourses.

Finally, the third key point has to do with explicit attention to "pedagogic affect" (Mulcahy, 2019; Watkins, 2006, 2016) not only in the classroom but also more broadly. Pedagogic affect is the idea of affect *as* pedagogy, namely, how affect serves as a material and political force that is impactful to teaching and learning, regardless of whether pedagogy takes place in the classroom or in public. As Watkins (2016) writes, pedagogic affect refers to "the ways in which different pedagogic practices possess differing affects that in turn affect learning" (p. 75). Attending to pedagogic affect, adds Mulcahy (2019), "brings into view the micropolitics through which knowledges are made" (p. 103), hence the pedagogic potential of this capacity to have knowledge materialize differently "requires a renewed engagement with affect in education" (p. 105).

In summary, the notion of affect as pedagogic and political practice offers a useful framework to understand pedagogy, politics and the formation of political subjectivity, because the self is not constituted top-down but rather by a tangle of forces that "run through us, we are made by them, and our decisions reflect the priorities of those forces rather than an abstract assessment of the world around us" (Schaefer, 2020, pp. 3–4). As Ott and Dickinson (2019) write in their analysis of Trump's Twitter responses, affects link "the sensual, immediate, and prediscursive responses of bodies to specific environmental energies with historically situated discursive processes and practices" (p. 31). Trump's affective style, which they refer to as "white rage," is reflective of the "fear and anxiety surrounding the social decentering of white privilege," (p. 29) leading to what DiAngelo (2011) calls "white fragility." Understanding the affective politics and technologies of whiteness (Leonardo & Zembylas, 2013; Matias, 2016a), therefore, is a crucial aspect of developing a critical and strategic pedagogical approach that includes *shame* (and, by extension, dignity and pride).

The Politics of Shame and Trump's Affective Rhetoric

Locke (2016) defines shame as a "*felt* ethic of obligation and regulation that involves an actual or internalized audience that judges one's thoughts and acts in terms of their relationship to norms or standards that one shares (or is expected to share) with others" (p. 19, original emphasis). Shame, then, is typically coded as a negative affect within a moral framework that sets moral standards and codes of conduct. Shame is the affect of dignity, according to psychologist Silvan Tomkins (1963); thus, shame is a painful feeling of social exclusion. In particular, Sedgwick-Kosofsky (2003), who draws on the work of Tomkins, argues that shame is not merely a painful feeling of social exclusion but a primary affect of intersubjective life. We feel shame, explains further Guenther (2011), because others matter to us in ways that are constitutive of our social and political identity. Given that shame is constitutive of social and political identity and being in the world, to approach shame as an individualized or psychologized feeling would be to miss something fundamental about the nature of social and political identity. As Benin and Cartwright (2006) write, "Shame is at the basis of a set of intersubjective, empathetic processes of identification that are constitute of both an individual sense of being and a sense of community and belonging in the world" (p. 158).

A key point here is the relationship between shame and interest. In fact, Tomkins (1995) defines shame in relation to pleasure, interest and enjoyment. In his account, shame "operates ordinarily only after interest or enjoyment has been activated, and inhibits one or the other or both. The innate activator of shame is the incomplete reduction of interest or joy" (p. 134). On this account, Nathanson (2008) explains that shame is the dominant negative affect of everyday life, because whatever interferes with the experience of pleasure and joy makes shame our constant companion. This understanding of shame contains a number of insights that are important for realizing how shame is politicized. Making the argument that shame needs to be identified in the context of political rhetoric (e.g., such as Trump's), for example, suggests that it is crucial to carefully examine the different types of shame that are manifested within a particular context and what could be done (Tarnopolsky, 2010) – politically and pedagogically – to address these different types productively.

In particular, shame is "resolutely political," suggests Schaefer (2020, p. 6), because the reduction of interest or joy is always experienced intersubjectively. In Tomkins's own words,

> whenever an individual, a class, or a nation wishes to maintain a hierarchical relationship, or to maintain aloofness, it will have resort to contempt of the other. Contempt is the mark of the oppressor. The hierarchical relationship is maintained either when the oppressed one assumes the attitude of contempt for himself or hangs his head in shame. (1995, p. 139)

Importantly, then, the politicization of shame functions not only in a negative manner but also in a "positive" way that forges mutuality in social groups – an affective economy of shame, as Ahmed (2004) put it – that brings shamed people together. For example, the nationalist, xenophobic or racist claims made by Trump draw affective energy from the aloofness of social groups in which shame circulates (e.g., working-class and poor Whites). Needless to say, my point here is not to turn attention to Trump as the "problem"; Trump is merely a manifestation, admittedly a powerful one, of the white supremacist logics that have long been in place prior to his presidency. Hence, it is important to understand how politicized mobilizations of hate, anger and fear are entangled with economies of shame; these economies are underpinned by feelings of estrangement and political disenfranchisement in which African Americans, other minorities, immigrants and refugees – "strangers" to use Hochschild's (2016) terminology – are deemed responsible for Whites' feelings of anxiety, resentment and fear:

> strangers step ahead of you in line, making you anxious, resentful, and afraid. A president [Obama] allies with the line cutters, making you feel distrustful, betrayed. A person ahead of you in line insults you as ignorant redneck, making you feel humiliated and mad. Economically, culturally, demographically, politically, you are suddenly a stranger in your own land. (p. 222)

As Probyn (2005) writes, shame provokes a profound emotional disturbance that questions one's sense of self: "[S]hame makes us question what we are feeling, the nature of the loss of interest, and fundamentally ... who we are, as a reevaluation of the self" (p. 64). Thus, shame is important to political discussions and debates about how to deal with social conditions that are considered the cause for some groups' feelings of shame. As such, shame is a source of political leverage that could offer "powerfully productive and powerfully metamorphic possibilities" (Sedgwick-Kosofsky, 2003, p. 65). This understanding of shame moves away from an orientation to negative self-assessment and offers a productive conceptualization of shame that is constitutive of new forms of political subjectivity (Zembylas, 2018b).

In fact, as Schaefer (2020) points out, a productive orientation to shame is a fundamental principle of progressive politics, in particular the politics of anti-racism as well as gender and queer emancipation: "Leftists use shame to challenge not only the politics of others, but also themselves, grinding away their own sense of comfort in a relentless project to become more sensitive, more thoughtful, more moral" (p. 6). However, the political right, and especially populist politicians such as Trump, also uses shame to generate an affective economy that transforms shame into rage toward those deemed responsible for a social group's poor economic, cultural and political status. Scheff and Retzinger (1991) argue that shame can give rise to repeated and ongoing feedback shame–anger loops: being ashamed of the fact that you are angry; or angry because you feel ashamed. These shame–anger loops are a crucial element of politics because they can constantly be reproduced and circulated, infecting others.

As Sedgwick-Kosofsky (2003) asks, "can anyone suppose that we'll ever figure out what happened around political correctness if we don't see it as, among other things, a highly politicized chain reaction of shame dynamics?" (p. 64). The political appeal of Trump, then, functions as an "affective ideology" (Peters & Protevi, 2017) that brings together people who "seek freedom from shame.... People get shamed, or lose their jobs, for example, when they're just having a little fun making fun. Anti-PC [political correctness] means 'I feel unfree'" (Berlant, 2016). Making a consonant point, Hochschild (2016) calls this a feeling of "collective effervescence ... a state of emotional excitation felt by those who join with others they take to be fellow members of a moral or biological tribe. They gather to affirm their unity and, united, they feel secure and respected" (p. 225). Mobilizing support through the social media (e.g., Twitter) and his public performances in campaign events, Trump establishes a particular affective style in politics that gives people – especially white supremacists – permission to not only express but also enjoy their anger and resentment against "others" and be free from shame, leading to a white defiance (Anderson, 2017b).

Many working-class and poor Whites, for example, are educated by Trump to think that "others" (e.g., African Americans, other minorities, immigrants) are responsible for their poor economic, political and cultural status: "Mexican migrants and African Americans become cast as lazy, stupid, parasitical, even criminal. Shame is transferred, enabling many Whites suffering precariousness to feel superior in their character and morals: hardworking, persevering, generous, God-loving" (Watkins, 2018, p. 30). The result, says Watkins, is a racist ideology that proclaims that getting rid of those seen as responsible for the shame and humiliation of Whites will bring them economic and social superiority. As Schaefer (2020) explains,

> Taking the side of whites who have been confronted with their complicity in a system of racial disparity, he [Trump] assures them that rather than feeling ashamed, they should take revenge on those who have sought to challenge their sense of ease. A racialized dynamic is skillfully converted into an affective battlefield, mobilizing political power. (p. 10)

This is precisely why, then, educators and academics need to pay careful attention to the affective complexities of the politics of shame – to understand how different manifestations of white shame are used by Trump (and, white supremacists, by extension) to become a resource of political power. But this is only the starting point, because the political and pedagogical questions that are raised are profound: What is the politically or pedagogically appropriate response to different types of white shame in the context of Trumpamerica? And, what are the political and pedagogical limits of shame and shaming in efforts to disrupt the affective economies of racism and white supremacy?

The Political and Pedagogical Limits of Shame and Shaming

The argument made so far introduced some fundamental questions of what (white) shame can do, politically and pedagogically, and whether this (multifaceted) shame can be directed in productive ways to benefit struggles for equality, social justice and antiracism. As Gray (2018) has put it, "As we lurch toward greater equality, the relevant question is not whether certain white Trump voters have an outsized persecution complex (they do), but whether adding shame to the powder keg of white resentment is likely to have the redemptive qualities we imagine."

A teleological account of redemption – that is often implicit in narratives of oppression, colonization and racism, suggesting that inducing shame to oppressors can work pedagogically and politically – is widespread in anti-racist literature (Locke, 2007, 2016; Milazzo, 2017; Sullivan, 2014; Zembylas, 2020c). In fact, as Milazzo writes, "Many scholars do not just posit shame as a valuable emotion, but *prescribe* shame to white people" (p. 6, original emphasis). The underlying assumption is that if Whites acknowledge and express shame for their racist ideas and behaviors, then this can work productively to transform themselves. However, as discussed earlier in the chapter, there are limits in engaging with shame and shaming. Tomkins (1995) emphasizes that shame is not an individual but a social and political affect; therefore, individual transformation, if or when it happens, does not automatically translate into a broad-based social and political change. In fact, Probyn (2005) acknowledges that there are great social and political obstacles for shame to bring a sort of self-transformation. In addition, Tarnopolsky (2010) points out that it is not shame *itself* that carries the potential for transformation but rather the different ways we are urged to engage with shame that could – under some circumstances – create transformative openings.

Other thinkers also express their deep skepticism about the alleged transformative effects of felt shame grounded in individualistic terms. This is not to dismiss the ethical value of individuals' experiences of shame and the potential of self-transformation, as Locke argues, but rather to be careful not "to place too much faith in the *world-changing impact* of shaming others" (2007, p. 156, added emphasis). As she further explains, "the case of shame as a common ethical framework perfectly attuned to address our otherwise conflicted and fragmented world, risks displacing disagreements as it offers up shame as a solace" (2007, p. 156). Locke's (2016) deep skepticism about the political value of shame is rooted in a historical assessment of discussions on shame in feminist, gay liberationist and anti-racist scholarship. As Button (2019) notes, Locke "rejects the political employment of shame on ontological grounds: for more pluralistic societies today, shame is incapable of providing a fixed guide or obligatory moral rule to help us govern ourselves" (p. 394).

Consider "white shame" in the context of Trump's politics and, by extension, in the broader sociopolitical setting of white supremacy and racial capitalism. Two crucial manifestations of white shame in this context are the shame that could be shown by Whites as a result of acknowledging their privilege, and the shame that could be felt by poor and working-class Whites for having lost (political, economic and cultural) ground and being left behind. Is there a political difference between these two types of white shame, given that working-class poor still benefit from white privilege? Although related, these types of shame may function differently and raise different pedagogical and political questions. Regarding the former, and assuming that Whites come to acknowledge their privilege, a set of crucial questions is, how do pedagogical engagements with white shame frame it as social and political affect, while highlighting systemic racism and racial inequality? What impact do these pedagogical engagements with white shame really have on the subjects whose lives have been traumatized by racism and racist views? Would African American suffering be ameliorated by white shame–inspired acknowledgments of racism in public and classroom pedagogies? Regarding the latter form of shame, namely, the shame felt by poor and working-class Whites for being left behind, a different set of questions may be raised: Does teaching about or showing empathy for poor and working-class Whites make them feel more included in the future or upgrade their political, economic and cultural status? Does this also imply showing empathy for the plight of poor Black and other minorities? How does acknowledgment of this type of white shame in politics or educational settings change the structural conditions that sustain social inequality and racism?

Sullivan (2014) describes shame as a narcissistic feeling that caters to white middle-class subjects, as it is grounded in the assumption that if white people acknowledge their shame about racism, they can be transformed. The problem is that insofar as the focus is on the "bad" character of the "shameless," the structural conditions of racism are not really challenged and racism is approached merely through the lens of individualized feelings (Locke, 2016). As Ahmed (2004), Cvetkovich (2012) and Ioanide (2015) show, however, it is possible to examine race and racism through the lens of affect, while making visible the workings of structural racism. Hence, a sense of shame for racism might be a vital source of some sort of transformation in educational settings, if this effort does not end up a sentimentalized attempt to make white students feel better about themselves because they acknowledge their shame and privilege. A pedagogical engagement with white shame, then, needs to be directed along two important directions simultaneously: First, a critical engagement with whiteness, white supremacy and white privilege that is *not* limited to changing individual attitude or reflecting upon what it feels to be a problem but rather focuses on examining and taking specific actions that challenge whiteness and promote social justice (Yancy, 2015); and, second, a critical engagement with Whites' feelings of shame for their political disenfranchisement and how to find ways to make the future more inclusive for them too, just as for all disenfranchised "others" (Gray, 2018).

As Gray (2018) suggests, reconsidering the strategy of shaming Whites may produce a more critical understanding of the role that shame and shaming play in combating racism and achieving social justice:

> Of course, the responsibility for bigotry lies squarely on the shoulders of bigots, but it's worth considering whether the language we use might influence whether whites see the future as one to be afraid of, or as an inclusive one in which equality benefits them too. There are humanistic reasons for that: everyone, regardless of race, should be able to feel a sense of community belonging and individual pride in an egalitarian future. But it is also in the self-interest of racial justice movements to think about the social factors that help drive the discontented in one direction or another.... It may not be our "job" to assist white people's adaptation to a new multicultural reality. But unless the political dynamics of backlash are carefully understood, important victories in the fight against racism may prove transient.

The pedagogical challenge here, then, is both theoretical and practical. There is still considerable theoretical work to be done to explore how different types of white shame are politicized and which pedagogies might be more productive for each type. In the last part of the chapter, a modest attempt is made to highlight some pedagogical strategies for doing so.

So What? Rethinking Our Pedagogical Strategies

I will briefly suggest two strategies to address the two types of white shame identified earlier in the chapter: the shame that could be shown by Whites as a result of acknowledging their privilege; and the shame that could be felt by poor and working-class Whites for being left behind. Needless to say, I am not saying that these are the only ones or the best strategies to address these types of white shame; however, my aim is to highlight some tactical moves, rather than specific teaching practices, that educators could utilize at the micropolitical level of educational settings – that is, strategies that are theoretically grounded in understanding the politics of shame as intertwined with (anti-)racism.

Before I start outlining these two strategies, it is useful to reiterate once again how important it is for educators and scholars to pay attention to the ambivalence of shame (Guenther, 2011) and identify the various manifestations of shame and its politicization in specific sociopolitical contexts. "The ambivalence of shame," writes Guenther, "attests to the irreducibility of our exposure to others, both as the site of relationality and ethical responsibility, and as the site of its exploitation through oppression" (2011, p. 38). Hence, applying shame to an entire category of people, as if shame or people are monolithic entities, "rather than conducting a more nuanced assessment of why people feel the way they do and did what they did," writes Gray (2018), "means we might miss those among the blameworthy who might be identified as something more mutable, more persuadable than a 'deplorable' – someone who might be convinced to join our side next time around." Ambivalence, then, is part of white shame, just as it is at the heart of white multiculturalism (Hage, 2000). Just as there are "evil" and "good" White nationalists, to use Hage's terminology, there are also different manifestations of white shame; undoubtedly, there are similarities between these categories, yet this nuance could be factored by educators into their pedagogical treatment of racism and the politics of shame. Doing so will raise crucial questions to be explored by educators and students in their attempts to examine and understand how and with what consequences white shame is differentially actualized in historically and politically specific circumstances (e.g., communities in the south of the United States compared to those in the north): How do feelings of white shame within particular sites attach to the ways through which racism is formed and moved? How are feelings of white shame differentially lived, that is, adjusted to, acquiesced to or disrupted? How and who do feelings of white shame harm or damage? These questions anticipate the work that needs to be done to create the necessary affective and pedagogical conditions in the classroom or beyond before even beginning to address different types of white shame as they are entangled with racism.

A strategy that I want to suggest, then, in response to white shame associated with acknowledging white privilege, is grounded in the realization that this type of shame is a deeply social and political affect rather than an individual one. As such, white shame associated with privilege is linked to structural legacies of racism; this understanding might help to not only trace shame's political complexities but also begin working toward a "reparative sensibility" (Sedgwick-Kosofsky, 2003, p. 141) in pedagogies, in particular, what have been called "reparative pedagogies" (Tarc, 2011; Zembylas, 2018a). Sedgwick's "reparative reading" is a critical practice that seeks to repair what may be broken – e.g., race relations as result of racism and Whites' failure to acknowledge their privilege. The pedagogical goal is to make visible "the hidden traces of oppression and persecution" (Sedgwick-Kosofsky, 2003, p. 141). Thus, adopting a reparative mode as a pedagogical practice – in tracing the experiences of white shame associated with acknowledging white privilege and racism – turns educators' and students' attention to how the world may be restored and repaired, beginning from everyday ordinary encounters that transform the micropolitical culture of racialized affects in classrooms and schools (Bonilla-Silva, 2019a, 2019b; Zembylas, 2015b).

Reparative pedagogies in democratic and anti-racist education address white shame associated with privilege by putting reparative sensibility at the center of teaching and learning. Reparative pedagogies would be unproductive, if they failed to take into consideration the complex affective implications of stories of suffering as a result of racism; these stories should be central to pedagogical activities addressing white shame and white privilege. However, the point of these pedagogical activities is not to blame individual white students for not feeling shame or to invoke shame to those who don't feel it (see also Chapter 9). Rather, the goal is to historicize oppression, settler colonialism, white supremacy, and racism and articulate how each and everyone's life is affectively and politically intertwined with the lives of others. Hence, reparative pedagogies aim to move the individual into the social and political space and his or her affective experiences to "make meaning from senselessly shattered sociality and social relations" (Tarc, 2011, p. 355), without idealizing or sentimentalizing those experiences or relations (Zembylas, 2018a). Reparative pedagogies, then, are deeply affective and political *practices* rather than merely a critical mode of teaching *about* or *through* shame; that is, practices that aim to inspire in students actions and activism that find ways of "repairing" shattered sociality and social relations as a result of ongoing racism and social injustice.

Another pedagogical strategy – this time in response to the shame that could be felt by poor and working-class Whites for being left behind – is how to invoke "pedagogies of shame" (Zembylas, 2008, 2020c) in the classroom that recognize the affective and political consequences of such feelings of shame for both white students whose families feel left behind and minority students who have life-long experiences of being marginalized. Pedagogies of shame essentially ask educators and students to engage in alternative ways of relating to others – not in order to make themselves or others feel "bad" or "good" but rather to seek a deeper understanding of the affective materialities of shame and racism, and particularly the complexities of white complicity and its entanglement with racism (see also Chapter 11). The goal of pedagogies of shame is not to offer any consolation, especially to Whites; to understand white complicity requires a great deal of processing of complex moments of entanglement with racism, both witting and unwitting (Straker, 2011). More importantly, suggests Straker (2011), educators need to question what it really means to request from Whites to publicly express shame about their racist views or their white privilege. How effective is it, for example, if educators use this tactic in anti-racist education to encourage or even demand expressions of shame from white students who openly share Trump's views or other racist views because they are feeling left behind? Can this work counterproductively by promoting a form of "promiscuous shame," in Straker's (2011) terms, that is, shame that is owned defensively, casually and prematurely, offering a solace to Whites that risks making invisible the workings of structural racism (Milazzo, 2017)? The point is to open up a critical space for examining the manifestations of shame associated with Trump's racism and white supremacy, e.g., communities affected by economic decline or that feel isolation for various reasons.

The pedagogical process of engaging with different types of white shame requires a strategic approach to empathizing with the plight of disenfranchised people, including poor and working-class Whites, not in the sense of offering Whites a solace or sentimental refuge but rather acknowledging different forms of human suffering with the aim to produce new vocabularies of hope and forms of community in which everyone feels included.

My point is that it is not a good idea for this sort of pedagogical engagement to be framed in self-absorbed and sentimental narratives that assume, for instance, that if I feel *enough* empathy for the other who suffers from racism, then my (white) shame will be erased or the other's suffering will disappear. A critical approach to working pedagogically with politics of shame needs to take into account both empathy's and shame's uneven natures and effects – that is, how claims for self-transformation via empathy or shame "can (re)constitute unequal affective subjects and relations of power" (Pedwell, 2012, p. 175). This implies problematizing claims that cultivating empathy or shame is an affective "solution" to complex structural and political problems such as racism and economic disparity. Once again, the pedagogical strategy that is utilized would need to consider the ambivalence and complexity of collective affects such as empathy and shame and what they might tell educators and students about the affective nature and workings of the "Trumping of politics" (Berlant, 2016) or the racialization of affects in educational settings (Bonilla-Silva, 2019a).

Regarding empathy, in particular, it "has to go both ways," as Gray (2018) emphasizes: "you have to understand why those who use shaming do it, and why the left's moral outrage isn't simply – as the right often suggests it is – an effort to seem righteous and superior" but rather "it comes from being genuinely disturbed and angered by the way marginalized people are treated." Hence, countering Trump's rhetoric to take political advantage of white shame requires empathizing – in critical and strategic ways – with views that educators may find unacceptable (Zembylas, 2012, 2018b). Yet, the goal is not to develop a common ground with racist views but rather to build a common world that is inclusive for all and benefits everyone (Biesta, 2010b). To the extent that educators in democratic and anti-racist education offer students possibilities to pay attention to how dynamics of shame and dignity play out in Trump's political theater and how students can engage critically and sensitively with those who have different views without dismissing them out of hand, then they will take a small but immensely important step toward countering not only Trump's rhetoric but also white supremacist views more generally.

All in all, experiences of shame are learned, and therefore, to unlearn these affects, educators and students need to begin *feeling differently*. As Hemmings (2012) explains, "Feeling that something is amiss in how one is recognized, feeling an ill fit with social descriptions, feeling undervalued, feeling that same sense in considering others ... can produce a politicized impetus to change," therefore, "in order to know differently we have to feel differently" (p. 150). The unlearning and transformation process has to work through affects, emotions and embodied understanding. However, forming new collective affects does not necessarily imply "overcoming" shame but rather engaging, critically and strategically, with its various manifestations – that is, a step-by-step process that involves a combination of institutional transformations and body trainings that redefine affective practices and affective economies within and beyond the classroom (Zembylas, 2019).

Concluding Remarks

The lens of affect theory and the acknowledgment of the politics of shame outlined in this chapter open up new possibilities to develop a political and pedagogical praxis that could advance struggles against racism and white supremacy. But the issue is not merely to recognize that race and racism are affective and therefore induce new feeling rules and (self)-management techniques that force shame upon Whites so that they recognize overt, subtle, symbolic, color-blind or institutional racism (Bonilla-Silva, 2019a). Shame cannot be forced on people, as Attwell, Pes and Zinato (2019) point out, and "we cannot decide to feel shame as shame is thrust upon us" (p. 27). Interest, as discussed earlier, plays a key role here, being a related affect. If we are not interested in something, we don't feel shame. Part of the reason for why shame may have such limited pedagogic effect at present is because people have been licensed not to care; they have no interest in the plight of disenfranchised others they see as outsiders as they have their own problems to focus on, a perspective manipulated by the political right to great effect. Conservative or defensive reactions (which are abundant by Trump and his supporters responding to racism) "are a clear sign of a dismaying lack of the necessary cultural conditions" (Attwell et al., 2019, p. 27) for working productively with different types of white shame.

This chapter has pointed out that paying attention to the dark consequences of Trump's affective rhetoric includes recognition of the affective and political complexities emerging from shame and shaming. For this reason, I have suggested some strategic moves – rather than specific pedagogical practices – that could identify and analyze these complexities, and I have discussed how this analysis could be beneficial for democratic and anti-racist education. However, there is a considerable risk, namely, how shame and shaming may be "translated" into moralizing stories or sentimental rhetoric that have little effect on anti-racist struggles; thus it is important for educators, scholars and citizens to be vigilant to the dangers of moralizing ethic. The political and pedagogical limits of shame and shaming teach us that shame or shaming – just as shamelessness or refusing to feel shame – on their own do not deliver democratic action (Locke, 2016), neither do they defeat the structures of racism and white supremacy. These limits are part and parcel of political and pedagogical efforts to (re)think and to (re)imagine ways of inhabiting the world differently. Unearthing these limits and inventing productive ways to address them may bring us a step closer to becoming better equipped pedagogically and politically to unpack the affective forces and consequences of the entanglements between politics of shame and racism. Chapter 2 focuses more specifically on how to analyze "Trump Pedagogy" in order to identify the affective modes of right-wing populism.

CHAPTER 2

Trump Pedagogy and the Affective Modes of Right-Wing Populism

I play to people's fantasies. People may not always think big themselves, but they can still get very excited by those who do. That's why a little hyperbole never hurts. People want to believe that something is the biggest and the greatest and the most spectacular. I call it truthful hyperbole. It's an innocent form of exaggeration – and a very effective form of promotion.

(Trump, 1987, p. 58)

We have 25,000, 30,000 people, they come [to Trump campaign events] with tremendous love and passion for the country [...] When they see what's going on in this country, they have anger that's unbelievable. They have anger. They love this country. They don't like seeing bad trade deals, higher taxes, they don't like seeing a loss of their jobs where our jobs have just been devastated. And I know – I mean, I see it. There is some anger. There's also great love for the country. It's a beautiful thing in many respects.

(Trump, 2016 in CNN)

Important questions may be raised about affectivity and right-wing populism in the case of Trump: In what specific ways is Trump's political mobilization of people carried out by an interplay of "emotional appeal" (Wahl-Jorgensen, 2018) and "affective dispositions" (Mühlhoff, 2019)? What are the affective underpinnings and implications of the so-called "Trump Pedagogy" (Ringrose, 2018) in the realm of democratic education, namely, how Trump "populariz[es], spread[s] and normalize[s] speech that is supposed to be hard hitting, honest and reflective of the 'common interest', but is actually hate-speech and a rejection of global equity and human rights" (p. 648)? To phrase the latter question more generally, are there any prospects to further democratic education by engaging in a critical interrogation of the affective modes of right-wing populism, including the possibility that populism itself may serve as a particular mode through "which teachers and students can articulate themselves in a democratic public" (Mårdh & Tryggvason, 2017, p. 603)? In an attempt to respond to these questions, the purpose of this chapter is to argue that a critical inquiry into the phenomenon of populism can provide opportunities for enriching democratic education (Petrie, McGregor & Crowther, 2019), especially when it opens up to a theoretical understanding of the affective modes of right-wing populism and its implications for democratic life.

To develop this argument, I first discuss in more details the phenomenon of populism and its core attributes, especially in relation to discussions in the literature whether populism is a movement, an ideology or a rhetoric. The next section will focus on the affective roots of right-wing populism, highlighting how modes of affecting and being affected are involved with discourses and power structures of right-wing populism. In the third section, I will utilize the concept of "affective ideology" (Peters & Protevi, 2017) to bring together the "affective investments" (Laclau, 2005a) that hold a group together with the affective attachment social agents experience toward a certain ideological vision; to illustrate this idea, I will analyze the case of Trump Pedagogy, building on some of the arguments presented in Chapter 1. In the last part of the chapter, I will conclude by outlining some of the pedagogical implications of this analysis for educators working in the context of democratic education, and I will argue for the importance of creating spaces and opportunities of affective counterpolitics in classrooms/schools/communities, while taking into consideration the possible risks emerging from this attempt.

What Is Populism?

The literature on populism is enormous, covering many disciplines and fields of study (e.g., De la Torre & Arnson, 2013; Laclau, 2005a; Mudde & Kaltwasser, 2012; Müller, 2016; Panizza, 2005). Not surprisingly, then, there is hardly any consensus in defining the concept of populism, as Freeden (2017) points out. If there is any consensus at all, it is that "populism is a slippery concept to define, attracting a range of cultural and geopolitical connotations that overlap only with difficulty" (Freeden, 2017, p. 2). In this sense, suggests Freeden, there are populisms, in the plural, just like there are liberalisms and socialisms. One of the major tensions in ongoing debates in the literature is whether populism is an ideology, a movement or merely a specific rhetorical logic that sees politics in terms of an opposition between "the people" and a powerful oppressive regime (Müller, 2016). Those advocating that populism is an ideology, for example, argue that there is an important distinction between left-wing populism – in which a political and economic establishment is deemed responsible for austerity politics – and right-wing populism – in which political and cultural elites are accused of favoring ethnic, religious and sexual out-groups at the expense of the neglected in-group (Salmela & von Scheve, 2018). Needless to say, the tension whether populism is an ideology, a movement or merely a specific rhetorical logic cannot be settled here, so I begin by discussing some core attributes of populism that appear to be shared by all three variants of populism.

There are, in my view, three core attributes of populism (Freeden, 2017; Müller, 2016):

(1) An understanding of society as a unitary body that is divided into two fractions – the people and the elites (e.g., political, economic, cultural). In the populist rhetoric, elites (who occupy positions of power) are considered to be corrupt, whereas ordinary, everyday people (who lack any significant power) are portrayed as pure.

(2) Populist politicians and parties claim to be the exclusive representatives of the people (Müller, 2016); this implies that populists have "the monopolistic ownership" (Freeden, 2017, p. 4) of representing the people in their name.

(3) The fight against the corrupted elites is considered by populists as a moral battle, namely, a battle between the "good" (true citizens, ordinary people) and the "evil" (elites). The construction of "we," the "people," or the "nation" is always articulated in comparison to "them" and "others," and hence antagonism is a fundamental element of populist logic (Panizza, 2005).

Looking at recent developments in Europe, the United States and the West more generally, for example, these features of populist trends seem to correspond with right-wing populism manifested through nationalism and nativism, racism, xenophobia and homophobia (Kinnvall, 2018). Nativism, for example, is "an ideology which holds that states should be inhabited exclusively by members of the native group (the 'nation') and the non-native elements (persons and ideas) are fundamentally threatening to the nation-state" (Mudde, 2007, p. 22). Nativism, according to Kinnvall (2018, p. 527), might also involve an economic element of welfare chauvinism, namely, the tendency to distinguish between the "pure people" who have their legitimate birthright to the nation-state's welfare system and those undeserving others, such as ethnic/racial/religious minorities who do not belong to the nation. Right-wing populist politicians and parties in several European countries in recent years (e.g., UK, Poland, France, Sweden, Denmark) have divided the society into the "sold out" and "unpatriotic" individuals and groups who are in favor of multiculturalism and the "pure people" who fight to get their country back from sympathizers of minorities (Mudde & Kaltwasser, 2017).

Laclau (2005a) is considered one of the leading theorists of populism; therefore, I draw here on some of his concepts to further clarify populist reason.[1] To begin with, Laclau makes an important distinction between the "logic of difference" and the "logic of equivalence." The logic of difference implies that social agents have different demands that are claimed through normal social and political processes (e.g., negotiation; construction of alliances and coalitions, etc.). Populism arises, argues Laclau, when a large number of these demands remain unfulfilled for a long time, and a political leader or movement emerges in the political scene and manages to portray all of these demands as equivalent and undifferentiated – this is the logic of equivalence. A relevant concept in Laclau's analysis of populist reason is the notion of "empty signifier," namely, the idea that the unity of the people is constructed around symbols that lack particular meaning (e.g., "equality" or "freedom"); as such, populism provides new meanings to empty signifiers, thus opening the way for populist leaders to invoke the logic of equivalence.

A fundamental question to ask, then, at this point is how one can distinguish a populist movement from one which is not. Laclau (2005b) argues that this is the wrong question to ask: "To ask oneself if a movement *is* or is *not* populist is, actually, to start with the wrong question. The question we should, instead, ask ourselves, is the following: *to what extent* is a movement populist?" (p. 45). In other words, Laclau implies that all movements as political practices entail some degree of populism, hence the question is not *whether* but *how* populism is manifested, even in political acts that might not look populist at first glance. Hence, Laclau's important contribution here is that he theorizes populism as an ontological category (Kinnvall, 2018) – that is, "its meaning is not to be found in any

---

[1] Needless to say, there have been several critiques of Laclau's theory of populism. It is beyond the scope of this chapter to discuss extensively these critiques; however, it is important to acknowledge some of those – e.g., that Laclau's account is based on an understanding of populism as rhetoric; that his account implicitly endorses an authoritarian view of power; that he portrays people as a homogeneous, passive and unreflective group; or that he ignores the complexity of horizontal antagonism among "the common people" (e.g., see Müller, 2016). However, as I discuss here, the value of Laclau's account is undeniable in terms of providing a number of concepts that help us theorize the form and content of populism as a deeply political phenomenon and act.

political or ideological content entering into the description of the practices of any particular group, but in a particular *mode of articulation* of whatever social, political or ideological contents" (Laclau, 2005b, p. 34). It is in this sense that Mårdh and Tryggvason (2017) correctly ask "to what degree is any democratic education enacted through the elements of populism?" (p. 607). No political act – and clearly, democratic education is one such example – can be exempt from the possibility of adhering to a populist logic, which must be considered as not only a glooming prospective but also a promising one, according to Mårdh and Tryggvason, because it encourages educators to reflect on "the risks and possibilities involved in conceptualizing education from the point of view of a populist logic" (p. 603). (I come back to this issue later in the chapter.)

Laclau's (2005a) theory of populism urges us to be attentive to the modes of articulation of social demands, particularly how social agents articulate social divisions *affectively* (Mårdh & Tryggvason, 2017). Whether understood as a discourse, a movement or an ideology, then, "populism would be unintelligible without the affective component" (Laclau, 2005a, p. 111). As Laclau writes, "Affect (that it, enjoyment) is the very essence of investment, while its contingent character accounts for the "radical" component of the formula. [...] there is no populism without affective investment in a partial object" (2005a, pp. 115–116). It is from this perspective that it seems imperative to explore how modes of affecting and being affected are entangled with discourses of right-wing populism (Anderson in Kemmer et al., 2019). In such discourses, for example (of hope and fear), there is a fundamental affective dimension that is constitutive to right-wing politics and the formation of antagonistic social categories (e.g., "Us" versus "Them"). The next part of the chapter focuses on the affective roots of right-wing populism, beginning to explore more specifically the affective dimension of Trump's populism.

Affect and Right-Wing Populism

The role of affect in politics and political movements has been studied for a long time (Clarke, Hoggett & Thompson, 2006; Demertzis, 2013; Goodwin, Jasper & Polletta, 2001; Hoggett & Thompson, 2012), but new theoretical and empirical research in the recent affective turn (Clough, 2007; Gregg & Seigworth, 2010; see also, Introduction) brings new perspectives in theorizing affect and right-wing populism. As Mühlhoff argues, "*Every* political movement and every critical project is driven by affects, so the point is not *whether* or not affect is relevant, but *how* it is involved" (in Kemmer et al., 2019, p. 26). Contemporary work in this area seeks an understanding of the affective dimensions of articulating right-wing populism and how those are entangled with right-wing discourses and power structures.[2]

Salmela and von Scheve (2017) have identified two mechanisms that drive emotional support for the populist right. The first mechanism is linked to feelings of resentment or *ressentiment*:

> [This mechanism] explains how negative emotions – fear and insecurity, in particular – transform, through repressed shame, into anger, resentment and hatred towards perceived "enemies" [...] such as refugees, immigrants, the long-term unemployed, political and cultural elites, and the "mainstream" media. (p. 567)

The close intertwining of anger, resentment and hatred with repressed shame (see Chapter 1) in right-wing populism, argue Salmela and von Scheve, "is characteristic for the emotional dynamics underlying support for populist parties in contemporary capitalist societies" (2017, p. 573). The second mechanism "relates to the emotional distancing from social identities that inflict shame and other negative emotions" in favor of social identities that are "perceived to be more stable and to some extent more exclusive, such as nationality, ethnicity, religion, language, and traditional gender roles" (p. 567).

"Angry populism" (Wahl-Jorgensen, 2018), as embodied by Trump, is a classic example showing how these two mechanisms drive emotional support for right-wing populism through the deliberate expression of anger. As such, explains Wahl-Jorgensen, "Trump's appeal is organized around a particular negative affective constellation representing coalescence of long-standing practices and trends" (p. 767). Similar to Salmela and von Scheve's (2017) analysis, this argument emphasizes the idea that Trump's supporters express anger emerging from their perceived long-standing exclusion from privilege, whether economic, social or cultural. To

---

[2] A fundamental assumption in which I ground my analysis here is Anderson's claim (in Kemmer et al., 2019) that we should not grant emotion or affect any special explanatory power or a special status by putting aside other modes of inquiry; rather, we need to explore how affective modes of inquiry "discern the geo-historically specific apparatuses, encounters, and conditions through which affective life becomes organized" (Kemmer et al., 2019, p. 26). In other words, one could engage in an analysis of right-wing populism from a variety of theoretical perspectives, none of which should be privileged; at the same time, it is important to acknowledge though that the affective turn creates openings for looking at the entanglements of power, politics and affectivity in educational theory and practice in ways that would have not been available in the absence of the affective turn.

this end, Hochschild's (2016) ethnographic work *Strangers in Their Own Land* – in which she follows supporters of the right-wing populist "Tea Party" – provides a compelling analysis of Trump's angry populism. As she writes:

> Trump is an "emotions candidate." More than any other presidential candidate in decades, Trump focuses on eliciting and praising emotional responses from his fans rather than on detailed policy prescriptions. His speeches – evoking dominance, bravado, clarity, national pride, and personal uplift – inspire an emotional transformation. [...] Not only does Trump evoke emotion, he makes an object of it, presenting it back to his fans as a sign of collective success. (Hochschild, 2016, p. 225)

Similar to Salmela and von Scheve's (2017) argument, Hochschild finds that ressentiment is one of the fundamental emotions emerging from Trump's supporters. They feel resentment for "liberal elites" who accuse them for not sympathizing enough with minorities, refugees and immigrants. As Pelinka (2013) explains, "right-wing populism sees multiculturalism as a recipe to denationalize one's (own) nation, to deconstruct one's own people" (p. 8). Hence, when Trump creates affective spaces for his supporters to express feelings of anger and resentment, he "plays to people's fantasies" and offers them "a bellicose fantasy of return and renewal" (Anderson, 2017b, p. 2).

The emergence of an "age of anger" (Mishra, 2017) suggests a fundamental change in the ways emotions are performed in public and political processes in recent years (Wahl-Jorgensen, 2018). Mobilizing support through the social media (e.g., Twitter) and his public performances in campaign events, Trump establishes particular "affective styles" in politics that give people permission to not only express but also enjoy their anger and resentment against "others" (Anderson, 2017b). Anderson describes an affective style as "an orientation to self and world that will repeat across, link, and blur the speech and bodily acts, images, stories, and pseudo-events that make up a campaign" (2017b, p. 4). Trump's affective style of anger, for example, highlights the affective connection between his expression of anger and his supporters' "affirmation of the validity and truth of those grievances and resentments" (2017b, p. 7). Similar to Ahmed's (2003) "point that right-wing nationalisms frequently claim to be acting out of love," Anderson (2017b) suggests that Trump valorizes and legitimizes anger, "as born from and standing in for love" (p. 7). As shown in the second epigraph of this chapter, Trump's renaming of hate as love is based on an "Us-versus-Them" binary, and it is presented as a form of redemption and dignity.

Importantly, notes Kinnvall (2018), at the heart of (right-wing) populist rhetoric is the promise of relief and redemption from fears and insecurities: "These ontological insecurities can be countered and salvaged through visions of a common future, implying a need to understand the discourses and narratives involved in populist rhetoric and their emotional reception" (p. 529). It is important to recognize, then, how a populist leader's affective styles create openings to his supporters for a better future. Circulating emotions of right-wing populism, argue Peters and Protevi (2017), aim at creating these affective spaces as forms of empowerment that will bring happiness and self-confidence back to a populist leader's supporters. Power works, then, *not* through "the manipulation or modulation of fear, anxiety, and other so-called 'negative' emotions"; rather, right-wing populism resonates with some people's affective lives (Anderson in Kemmer et al., 2019, p. 28). As Anderson points out once again about Trump's affective styles,

> It's the fun of feeling liberated as finally someone other than you is publically saying everything you were told you couldn't or shouldn't. The fun of not conforming to norms of action and thought that you never fully believed in or felt like you consented to. Often, it's the fun inseparable from violence. It's the fun of being on the side of the bully. Perhaps Trump gives people permission to have fun again in a mood and situation of too serious crisis ordinariness, permission to enjoy their resentment and grievances, permission to enjoy hate. (2017b, p. 14)

Theoretically speaking, the enjoyment of resentment and anger is connected to Massumi's (2002a) notion of power as primarily affective. As Massumi asserts, "Power is no longer fundamentally normative, like it was in its disciplinary forms – it is affective" (p. 232), hence "the crucial political question is whether there are ways of practicing politics that takes stock of the affective way power operates" (p. 235). For example, while disciplinary power works micropolitically to increase a body's docility (Anderson, 2017a), affective power works by opening possibilities for new relations and potentials, e.g., for a better life with less fear and anxiety (Peters & Protevi, 2017). Importantly, then, affective politics work not only through negative emotions (e.g., anger and resentment) but also through positive ones such as the promise of redemption, hope and love for one's country. This "positive framing" of affect explains something very important about the appeal of right-wing populism to a broad swathe of citizens who do not perceive themselves to be hate-filled and resentful.

Consequently, to comprehend how power works through right-wing populism, it is important to consider how it works affectively, condoning particular affects and emotions (both positive and negative) that build a new imagination of a contemporary strong nationality without those (e.g., immigrants, minorities, unemployed) who are considered the "origin of danger" (Ahmed, 2014, p. 4). Hence, it is important that affects and emotions related to right-wing populism are *not* reduced to negative emotions and primarily hatred – the emotion that is conveniently and most frequently identified with right-wing populism and nationalism (Baldacchino, 2011; Krauel, 2014). In doing so, I am extending the work of those who have interrogated the charge that right-wing populism and nationalism are largely constituted by negative emotions (e.g., hatred) and that these movements invariably cater to our dark side, by bringing to the fore the affective power of positive emotions that fuel these movements (e.g., see Damluji, 2019).[3] To understand further the pedagogical implications of the affective power of right-wing populism, it is necessary to look at more closely how "Trump Pedagogy" functions affectively.

The Affective Ideology of "Trump Pedagogy"

"Trump Pedagogy" (Ringrose, 2018) is understood here as Trump's pedagogical dynamic that legitimates affects and emotions such as anger and resentment but also hope and redemption for his supporters. Not only does Trump Pedagogy legitimize "a white rage that ignores, minimizes and trivializes" oppression, but it also encourages hate speech against all "others" (women, minorities and immigrants) or those who sympathize with them (liberals) (Martin, Nickels & Sharp-Grier, 2017, p. xxiii). As Giroux (2019) points out:

> Trump has managed to shape the cultural landscape in ways that have unleashed what I term a poisonous public pedagogy of sensationalism, easy consumption, bigotry, fear, and distraction. All the while, Trump fills the Twitter world with an ongoing bombast of emotional drivel. [...] Trump's pedagogy is largely fashioned through his use of the social media, his support by conservative diffusion outlets [...], all of which function as thinly veiled propaganda and disimagination machines. Trump's unrelenting pedagogical shocks to the body politics and civic culture have done more than lower the bar of civic discourse and the rules of governing, they have normalized the unimaginable. (pp. 9, 10)

---

[3] As Damluji (2019) argues, learning the lessons of nation-building in the past (e.g., national identities are important for people and are not going to be given up easily; those who value national identities are not all of them racists or nationalists) can actually help us create globalist identities that are more inclusive than they have been so far.

This is not to say that Trump's populism and pedagogy "is only about finding culprits and constructing others onto which rage and fear can be projected" (Kinnvall, 2018, p. 533). As discussed in the previous section, Trump and his supporters "are united in more general antiestablishment sentiments" (Kinnvall, 2018, p. 533) and fantasies of renewal, hope and redemption (i.e., positive emotions). It would be a mistake for scholars to fall into the "residual tendency" (Anderson in Kemmer et al., 2019, p. 28) and presume that Trump's supporters are merely manipulated through "negative" emotions. Trump's tactics catalyze interpersonal and transformative emotional processes of hope and redemption (Peters & Protevi, 2017). To deconstruct Trump Pedagogy, then, means going back to the question set from the beginning of this chapter: What kinds of affective modalities does Trump Pedagogy take/enable and what are the implications for democratic education?

Following my earlier analysis on the affective roots of populism, two features of Trump Pedagogy become especially important to highlight: (1) the ideological and moral division of "Us-the-Good-People" and "Them-the-Evil"; and (2) the affective investments of Trump's populism in particular ideas that take the shape of politically orchestrated forms of nostalgia for a "great" and glorious ethnic past (Kinnvall, 2018). If we want to understand Trump Pedagogy, our focus should be on how these two features are manifested into new modes of racist, sexist, misogynist and otherwise violent political movements. Trump's sexism and racism, for example, "pedagogize" – to use Bernstein's (2001) famous term – his supporters into a certain type of social relations that involve attempts to modify the expected affective frameworks through which social agents engage in politics (Zembylas, 2018c). Trump's sexism and racism are "successful" pedagogical tactics, because they resonate with his supporters' affective dispositions (Mühlhoff in Kemmer et al., 2019). In this sense, Trump Pedagogy shows how social control operates not by coerced social reproduction but rather through specific affective relations with his supporters.

I want to further discuss at this point the concept of "affective ideology" (Peters & Protevi, 2017; see also Chapter 1) because it brings together the affective investments that hold a group together with the affective attachment social agents experience toward a certain ideological vision of the ideal society, such as for example, Trump's vision of "Make America Great Again." These affective investments and attachments should be seen as attunement between Trump and his supporters (Anderson, 2017b), because his supporters desire what he promises to deliver: an America that is great again, a redemption of the "crippled" nation (Trump, 2015). It is important, then, to focus on how affective ideology works in the case of Trump Pedagogy, or, more explicitly, to examine the affective force of Trump Pedagogy and its implications for democratic education. To put this differently, I am interested in understanding "the grip" (Glynos, 2001) of Trump Pedagogy, that is, "how or why social agents are made (or 'seduced') to join and adhere" (Kølvraa & Ifversen, 2017, p. 182) to Trump's populist rhetoric and whether, eventually, there is a way to challenge this affective ideology.

First, affective ideology has two dimensions, according to Peters and Protevi (2017): the psychological and the functional. Psychologically, "ideology is the process that produces a rough coincidence of body political affective-cognitive patterns of an entire society. What is shared is an orientation to the world such that objects appear with characteristic affective tones" (p. 5). Functionally, "the sharing of affective-cognitive orientation we call 'ideology' contributes to the stability and reproducibility of social patterns of thought and practice on daily, lifespan, and generational scales" (p. 5). To understand Trump Pedagogy as an affective ideology, then, it is important to examine how it is connected to the realm of the body and its enjoyment of certain modes of transgression. Trump Pedagogy is an embodied pedagogy that circulates specific affects and "affective relations of bemused or indignant fascination" (Anderson in Kemmer et al., 2019, p. 28). Hence, it might be argued that the affects produced through/in Trump Pedagogy "are part of the reproduction of the practice of white supremacy"; they are

> not simply accounted for by instilling in children beliefs with the propositional content of racial superiority and inferiority and binding them to those identities by love for friends and parents who participate in that practice. The reproduction of the practice of white supremacy is also constituted by an affective structure of white pride and vengeance motivated by white vulnerability, and hatred, fear, and contempt for blacks that is encoded along with the representational content of the scenes of humiliation, torture, and death that constitute the daily practices of the coercive reproduction side of plantation white supremacy. (Peters & Protevi, 2017, p. 6)

In other words, if we understand Trump Pedagogy as merely a set of racist/sexist/xenophobic ideas, then we risk missing the reproduction of affective investments that allow Trump's supporters to appear even "stronger" by way of enacting these ideas in their everyday life as white supremacy practices (Mühlhoff in Kemmer et al., 2019, p. 27). The difference, then, between social reproduction of white supremacy and the idea of white supremacy as affective ideology is that the latter shows precisely how affective politics plays a fundamental role in the former idea, namely, the social reproduction of white supremacy.

From this reading of Trump Pedagogy, there are some important implications for how democratic education may respond. To begin with, an important implication is for scholarship in democratic education to explore the different modes of articulation of populism within specific circumstances. This analytical and conceptual exploration "is the essential precursor for addressing what educators can do, in these circumstances, to enhance democracy" (Petrie et al., 2019, p. 490). By this, Petrie et al. "mean the capacity of people to engage in political institutions and procedures as well as to participate actively and critically in political thinking, analysis and debate" (2019, p. 490). For example, Mårdh and Tryggvason (2017) suggest that "the possibility of posing and answering the questions 'who are we?' and 'who are we not?' can be seen as constitutive for both the definition of the people and for the people's definition of itself as a democratic public" (p. 610). Educators wishing, then, to intervene and interrogate populism "ought to be equipped with a critical understanding of populism – its functions and features – in order to practice skillfully, reflexively and creatively" (Petrie et al., 2019, p. 3).

More importantly, though, as I have argued throughout this chapter, educators and students need to pay close attention to how Trump uses affective styles as rhetorical devices to invoke the logic of equivalence in building a new imagination for America. Identifying and engaging critically with the ways in which right-wing populism in America and elsewhere works affectively to construct certain portrayals of "Us" and "Them" will make an important contribution to understanding how racism, sexism and xenophobia are enacted and reproduced through affective ideologies such as Trump Pedagogy (see also Zembylas, 2019; Chapter 11). For example, educators and students need a much better understanding of "how media is constitutive and generative of modes of affectivity and political speech, of subjectivity and intersubjectivity" (Mühlhoff in Kemmer et al., 2019, p. 26). The challenge for educators is to create spaces and opportunities for critical dialogue with students that acknowledge how and why different people articulate themselves affectively in certain ways and what can be done to respond productively to those affective investments. Democratic education cannot stop populism, but it can work with disaffected people who have been alienated from traditional politics to enact democracy in renewed ways (Petrie et al., 2019).

A Pedagogy of Affective Counter-politics in Democratic Education

If democratic education cannot stop populism, then it can make a contribution at the micropolitical level to cultivate "hopeful criticism" (Anderson in Kemmer et al., 2019) – namely, dispositions and practices that disclose potentialities for sustained action against the affective infrastructures of right-wing populism. In the last part of this chapter, I consider how a renewed form of democratic education may contribute toward the cultivation of hopeful criticism, especially by creating spaces for educators and their students to enact affective counterpolitics.

First of all, it is crucial to acknowledge that the micropolitical level at which a pedagogy of affective counterpolitics works is extremely significant and, therefore, its impact should not be underestimated. Importantly, the micropolitical is not synonymous with the resistant or the private level (Anderson, 2017a). A micropolitical dimension, explains Anderson, is a constitutive dimension of all political activity and allows us to notice the affective tones that animate political action in everyday life. For example, Anderson reminds us of Deleuze and Guattari's (1987) analysis of the micropolitics of Nazi fascism, pointing out that the fine segmentations in everyday life are as harmful as rigid segments (for more details, see Chapter 4). Similarly, Massumi (2015a) shows how the militarized "ontopower" of the United States involves "a colonization of the micro-political" (p. 65), that is, the militarization of everyday life such as the proliferation of guns and violence, the invisible surveillance and so on (see Scheper-Hughes, 2014). Power, then, works affectively and micropolitically to organize intensive forces in order to increase a body's pleasure and/or docility (Anderson in Kemmer et al., 2019).

Therefore, a point of departure for democratic education is to understand how affective dynamics work micropolitically to organize people's responses to Trump's racism, sexism and xenophobia and under which circumstances there can be an antidote to the affective ideology of right-wing populism and its practices in everyday life. A key pedagogical question becomes, then, how and with what resources can educators and their students first of all *identify* the forms of damage and harm done by Trump Pedagogy micropolitically? For example, a counterpolitical response and resource, Anderson suggests, could take the forms of draining the eventfulness from Trump's social media interventions every once a while:

> This would be a counterpublic that responded with indifference, with a shrug, rather than in a manner that amplified attention and fascination. It

would be a counterpublic that didn't laugh at jokes about Trump on late-night comedy shows, who didn't retweet amusing Trump-related memes or GIFs. (in Kemmer et al., 2019, p. 36)

Similarly, in the context of democratic education, a concrete pedagogical action as a consequence of exploring the forms of harm done by Trump Pedagogy is for educators and students not simply to concede or be amused by jokes about Trump but to move a step further and seek to open up a critical space for examining the negative and positive affects and emotions of those who feel attachment to Trump's politics, e.g., communities affected by economic decline or that feel isolation for various reasons. The pedagogical goal, then, is to reflexively examine *how* peoples' affective attachments to Trump's politics are rooted in *both* feelings of anger and resentment (negative emotions) *and* the promise of redemption and hope (positive emotions).

Hence, if there is one lesson to learn from interrogating right-wing populism and its implications in the context of democratic education, it is that dreams and fantasies for an ideal society, no matter where they come from, are intertwined with forms of harm and damage in ways that create unexpected openings for critical work on affect. One such opening of immense political value is how educators and students may identify the ways right-wing populism remains "cruel" in Berlant's (2011) sense of "cruel optimism." Cruel optimism exists "when something you desire is actually an obstacle to your flourishing" (p. 1), writes Berlant. Affective attachments to what is desired offering promise for satisfaction can be persons, objects, norms and ideals. Why, she asks, do people stay attached to such fantasies "when the evidence of their instability, fragility and dear cost abounds?" (p. 3). The reason, Berlant explains, is because "the loss of what's not working is more unbearable than the having of it" (p. 27). The optimistic affective attachment of supporters to a populist leader involves an inclination to return to a fantasy that will never fulfill the transformation they desire. It is very unlikely or rather impossible, for example, that Trump's affective politics of fear and hatred "will satisfy the desires and hopes of all of his supporters" (Peters & Protevi, 2017, p. 14). This is why Trump Pedagogy will remain "cruel," because it will not solve the different and complex problems of Trump's supporters. "This cruelty of right-wing populism," point out Peters and Protevi, could in fact "be the starting point in the struggle against it" (2017, p. 15). This line of thinking, i.e., the exploration of Trump Pedagogy as a form of cruel optimism, offers an insightful, albeit critical, invitation to look closely at the ways in which the affective attachments of right-wing populists work to the detriment of those swept up in this movement.

Learning in democratic education how to look closely at the ways in which right-wing populism works affectively does something more, though, than just expanding educators and students' understanding of how power works affectively through cruel optimism. To use Anderson's (2017a) words, I would argue that this effort invites educators and students "to learn how to act in the midst of ongoing, unforeclosed situations and experiment with ways of discerning and tending to the 'otherwise'" (p. 594). "Negative" critique of right-wing populism, its affective ideology and its consequences are obviously necessary in democratic education but not sufficient for developing a productive counterpolitics. An "affirmative critique" (Braidotti, 2013) is also needed to highlight "positive" and hopeful stories of "alternative" belongings that embody in practice the hope for other futures. An affirmative critique is the critique that focuses on the search for an alternative to a negative reality and requires a capacity to reimagine reality and open new potentials (Rebughini, 2018). As Rebughini clarifies further, "While the emphasis on negation seeks to establish why critique could lead to an emancipatory reality, the emphasis on affirmation endeavors to demonstrate how the complexity and unpredictability of reality engages imagination to offer new solutions to common needs" (p. 5). As Staunæs (2016) also explains,

> An affirmative critique reflects an ambition of transcending the idea of analysis as reflections of reality and instead analyzing tendencies with the purpose of reconfiguring the world. However, the direction for change or not-change is not pre-ordained. An affirmative critique unfolds like a curious form of critique, defending itself from moralism. That means scientifically reconfiguring what we think we know with certainty by pointing out what could be different, while simultaneously consulting common concerns and hopes for what the future may bring whom. (pp. 66–67)

An example of a more concrete pedagogical action for countering the cruel optimism of Trump Pedagogy through the lens of affirmative critique could be to have students identify positive and hopeful narratives such as "love for the world," which "is not an acceptance of how things are, but an affirmation of the value of what we do in the present and thus of things that we value as worth passing on" (Hodgson, Vlieghe & Zamojski, 2017, p. 18). Needless to say, advocating for a pedagogy of love, compassion or solidarity is not a new idea in educational philosophy and theory (e.g., see Goldstein, 2009; Loreman, 2011; Zembylas, 2017a). However, what is new here is that an analysis of the ways in which cruel optimism circulates in the various affective modes of Trump Pedagogy will not be enough. The ethical and political framing of Trump Pedagogy – a form of "poisonous pedagogy" (Goldstein, 2009; Miller, 1983) – will not simply go away by negative critique (for a more in-depth discussion of affirmative critique, see Chapter 5). A different ethical and political framing of pedagogy of affective counterpolitics will be needed, one that involves a reorientation of knowledge practices so that educators and students explore what it would take and how to invent and circulate new modes of relation and belonging – that are more inclusive and hopeful – in replacement of the affective modes of Trump Pedagogy.

Finally, it is important to acknowledge that a pedagogy of affective counterpolitics in democratic education entails several risks. First, there is the risk of how to "translate" the conceptual analysis done here into a set of dispositions and practices that move and inspire educators and students, while recognizing that all education inevitably involves some sort of work on affect as a way of understanding people's affective investments in the world (Zembylas, 2018d). If democratic education cannot fully eliminate the possibility that it may engage itself in practices of populism by creating openings for affects and demands that are not directed toward a democratic life (Mårdh & Tryggvason, 2017), then it is important that educators are constantly vigilant about the possibility of employing moralistic and populist pedagogic tactics.

In addition to this risk, there is also the danger that educators may be accused of politicizing democratic education if they touch on issues of right-wing populism especially in connection with specific leaders (e.g., Trump in the United States). This is a serious challenge, given the dangers of polarization in and beyond the classroom, so educators need to be careful and strategic how they choose to address issues of right-wing populism. However, it should be clear that the goal of democratic education is *not* to criticize individual populist leaders as such (i.e., Trump) because this effort can easily backfire; rather, the focus should be on critically examining the affective dimension of right-wing populism and its complex and multifaceted consequences for democratic life. Hence, it is important *not* to establish an a priori form of critical practice/ethos of democratic life as a response to "negative" critiques of right-wing populism. The question of "translating" democratic ideas into practice is always *specific*, argues Anderson (in Kemmer et al., 2019), and therefore, it is important that it is not "reduced to a unidirectional process" (Kemmer et al., 2019, p. 38) between a set of conceptual ideas and a set of dispositions that "ought" to be developed by students. Rather, democratic education should create "sparks of hope" (Anderson, 2017a, p. 595) for a more inclusive and socially just future, when issues of right-wing populism are addressed (see also Chapter 6).

The question, of course, whether a pedagogy of affective counterpolitics in democratic education will indeed work with disaffected people in the way it is envisaged in this chapter remains open. As empirical research on right-wing populism and its affective implications demonstrates (e.g., Hochschild, 2016), the success of any public intervention is always dependent on the articulation of "alternative" belongings that are inclusive and offer hope to citizens for the future. This point is politically *and* pedagogically significant because the association of right-wing populism merely with negative emotions will obscure efforts to find new ways to include those who feel excluded or are labeled as nationalist. A solid analysis and understanding of the ways that various affective modes of Trump Pedagogy circulate offers points of intervention to further the spaces for democratic education without implying that a pedagogy of affective counterpolitics will always work in both disruptive and productive ways.

Conclusion

This chapter has argued that it is important for educators in democratic education to understand how the rise of right-wing populism in Europe, the United States and around the world can never be viewed apart from the affective investments of populist leaders and their supporters to essentialist ideological visions of nationalism, racism, sexism and xenophobia. The fear and anxiety that are invoked by right-wing populist movements are not simply psychological but also social and political practices embodying and enabling specific visions for an ideal society that is oppressive and exclusionary to "others" (Kinnvall, 2018). Democratic education can provide the space for educators and students to think critically and productively about people's affects, in order to identify the implications of different affective modes through which right-wing populism is articulated.

CHAPTER 3

The Affective Grounding of Post-truth Claims

> I found one thing missing in them [theories] all – a full understanding of emotion in politics. What, I wanted to know, did people *want to feel*, think they *should or shouldn't feel*, and what *do they feel* about a range of issues?
>
> (Hochschild, 2016, p. 15, original emphasis)

In Chapters 1 and 2, the focus has been on the example of Trump's right-wing populism as illustrative of a wider phenomenon and its affective and educational implications. This new populism is underpinned by the phenomenon of *post-truth* that is especially manifested in the use of social media as a mouthpiece for "fake news" and "alternative facts" (Mejia, Beckermann & Sullivan, 2018).[1] The term "post-truth," which became word of the year in 2016 by Oxford Dictionaries, is defined as "relating to or denoting circumstances in which objective facts are less influential in shaping public opinion than appeals to *emotion* and personal belief" (Oxford Dictionaries, n.d.a, added emphasis). A decade earlier, the word "truthiness," coined by American comedian Stephen Colbert, was selected by Merriam-Webster as its 2006 word of the year; truthiness is understood as that which is being *felt* to be true, even if it is not necessarily so. Both "truthiness" and "post-truth" have become trademarks of the contemporary zeitgeist in which individuals or groups have affective investments in a truth claim rather than to the proof of its truthfulness as such (Gilbert, 2016). Both terms exemplify the significance of emotion/affect in politics and the media, and particularly an understanding of truth as a

---

[1] "Post-truth" is not a new phenomenon. The reader is reminded that the term "post-truth" was first used by Steve Tesich in his article "A Government of Lies" (1992) in *The Nation*, where he discussed the Watergate syndrome, arguing that American society seemed to have consciously decided to move into a post-truth world at the expense of democracy. The current iteration of post-truth needs to be traced at those moments in which certain truth claims (which include "fake news" and "alternative facts") are used to effect political power.

function of the ways through which we constitute, experience and express public feelings.

The centrality of emotion/affect in truth claims is not new, of course. Feminist, affect and critical social theories have long exposed the affective grounding of truth-making claims in politics and the media (Ahmed, 2004; Leys, 2011; Seigworth & Gregg, 2010; see also, Chapter 2). What has changed recently that makes the present into a "post-truth" era, according to Boler and Davis (2018), is "that there has been a shift in *awareness* of emotion as a determining factor" (p. 75, original emphasis). In particular, argue Boler and Davis, this increased awareness of the determining role of emotion is visible in many examples in politics and media, including "the crisis of trust in news media and government; filter bubbles and information silos shaping public sentiment and partisan politics; and the embattled discourse surrounding 'fake news'" (Boler & Davis, 2018). The ultimate example of present post-truth politics is perhaps the polarized politics in the United States with the campaign election and the authoritarian presidency of Donald Trump, as shown in Chapters 1 and 2. Although politics has never been about a correspondence with truth, either in the United States or elsewhere in the world, as Ford (2019) points out, post-truth must not be understood as negation or as anti-truth, but rather as "an occasion to refuse the liberal nostalgia for the democratic and civic public sphere based on truthful exchange at the marketplace of ideas" (p. 2).

Within this conceptualization of post-truth, and the centrality of emotion/affect in politics and the media, there is no shortage of questions for those of us concerned with the ethical, political and pedagogical implications of contemporary post-truth claims that reiterate racism, sexism and xenophobia: What exactly, if anything, new do we learn from this entanglement of post-truth, emotion/affect and politics? How can we – educators, academics, citizens – become more critically responsive to post-truth politics, especially in using feelings as a guide for socially transformative praxis? What are the potential pedagogical risks of such efforts, particularly the failure to acknowledge that even "critical" pedagogical approaches are not immune from critique? (see also Chapter 4).

Such questions arise at a significant historical juncture at which post-truth "has achieved zeitgeist status" (Boler & Davis, 2018, p. 75), creating an urgency for rethinking and perhaps reframing what could possibly turn post-truth experiences into *productive* engagements – not only in the arena of politics and media (Boler & Davis, 2018; Mejia et al., 2018) but also in education (Horsthemke, 2017; Peters, 2017; Ringrose, 2018;

Samayoa & Nicolazzo, 2017). Although the role of emotion/affect and its implications has been acknowledged in education, particularly in relation to democratic education (Ruitenberg, 2009; Tryggvason, 2017, 2018; Zembylas, 2009, 2014, 2018c), little attention has been paid to theorizing the pedagogical risks as well as the transformative possibilities of engaging with affect to counter post-truth claims. The aim of this chapter, then, is to map a line of theorizing affect and its entanglement with post-truth and use this theorization to think about what it could mean for the role of educators – that is, what can be done in education to respond critically to the affective infrastructures of post-truth politics?

The chapter proceeds as follows. In the first section, I discuss the notions of truthiness and post-truth, highlighting their affective grounding; this section examines how affect circulates within political discourses constructing "falsehoods" that nevertheless *feel* true. The second section summarizes briefly some ideas on affect theory discussed in the Introduction focusing in particular on the entanglement of affect and governmentality; this section shows how the affective grounding of post-truth claims works to govern our subjectivities and thus it has important ethical, political and pedagogical implications. In the third section, I analyze how this nuanced understanding of affect, governmentality and post-truth offered by affect theory can be helpful in educational settings to respond critically to post-truth politics. The last section of the chapter addresses potential risks of pedagogical interventions that attempt to counter post-truth.

The Affective Grounding of Truthiness and Post-truth

American comedian Stephen Colbert coined the term "truthiness" in 2005 "to identify the emotional and selfish quality of perceived realities, which are derived from passionate preferences rather than scientific, logical or even journalistic certainties" (Gilbert, 2016, p. 96). The neologism "truthiness" highlights the idea of truth as "gut feelings" and "affectively legitimated fact(s)" (Massumi, 2010, pp. 54, 55), namely, that affective facts become the measures of truth. Truthiness is a feeling that shapes judgments that are based on the pervasive sense that all unwanted facts are questionable and unfounded (Gilbert, 2016). In other words, "we *know* to be true what we *want* or *feel* to be true," as Gilbert (2016, p. 98, original emphasis) poignantly says – a claim that raises many concerns about the ethical and political consequences of affectively legitimated facts.

Along similar lines, the notion of "post-truth" denotes the declining value of truth and its replacement with emotion and personal belief (d'Ancona, 2017). The "post-" prefix does not mean "after" – as the assumption that we once enjoyed an "era of truth" that has been replaced would be deeply problematic – but rather it marks a political shift toward a situation in which facts have become less important than emotional persuasion. Donald Trump's numerous claims throughout his political campaign and in his presidency constitute prime examples of "post-truth." Trump made multiple false claims concerning every possible issue; the newspaper *Washington Post* even created a website called Fact Checker (www.washingtonpost.com/news/fact-checker/) that was devoted to debunking Trump's false claims. For instance, Trump made false claims about global warming, saying that "the concept of global warming was created by and for the Chinese in order to make U.S. manufacturing non-competitive"; he claimed that "inner-city crime is reaching record levels," which is false; he falsely claimed that "it could be 30 million undocumented immigrants currently residing in the United States." Also, the main slogans of his campaign and presidency ("America First," "Make America Great Again") allude to the idea that American values have been neglected, and thereby he serves as a vehicle to revive them. What is important in his Twittered emotional appeals and irrational personal beliefs is not so much their meaning but rather the affective force they unleash (Krasmann, 2019). Trump appeals to feelings, because he wants to create identity and forge alliances among his supporters by drawing a clear divide between "Us" and "Them"; in this manner, he creates his own truth "of asserting voters and abiding members of the party who want to have a share in the feeling of strength and power" (Krasmann, 2019, p. 13).

Truth, of course, never stands alone as some "real" thing. Hence, there are different manifestations of post-truth, as post-truth might refer to a wide range of issues – from information asymmetries, to agnotological campaigns, to the "expert lies" of economies, to state denials of atrocities, etc. As Foucault (1997a, 2010, 2014) has pointed out all along, what "truth" is requires some truth regime to give it meaning. Therefore, it is important to remember that prior to our "post-truth" moment, there wasn't a time that "truth" was respected. Many are struggling with the advent of Trump, especially liberals who thought that all was much better prior to Trump. However, the "all" that was better only applies to a certain segment of the US population. Police were killing black men with impunity prior to Trump. Much of the racism, sexism, classism and xenophobia highlighted or expanded by Trump were already in place and systematically damaging people. The same is true of truth. What was true before post-truth was not truth but a truth regime that was highly prejudiced and biased itself, whether the "truth" regime of the liberal state or the "truth" regime of experts in economics or information systems. In all of these different manifestations of post-truth – that remind us that post-truths are not undifferentiated wholes – what is common, according to Keyes (2004), is that borders blur between truth and lies, honesty and dishonesty, fiction and nonfiction.

To return to my earlier point though, truth has never been free from affect and politics. What makes this the era of "post-truth politics," as is evident in the example of Donald Trump's politics and social media tactics, is the victory of emotion over reason – an era where facts/facticity are not as important or do not have the same political currency as the emotions beneath (Crilley, 2018). In this sense, emotions are considered to be above and beyond truth and rationality, and any factual counter-evidence is disregarded as unimportant. Hence, arguing with post-truth claims, points out Davis (2017, p. 40), is both futile and counterproductive for two reasons: First, if the communicator had wanted to convey more accurate information, they would have double-checked their claims, so engaging in correcting their claims is pointless; second, by arguing with those who make post-truth claims, one only draws more attention to their persona rather than to the falsehood of their claims.

The popular uptake of truthiness and post-truth reveals how the relationship between emotion and politics has become front and center over the last decade (Boler & Davis, 2018). However, the idea that emotions/affects are fundamental to political life, especially to the formation of political community and identity, is not new (Clarke, Hoggett & Thompson, 2006; Demertzis, 2013; Ferry & Kingston, 2008; Goodwin, Jasper & Polletta, 2001; Hoggett & Thompson, 2012; see also, Chapter 2). In particular, sociological theories have emphasized for some time now that emotions are social and cultural constructs that have significant links to the body, social norms and values, and habituated action. In other words, emotions are not understood as subjective inner states but rather as products of social and political relations. Therefore, there are two serious problems with recent claims in the post-truth era that emotions have replaced reason: First, there is a problematic distinction of rationality and emotion that is rejected by political and sociological theories; and, second, the suggestion that the age of emotion has replaced the age of reason is rather simplistic and ignores a historicized understanding of the resurgence of emotional narratives (d'Ancona, 2017). As Crilley explains,

> [T]here has been no sudden shift towards people making decisions and voting with their hearts rather than heads. Emotions have always been important in politics, economics and society. Feminists, critical theorists and others outside the mainstream of academic inquiry have argued so for decades. What is new is the recognition, both within the study of these respective fields and within wider public discourse, that emotions matter. (2018, p. 419)

Emotions matter, but not at the expense of rationality, as it is often assumed in wider public discourses. Seeing emotion and rationality as oppositional constructs a false dichotomy that ignores the ways in which emotions and rationality are intertwined (Hutchison, 2016).

Therefore, what seems to be important in understanding post-truth politics and its implications is not simply to realize that emotions/affects matter but rather to examine precisely *how* emotions/affects matter in constructing certain truths that reproduce social and political evils such as racism, sexism and xenophobia. It is important to pay attention to the specifics of the everyday and interrogate how individuals and groups make certain emotional truths a compelling explanatory framework that ignores and thus reinscribes hegemonic power relations and existing social inequalities. Such an analysis of post-truth is necessary in both politics and education, if we wish to avoid reproducing the myth that we once lived in an era of unproblematic truth or the reign of reason, and now there has been a shift to the age of emotion – a rather naive and quite unconvincing story (Crilley, 2018).

Therefore, it is not enough to analyze Donald Trump's Twittered emotional appeals, for example; it is equally important to examine the feelings of those in the receiving end of his post-truth tactics, as I emphasize in Chapters 1 and 2. In other words, we need to interrogate the social and political processes that produce post-truths and specifically how emotions are formed and reproduced in relation to post-truth issues. To this end, Hochschild's (2016) book *Strangers in Their Own Land* – which has been introduced in Chapters 1 and 2 – offers a compelling example of how and why (white) Tea Party Republican voters in the American South feel anger, bitterness and resentment for people of color, immigrants and refugees. Hochschild's book is relevant to post-truth issues because it shows how the polarization of emotionality takes place in US politics, providing opportunities to politicians such as Donald Trump to appeal emotionally to rural Whites who feel marginalized. As Hochschild explains, people form political decisions on the basis of what she calls a "deep story" that "tells us how things feel" (2016, p. 135). The deep story that Hochschild creates for the Tea Party supports is a parable of the white American Dream. It begins with the metaphor of a long line of people marching across a vast landscape. The Tea Party supporters (white, older, Christian, predominantly male, many lacking college degrees) are somewhat in the middle of the line; far behind them, there are people of color, immigrants and refugees. However, for various reasons (e.g., welfare, immigration, globalization, identity politics), the rules of waiting in line to fulfill the American Dream are not properly upheld; some people are cutting in, sometimes the line seems to be moving backward, and those overseeing the line (federal government) do not seem to care much (Davies, 2017). In the view of Tea Party supporters, liberals seem to feel more sympathy for every demographic group but theirs. "People think we're not good people if we don't feel sorry for blacks and immigrants and Syrian refugees," one Tea Party supporter tells Hochschild; "But I am a good person and I *don't* feel sorry for them" (2016, p. 227, original emphasis).

In another example, Hochschild (2016) describes the emotional reaction of a woman (Tea Partier) to news media and particularly a well-known CNN journalist who implied that everyone should feel sympathy for children who suffer in Africa and India. Hochschild writes how this woman felt that the journalist "was imposing liberal feeling rules about whom to feel sorry for"; however, Hochschild explains, "The woman didn't want to be told she should be sorry for, or responsible for, the fate of the child," and thus she felt that the journalist "was overstepping her role as commentator by suggesting how to feel" (2016, p. 128). Hochschild's turn to "the deep story" is a brilliant means of helping us understand what she calls the "empathy wall" that separates political groups preventing mutual understanding. Hochschild's analysis seems to be suggesting that moralizing approaches on behalf of liberals who wish to make it obligatory for everyone to feel sympathy for some groups may backfire and lead to "sympathy fatigue," because these approaches try to enforce their feeling rules on others. As Hochschild writes toward the end of her book: "Those on the far right [...] felt two things. First, they felt the [ir] deep story was true. Second, they felt that liberals were saying it was not true, and that they themselves *were not feeling the right feelings*" (2016, p. 227, original emphasis).

My references to Donald Trump's post-truth politics and Hochschild's account on rural Whites in Louisiana highlight the complexities emerging from the entanglement of post-truth, emotion/affect and politics, and suggests that it is necessary to delve deeper into the ways that social and political realities (e.g., racism, sexism and xenophobia) are articulated as feeling rules in people's everyday life (Boler & Davis, 2018). The explanation that post-truth claims are held because of people's ignorance, faulty reasoning and failure to take into account relevant evidence fails to take into consideration the power of affective truths (Mejia et al., 2018). Hence, the solutions that are frequently offered – e.g., to provide more media literacy, a course on critical thinking or better education in general – fail to consider that the issue is not a problem of individual irrationality and ignorance, that is, an epistemological problem (Shelby, 2003). Rather, the problem is deeply ethical and political and thus what needs to be explored is how affective truths are formulated and entangled with underlying socioeconomic structures that keep some social groups in the margins. The next section of the chapter draws on affect theory to delve into a deeper understanding of affective truths and how they are used for (self-) management purposes and discusses the implications for post-truth politics.

Affect and Governmentality in Post-truth Politics

As noted in the Introduction, there are at least two important advantages in paying attention to affect (Buser, 2014), especially in the context of efforts to explore and counter post-truth politics. First, affects are understood as transpersonal, which means that they are positioned within and between bodies and nonhuman actors, rather than within the frame of personal experiences. Politically, this is important because it focuses our attention on the ways in which affects/affectivity may be organized in an affective economy (Ahmed, 2004). In an affective economy, affects are circulated, exchanged, capitalized, cultivated, managed and (self-)governed. For example, this means interpreting Trump's frequent toxic tweets as part of a wider affective economy in post-truth politics that circulates certain affects (e.g., resentment, hatred) rather than as erratic responses of a confused administration.

Second, affects are forces and intensities that are continually made and remade, as they are the outcomes of encounters between bodies within specific places. As affects are not individual but performative, relational and political, it implies that there are always possibilities to interrogate and rupture affective economies. To challenge the material-affective infrastructure of post-truth regimes, for example, new affects need to be felt in actual bodies, organizations, mechanisms and social agents. Solidarity and empathy are not abstract feelings that are talked about in intellectual conversations; they must be felt in the context of affective economies that grow such affects. Affectivity, then, can be deployed politically to make us aware of how the management or governmentality of affect takes place (at the micro or macropolitical level), and how affects can be transformed (Thrift, 2008). As Bjerg and Staunæs (2011) argue, bringing together the notions of governmentality and affect can help us understand affective management "as a strategic endeavor to capture, generate and seize intensity in certain ways to allow the subject to create himself or herself" (p. 143). Thus by understanding the (self)-management of affects in post-truth politics, we are enabled to see how certain "truths" are reproduced or can be challenged; for this to happen, we need to interrupt the mechanisms and practices that governed subjectivities use to affect and be affected. The risk of this interruption, of course, as I highlight next in the chapter, is replacing one regime of truth with another that claims to be more "critical" and "emancipatory"; this is an important reminder of how subjectivities are always produced and embedded within certain regimes.

In particular, governmentality studies teach us how governmentality, defined as the art of governing ourselves and others (Foucault, 1997a, 2010), is entangled with affectivity and the management of the heart (Brøgger & Staunæs, 2016; Staunæs, 2011). In this sense, affective (self)-management is part of everyday life as a social technology of control, that is, a set of acts to act on ourselves and on others. As Staunæs explains, "Managing how you are affected and affect others becomes the instrument of managing the conditions of others. [...] You must learn to manage the affective intensity and quality strategically [...] correct your own emotional reactions [...]" (2011, pp. 241–242). Thus, expanding governmentality studies into studies of affectivity, suggest Juelskjær and Staunæs (2016a), enables us to realize – in politics, media, education – how governance and everyday (self)-management technologies "turn into strategic endeavors to capture, generate, and maintain affectivity" (p. 188), thus producing particular subjectivities (e.g., a "patriotic" citizen).

Importantly, what distinguishes affective (self)-management from other kinds of self-management (e.g., reflexivity) is its focus on the *intensity* of affectivity rather than the *identity* of subjects (Bjerg & Staunæs, 2011; Juelskjær & Staunæs, 2016a; Staunæs, 2011). This shift means that "management works strategically with affect and intensity, where the management of intensity regards the way in which something or someone is strategically attuned" (Juelskjær, Staunæs & Ratner, 2013, p. 1134).

Understanding affective management in particular contexts (e.g., schools, communities, political arenas, etc.) helps us reframe theorization of subjectivity as a process of entanglement with affectivity and thus urges us to rethink categories previously associated with identity. For example, by moving beyond identity categories as fixed and focusing upon the intensity of affectivity, it becomes possible to understand how affective technologies are used (e.g., by post-truth politicians as well as by others, including "critical" voices) to invoke particular effects and affects on individuals and social groups. This understanding helps us see how "good" and "bad" feelings are entangled with moral perceptions and obligations that form the affective infrastructure of post-truth politics. A fundamental question, then, is, how possible is it – especially for educators – to counter the affective infrastructures of post-truth without invoking moralization or indoctrination?

Countering Post-truth in Educational Settings

The lens of affect theory opens up possibilities to acknowledge the complex affective conditions, intensities and tensions involved in efforts to explore the ethical, political and affective consequences of post-truth. But the issue is not merely to recognize that post-truth is affective and induces specific feeling rules, affective practices and (self-)management techniques but rather *how* these rules, practices and techniques may be challenged and perhaps interrupted. Importantly, though, one needs to keep in mind that even such interventions are not free of the same critique as post-truth technologies – i.e., they also invoke particular effects and affects on people and groups and entail certain risks – therefore, constant vigilance is of the essence.

Admittedly, it is not easy for adults, let alone for children and teenagers, to distinguish between news and "fake news" or post-truth claims. To address this challenge, it has been suggested that media literacy and the cultivation of critical thinking are important pedagogical tools in schools and universities (Ball, 2017; d'Ancona, 2017). Emphasizing media literacy is certainly laudable and has its place in combating post-truth, but it is *also* important to understand that post-truth operates through powerful affective means that need to be *explicitly* interrogated. Unless there is recognition and critical engagement with the affective, political and ethical complexities of post-truth in all aspects of everyday life – e.g., the affective grounding of post-truth regimes; the different manifestations of post-truth in politics and media; the ethical implications of making us/them divides – it will be difficult to appreciate the full consequences of post-truth in politics and education. For example, it is important to understand that racism is not the symptom of post-truth; rather, post-truth is the symptom of racism (Mejia et al., 2018) – a form of racism for which truth claims are no longer an adequate resource. Hence, unless students and citizens learn to "see" in their everyday lives how and why racism, sexism and xenophobia operate through affective, political and ethical forces that induce divisions among different peoples (Zembylas, 2018d), the broader complexities of post-truth will not be adequately recognized and interrogated.

Cultivating critical thinking is another pedagogical tool that is suggested "as transformative and as a source of empowerment, a means of acquiring knowledge and habits of mind that enable one to speak truth to power" (Bowell, 2017, p. 583). As Bowell explains in further details,

> We need a critical thinking pedagogy that teaches not only the skills of good reasoning and critical analysis of others' reasoning, but that enculturates the values of which responsible enquiry is comprised, values such as open-mindedness [...] and epistemic humility [...]. We need a critical thinking pedagogy that teaches that the *ad hominem* attack is not a legitimate form of political discourse, but a rhetorical strategy designed to undermine our right to think critically and make up our minds on the basis of evidence. We need a critical thinking pedagogy that [...] leads away from and enables the awareness of Intellectual vices – gullibility, close mindedness, intellectual arrogance and wishful thinking, a critical thinking pedagogy that teaches us how to recognize rhetorical ploys and the affective responses they are intended to elicit from us. (p. 584)

Once again, however, it is important to move beyond critical thinking pedagogy and interrogate the affective force of (post)-truth claims, their complexities as well as their consequences. This means recognizing that the infrastructures of post-truth politics instill certain affective modalities; therefore, the question is how educators can challenge these affective infrastructures without assuming that such efforts are immune from critique.

Samayoa and Nicolazzo (2017) suggest what they are calling "an *affect of collectivity*, or communal feelings of solidarity through which we can create microclimates of love and support and, as a result, find the strength and space to persist, thrive, and live amidst the rubble of the current post-truth regime" (p. 991, original emphasis). In particular, they argue that our pedagogical interventions need to challenge the boundaries between "us" and "them" invoked by post-truth politics by thinking about opportunities for connection as the road map for resistance and emancipatory futures. These suggestions highlight the importance of cultivating the affect of collectivity (e.g., through school projects and other activities) as a means of instilling cracks to the affective-material infrastructures of post-truth politics.

There are, however, deeper affective complexities behind the rise of post-truth conditions that need to be critically exposed through pedagogic work, if the collective affects that are aimed to be cultivated among students are going to be "deep" rather than superficial and sentimental (Zembylas, 2016). For this reason, it is important to remember Thrift's (2008) emphasis that forming new collective affects and criticality involves a combination of institutional transformations and body trainings that redefine our affective practices and affective economies. Rather than claiming that cultivating empathy is an affective "solution" to complex structural, political and economic problems, our pedagogical approach would need to interrogate what collective affects such as empathy and solidarity might tell us about the affective nature and workings of contemporary post-truth politics or how the affective aftermaths of post-truth regimes shape both politico-economic and psycho-social relations. Our pedagogic work would need to emphasize action-oriented empathy and solidarity relationships that seriously engage the demands posed by countering post-truth claims without falling into the traps of naïve multiculturalism or liberal cosmopolitanism.

To promote action-oriented empathy and solidarity, there has to be a systematic investigation of the different ways in which feelings of empathy and solidarity are evoked and have differential implications for those who suffer (Zembylas, 2018b, 2018d). Empathy takes place, if students begin to understand the conditions (structural inequalities, poverty, globalization, etc.) that give rise to the suffering of different groups and create realistic opportunities for affective solidarity between themselves and others (see Hemmings, 2012). But mere "understanding" is not enough; students will become more susceptible to affective transformation when they *enact* empathetic action early on in their lives (Zembylas, 2013a). As they grow up, children can be offered varied opportunities to enact more complex manifestations of empathy that include specific actions to alleviate the suffering of people who experience the consequences of marginalization. At the same time, it is equally important to explore why showing empathy toward some people or groups is difficult and what would take to overcome the obstacles that create the "empathy wall."

I suggest, then, that we need pedagogical approaches that understand the complexities and ambivalences of affective technologies that operate in post-truth regimes and the consequences they produce. These approaches will not pretend to be "just descriptive" or leaving aside issues of power but confront modes of affective (self)-management critically (Staunæs, 2016). These pedagogical approaches may be thought to be composed of two closely related components (Zembylas, 2018e). The first may be the educator's ability to design and produce critical sensitivity toward the affective implications of mechanisms and techniques of discipline and normalization, as those take place in post-truth regimes and beyond. The second is pedagogy as an "ethics of cultivation" (Thrift, 2008), namely, the cultivation of an ethico-political perspective that attempts to instill an "affirmative critique" (Braidotti, 2013; Juelskjær & Staunæs, 2016b; Staunæs, 2016; see also Chapters 2 and 5) in teachers and students. An affirmative critique in the case of pedagogical interventions to counter post-truth is the strategic design of alternative counter-practices toward post-truth that reconfigure taken-for-granted assumptions about the present and the future. Let me offer an example to make these ideas clearer.

For instance, if we want to teach our students to recognize and assess truth and its value – about oneself, what one feels, what one did or experienced – sincerity and accuracy are not enough; ethical commitment, sensitivity and passion need to be also cultivated (Krasmann, 2019). Most importantly, Krasmann suggests, the appealing affective force of truth needs to be approached historically, just as Foucault (2014) argued, because truth is accessible only within a particular regime of thought. As something that is deeply ingrained in our conception of the world, truth has an affective force that ties the subject to itself and the world. To crack the empathy wall among different people and groups – to the degree, of course, that this is possible within the limits of a classroom – educators would need to explore first the power-effects of truth regimes and the affective technologies that are used to affirm or reject particular truths. This perspective will enable educators to unpack the relationship between affects and truth regimes (including post-truth ones) and to figure out small everyday practices in the classroom and beyond that could overcome the empathy wall. Essentially, it is about relearning "to listen and to watch, it is to read and decipher signs, but also to sense and to grasp [...] [it is] to recognize that public opinion and truth also rely on sensual experience," writes Krasmann (2019, p. 702). Needless to say, these pedagogical interventions come with considerable risks that need to be carefully analyzed. The last section of the chapter discusses the potential pedagogical risks and possible ways to address those risks.

Potential Pedagogical Risks

So far I have discussed some ideas of how educators could challenge post-truth claims in educational settings, while at the same time being vigilant about the risks involved and taking into consideration that even "critical" approaches are not immune from critique. In the last section of the chapter, I provide a deeper analysis of these risks focusing specifically on the question of how educators can enhance a sense of democracy, engagement and possibility for socially transformative praxis as a response to post-truth regimes, while avoiding the pitfalls of sentimentalization, moralization and indoctrination. In particular, I will discuss three important risks emerging from attempts to counter post-truth claims in educational settings; there are clearly many more risks, but I focus on those three, because they seem to me to be the most serious. These are the backfire effect; the ignorance explanation; and sympathy fatigue.

First, the backfire effect refers to students' anger toward educators' attempts to instill guilt or shame because they might subscribe to post-truth claims (see also, Chapter 9). When students get exposed to ideas contradicting their deeply held beliefs, pedagogical efforts to debunk those beliefs may actually become counterproductive, entrenching them in their preexisting positions even more deeply, if educators fail to show "strategic empathy" toward their students' beliefs (Zembylas, 2012, 2013a, 2018c). Strategic empathy refers to the willingness of the educator to make herself strategically skeptic (working sometimes against her own feelings) in order to empathize with students' beliefs, even when these beliefs are disturbing to other students or to the educator herself (Lindquist, 2004). Strategic empathy can function as a valuable pedagogical tool that opens up affective spaces that might eventually disrupt the affective force of post-truth claims – a process that is long and difficult, yet necessary, if the affective roots of post-truth claims are going to be challenged step by step rather than superficially. Undermining the affective roots of post-truth claims without backfiring – and particularly, without educators being accused for indoctrination – will require developing pedagogical strategies that do not alienate those students who might adopt post-truth claims. If students are simply bombarded with material teaching them that their (post-truth) beliefs are "stupid" or "morally bankrupt," it would amount to telling them they are morally complicit to post-truth regime (see also, Chapter 11) – a logic that would inevitably bounce back and would have the opposite results from the ones envisioned.

Second, the ignorance explanation refers to the tendency to blame students for being gullible and uncritical and for believing in post-truth claims and false narratives because they are ignorant. Notwithstanding the fact that this message lets those who strategically stretch the truth off the hook in post-truth regimes (Crilley, 2018), blaming the individual rather than engaging critically with the affective roots and consequences of post-truth regimes seems to be rather short-sighted. Understanding students' ignorance as a cognitive or psychologized disposition would more likely "correct" it by offering opportunities for conscious reflection and argumentation in the classroom. This could, then, justify the emphasis on media literacy, for example, as a treatment of the problem in epistemological terms; however, it would fail to address the problem in its roots, because post-truth regimes – just like any truth regime – constitute an ontological problem and thus require ontological rupture rather than (merely) an epistemological one (Mejia et al., 2018). Hence, by treating ignorance as not primarily a cognitive difficulty but rather a deeply affective and ontological one (Steyn, 2012; Tate, 2014) – namely, a practice and a habit – it means that to un-make this practice, it would require developing counter-practices that invest in truth as a practice and habit of everyday life.

Finally, the sympathy fatigue refers to the condition of majoritized students' fatigue and indifference toward showing sympathy for the suffering of minoritized others (e.g., immigrants, refugees), because they may believe that they receive no sympathy from anyone for their own suffering (see Hochschild, 2016). As noted earlier, moralizing approaches that aim at making it obligatory for everyone to feel sympathy for some groups may backfire and lead to sympathy fatigue, because these approaches try to enforce their feeling rules on others. A similar thing may happen when moralizing pedagogical approaches are used to convince (majoritized or minoritized) students that they ought to reserve their sympathy for some groups only, while rejecting a deeper understanding of those who are taken in by post-truth claims. The pedagogical spaces that educators may need to consider when engaging in these practices when these spaces are simultaneously inhabited by students who may have a disposition toward internalizing/believing these post-truth rhetorics and those whose own bodily experiences and memories contest/deny these post-truth statements become further complicated. For example, showing strategic empathy to post-truth claims – without implying that they are condoned – might be an important step for recognizing the affective complexities of post-truth claims and their consequences, thus creating spaces for acknowledging the affective experiences of all those who become victims of post-truth politics. In general, some of the ideas discussed here – e.g., strategic empathy, historicization of truth claims, affirmative critique – offer a path to engage in these terrains.

The implications of the three risks discussed here, in light of the conceptual framework sketched earlier about affect and governmentality, are twofold. The first implication is the importance of recognizing that the discourse and practice of post-truth claims produce certain affects that have profound effects in teachers and students' lives. Post-truths do not come into existence abstractly or merely as a matter of language; they become alive through specific practices, mechanisms and techniques that are deeply affective and have normalizing effects. Therefore, educators need to provide contexts where students are exposed to historicizing the affective roots and effects of various truth claims. This means investigating truth-telling practices in specific contexts, including looking at what happens to subjects who apparently no longer see themselves as bound to particular truths (Krasmann, 2019). For example, the problem with developing collective affects of empathy and solidarity – as well as with countering sympathy fatigue – is that we often assume that we can simply (and comfortably) take the position of the other, thus denying both our own and the other's situatedness (Biesta, 2010b). Pedagogical approaches that fail to take into consideration these risks are likely to fall prey to sentimentalization, indoctrination or moralization.

The second implication is that in addition to providing opportunities for critical thinking and engagement with post-truth claims, students need affective spaces that enhance their sense of democracy and possibility for socially transformative praxis. This argument does not entail moralizing approaches that cultivate empathy and solidarity for the sake of it but rather the creation of experiences that enable students to feel the plight of others, regardless of their own or the others' social position and ideological views. Countering post-truth claims are embodied and affective practices that require sympathizing with views that we may find unacceptable. Yet, the goal is not to develop a common ground or agreement with such claims – e.g., it would be impossible to find common ground with racist views – but rather to find ways to live in a common world (Biesta, 2010b). To the extent that students are enabled to pay attention to the affective force of post-truth claims and their normalizing effects and take action that engages them critically and sensitively with those who have different views, they may take a small step toward countering post-truths.

Concluding Remarks

This chapter has focused on the ethical, political and pedagogical implications of post-truth claims and how affect theory contributes to theorizing these implications and exploring counter-practices in educational settings. Some may question whether it is necessary to engage with post-truths in educational settings, in light of the risks involved, or the concerns of politicizing teaching and learning. I would respond by arguing that education is already political, and therefore, it is important to explore in educational settings the value of truth in its historical and political context, including those moments where commitment to certain truths is explicitly or implicitly dismissed. There is no doubt that this is a truly daunting task for educators, especially in the toxic political environment created by post-truth regimes; it's not easy to create learning environments in which students learn to hear all stories with sympathy and understanding, even the ones that are upsetting.

However, what is important to understand when attending to post-truth claims in educational settings is not so much their symbolic meaning or the fact that they disregard the value of some truths subscribing to a different truth regime but rather the affective force they unleash: "the enactment of superiority and the license to act superiority out, naturally at the cost of those who are thus put in the inferior position" (Krasmann, 2019, p. 703). Pedagogies that emphasize media literacy and critical thinking are important, but they are not enough unless they explicitly acknowledge and interrogate the affective infrastructures of (post-)truth regimes. Post-truth claims, in particular, operate and forge alliances through their affective force. Contrary to those who position post-truth as an epistemological rupture with past forms of truth-telling, I would argue that the issue is deeply affective and ontological (Mejia et al., 2018), which means that there is considerable pedagogic work to be done to unpack the affective force and consequences of post-truth claims.

CHAPTER 4

The (Un-)Making of Microfascism in Schools and Classrooms

[N]ot only historical fascism, the fascism of Hitler and Mussolini – which was able to mobilize and use the desire of the masses so effectively – but also the fascism in us all, in our heads, and in our everyday behavior, the fascism that causes us to love power, to desire the very thing that dominates and exploits us.

(Foucault, 1983, p. xiii)

Only microfascism provides an answer to the global questions: Why does desire desire its own repression, how can it desire its own depression? The masses certainly do not passively submit to power, nor do they "want" to be repressed [...] nor are they tricked by an ideological lure. Desire is never separable from complex assemblages that necessarily tie into molecular levels [...]. It's too easy to be antifascist on the molar level, and not even see *the fascist inside you*, the fascist you yourself sustain and nourish and cherish with molecules both personal and collective.

(Deleuze & Guattari, 1987, p. 215, added emphasis)

In the last chapter of Part I of the book, I move from the macropolitical level that has (mostly) dominated my analysis in previous chapters toward the micropolitics of schools and classrooms. In particular, I focus on how *microfascism* is done or can be undone in educational settings. First of all, it is admittedly difficult to define and analyze *fascism*, as there are various theoretical approaches to understand fascism as well as different manifestations of what we may call "fascist" (Griffin, 1991; Paxton, 2004; Stanley, 2018; Woodley, 2010). Some argue that fascism can be understood as "a genus of political ideology whose mythic core in its various permutations is a palingenetic form of populist ultanationalism" (Griffin, 1991, p. 26). Others suggest that "fascism does not rest explicitly upon an elaborated philosophical system, but rather upon popular feeling about master races, their unjust lot, and their rightful predominance over inferior people" (Paxton, 2004, p. 17). Importantly, what most of these understandings acknowledge is the affective power of fascism over people, that is, how people invest emotionally in ideas of ultranationalism and superiority. By now, it is well established how the two classic examples of historical fascism – the nationalist political movements during the 1920s and 1930s in Italy (Mussolini) and Germany (Hitler) – canalized people's feelings into a collective and political force (Berezin, 1997).

However, when Deleuze and Guattari talk about *microfascism*, as seen in both epigraphs of this chapter – Foucault's (1983) preface to Deleuze and Guattari's *Anti-Oedipus*; and, Deleuze and Guattari's (1987) analysis of "molecular fascism" or "microfascism" in *A Thousand Plateaus* – they refer to fascism from a different perspective: They are wondering why people willingly desire their own oppression. Deleuze and Guattari as well as Foucault want us to consider not the fascism of governments and political movements (i.e., molar fascism) but rather the fascist tendencies that exist within all members of a society, that is, all of us (i.e., molecular fascism) – the yearning that all of us have to want others to conform to our own rules. As Deleuze and Guattari explain, these two forms of fascism at the macropolitical and micropolitical levels are inseparable:

> [F]ascism is inseparable from a proliferation of molecular focuses in interaction [...] Rural fascism and city of neighborhood fascism, youth fascism and war veteran's fascism, fascism of the Left and fascism of the Right, fascism of the couple, family, school, and office. (1987, p. 214)

Hence, Deleuze and Guattari view fascism as a phenomenon in which the masses are not somehow tricked into fascism, but they willingly participate in it, because it is something they desire. Desire, rather than ideology, is central in Deleuze and Guattari's understanding of everyday fascism at the micropolitical level (May, 2013). The notion of microfascism, therefore, connects the preconscious (needs and interest) with the unconscious (desire) (jagodzinski, 2019), that is, the zone "between moral repression and the creative power of the molecular" (Deleuze & Guattari, 1983, p. 69).

I argue that Deleuze and Guattari's analysis of microfascism is extremely valuable in contemporary times, when populist, far-right and neo-fascist movements are springing all around the world from the United States to Russia, Turkey, Hungary, and the Philippines, to name a few (Connolly, 2017; jagodzinski, 2019). One of the most vexing questions this contemporary reality opens up is how educators can understand and respond to the rise of right-wing populism and neo-fascism in Europe, the United States and around the world (Mårdh & Tryggvason, 2017; Miller-Idriss, 2018; see

The Micropolitics of Fascism

also, Chapters 1, 2 and 6). This chapter utilizes the work of Deleuze and Guattari on microfascism to illustrate how the formation of subjectivities in schools and classrooms, especially that which reinforce the discipline and control of the body and affect, may function as a microfascist practice. The tendency to follow rules and see others conform to them that operates throughout everyday school life – from promoting particular messages about health to teaching national(ist) perspectives about citizenship – shapes how students participate in, feel about, and understand social and political organization.

What this chapter suggests, then, is that the question of microfascism and its consequences for democratic education cannot be fully appreciated unless it is better attuned to this particular psychosocial complexity, namely, how the draw of affect and power in the everyday, the desire to follow rules and see others conform to them, is inextricably linked to the macropolitical phenomenon of state fascism (Mohammed, 2020). In this chapter, I draw connections between Deleuze and Guattari's notion of microfascism and understandings of how forms of biopower work through affect (Anderson, 2012, 2014) in the context of education (see also Zembylas, 2018e). By bringing together microfascism, affect and biopower, I argue that attending to the affective dynamics of microfascism as practice, it is possible to develop new relations that unmake the microfascist subjectivities that are worked through processes of discipline and control in everyday school life.

My argument unfolds in four sections. The first section offers an overview of Deleuze and Guattari's notion of microfascism and how it can be used to understand the molecular elements of fascism in everyday life. In the second section, I discuss how affect and biopower are entangled in everyday processes of discipline and control; here I argue that affect and biopower are pivotal for appreciating the affective relations and capacities of microfascism. The third section takes on two examples from school curriculum – health education and citizenship education – to show how the concepts of microfascism, affect and biopower could shed light in understanding these school subjects as manifestations of microfascism. In the concluding section, I theorize how the creation of microfascist subjectivities in schools and classrooms may be challenged and undone.

The Micropolitics of Fascism

My point of departure is Deleuze and Guattari's (1987) observation that "what makes fascism dangerous is its molecular or micropolitical power" (p. 215). As Guattari (2016) clarifies elsewhere, "micro-fascist conjunctions of power can spring up all over the place" (p. 104). Deleuze explains why it is crucial to develop this micropolitical understanding of fascism:

> Oldstyle fascism, however real and powerful it may still be in many countries, is not the real problem facing us today. New fascisms are being born. The old-style fascism looks almost quaint [...] compared to the new fascism being prepared for us. All our petty fears will be organized in concert, all our petty anxieties will be harnessed to make micro-fascists of us; we will be called upon to stifle every little thing, every suspicious face, every dissonant voice, in our streets, in our neighborhoods, in our local theaters. (2006, p. 137)

As Deleuze points out here, the fascism to be feared is not the Nazi-like fascism but rather the everyday microfascism spread everywhere. This fascism on the level of the everyday finds expression in a number of simple examples, suggests Mohammed: "the anger that we feel when someone cuts in front of us in traffic on the drive to work, when they don't wait for us to get off the elevator before trying to get on, when they don't replace the chapter in the communal printer" (2020, p. 203). Importantly, Adkins (2015) notes a crucial difference between macropolitical and micropolitical fascism that makes the latter much more intensive and pervasive in everyday life: "[M]olar organization [of fascism] is more calcified; it describes the relations among discrete objects. Molecular organization is more fluid; it describes the relations among flows or intensities" (p. 131). Evans and Reid (2013), commenting on Deleuze and Guattari's thoughts on microfascism, put it even more forcefully: "Relations, fundamentally understood, in all their endless variations simply are fascist. Life, as well, is, [...] fascist. There is always the desire for power underwriting life" (p. 1).

As the second epigraph of this chapter suggests, Deleuze and Guattari (1983, 1987) argue that only microfascism provides answers to the fundamental question of why masses desire fascism, when for many of them, their material interests are not served well by fascism. Deleuze and Guattari explain that unlike psychoanalysis (e.g., Wilhelm Reich), which explains things in terms of repressed desire, microfascism provides a more robust conceptualization of desire as a psychosocial force:

> Reich is at his profoundest as a political thinker when he refuses to accept ignorance or illusion on the part of the masses as an explanation of fascism, and demands an explanation that will take their desires into account, an explanation formulated in terms of desire: no, the masses were not innocent dupes, at a certain point, under a certain set of conditions, they wanted fascism, and it is this perversion of the desire of the masses that needs to be accounted for. (1983, p. 29)

Deleuze and Guattari, then, understand fascism not in terms of ignorance or ideology but rather in terms of *desire*. However, desire, which has an affective basis, "does not express a molar lack within the subject" (Deleuze & Guattari, 1983, p. 27), namely, it is not contained within an individual as a form of repression. Rather, it is a productive, disindividuated, psychosocial force (Mohammed, 2020) that runs through the social fabric and drives "molecular energies" giving desire its "fascist determination" (Deleuze & Guattari, 1987, p. 215). In other words, Deleuze and Guattari do not understand desire as preexisting or as lacking within a subject but as socially produced. This implies that the problem of fascism is best understood not in psychoanalytic terms but rather in terms that draw attention to the molecular energies and affective flows through which desire moves.

In his own writings, Guattari (1984, 2009) analyzes further the relationship between desire and fascism. For Guattari, desire at the micropolitical level is understood as multiple and different, and consists of singular intensities that combine with one another in different ways rather than as identities that may be totalized by a party apparatus, namely, "by the totalitarian machine of a representative party" (2009, p. 159). As he further argues, fascism is irreducible to historical phenomena such as National Socialism, yet he wants to avoid simplifications that make us blind to how certain historical forms of fascism continue to exist (Genosko, 2017). For this reason, Guattari suggests that "what set fascism in motion yesterday continues to proliferate in other forms, within the complex of contemporary social space" (2009, p. 163). In other words, there is connection and continuity between the past and the present, when it comes to the proliferation of fascist forms. It is precisely in this context that desire emerges and flows in various assemblages, namely, in ways that fascist potentials never really disappear but change and modulate into other forms (jagodzinski, 2019). As Guattari puts it, "fascism, like desire, is scattered everywhere, in separate bits and pieces, within the whole social realm; it crystallizes in one place or another, depending on the relationships of force" (2009, p. 165). Deleuze and Guattari explain further:

> [E]very fascism is defined by a micro-black hole that stands on its own and communicates with the others, before resonating in a great, generalized central black hole. There is fascism when a war machine is installed in each hole, in every niche. Even after the National Socialist State had been established, microfascisms persisted that gave it unequaled ability to act upon the "masses." (1987, p. 214)

The consideration of the relationship between microfascism and desire in Deleuze and Guattari's theorization, then, entails an understanding of politics and desire that goes beyond the micro/macro or psychoanalytic/political distinctions, "thus enabling the consideration of a politics on the level of the individual and a treatment of desire on the societal level" (Mohammed, 2020, p. 201).

Consequently, it is important to realize that the mass macropolitical fascism that swept across Europe in the mid-twentieth century (particularly in Italy and Germany) "was not an accident, or the product of a malevolent and destructive few, but rather was the result of a deeply held desire for power [...] common to all" (Mohammed, 2020, p. 201). Fascism at the macropolitical level cannot be fully understood unless it is seen as inextricably linked to microfascism. As Holland (2008) explains, "mid-century European masses weren't ideologically tricked into fascism: they actively desired it because it augmented their feelings of power" (p. 76). Affect, then, is extremely important, because the masses "feel" as if their power is augmented. Once again, these feelings are not psychological or subjective, but they are socially produced and circulated (see also, Introduction). It is this micropolitical power of fascism that makes it so dangerous, according to Deleuze and Guattari (1987), "for it is a mass movement: a cancerous body rather than a totalitarian organism" (p. 215). Unlike totalitarianism, which comes to power through the actions of a vanguard, or in the case of a military dictatorship that mobilizes the army, fascism becomes a mass movement that transforms the social body (jagodzinski, 2019). Adopting the (biological) language of mutation and proliferation that shows how cancer is spread allows Deleuze and Guattari to highlight the capacity of fascism to spread throughout the social body, and eventually to overwhelm it (Genosko, 2017). This happens, explains Genosko, because Deleuze and Guattari theorize desire as "not undifferentiated and instinctual" but as resulting "from highly complex and supple micro-formations and refined interactions" (2017, p. 64).

All in all, it is important to understand and engage a micropolitical theorizing of fascism in various social and political sectors of everyday life (e.g., education), especially nowadays that there are increasing concerns about neo-fascism, populism and right-wing extremism. As Deleuze and Guattari (1987) remind us, it is easy to oppose macro-level fascism "and not even see the fascist inside you, the fascist you yourself sustain and nourish and cherish with molecules both personal and collective" (p. 215). It is this "fascism in us all, in our heads, and in our everyday behavior" that

Foucault (1983, p. xiii) calls out to turn our attention to and consider its consequences. Deleuze and Guattari put this powerfully as follows:

> [M]icrofascisms have a specificity of their own that can crystallize into a macro fascism [...] Instead of the great paranoid fear, we are trapped in a thousand little monomanias, self-evident truths, and clarities that gush from every black hole and no longer form a system, but are only rumble and buzz, blinding lights giving any and everybody the mission of self-appointed judge, dispenser of justice, policeman, neighborhood SS man. (1987, p. 228)

The force of Deleuze and Guattari's argument is in their claim that every individual can be turned into a "neighborhood SS man." This fascism on the level of everyday life in schools and classrooms is expressed in simple examples: the anger that a teacher may feel when a student talks in class while he or she is trying to explain a concept; the resentment of a student when another student cuts the line in front of them to get lunch; the irritation that a teacher feels at a faculty meeting when colleagues fail to share their viewpoint. Microfascism provides insights into how such behaviors and practices are affectively formed – which is why theorizing how affect and biopower are entangled in everyday life is of crucial importance.

Affect and Biopower in Microfascism

As noted so far, microfascisms are very much entangled with people's emotions and feelings; thus, the affective forces of fascism turn scholarly attention to the ways in which fascist affects of power emerge and are channeled toward particular directions. Deleuze and Guattari (1987) do not use the term "feeling" but rather they refer to "affect," which, following Spinoza, they understand as not emerging in individuals but between and through them, as part of assemblages. In his introduction to *A Thousand Plateaus*, Massumi (1987) explains that for Deleuze and Guattari, affect is not "a personal feeling"; it is "an ability to affect and be affected. It is a prepersonal intensity corresponding to the passage from one experiential state of the body to another and implying an augmentation of diminution in that body's capacity to act" (p. xvii). Affect, then, is the capacity of bodies in social space to affect one another and thus it is understood in terms of intensities, flows of energy and life forces that are not contained within an individual as discursive meaning-making but flow and impact the social (Massumi, 2002b).

The dual capacity of bodies to affect and be affected, as theorized by Deleuze and Guattari and further elaborated by Massumi, suggests that affect and power are entangled – that is, affects need to be understood as forces of becoming rather than governed by an overarching logic or regime (Schaefer, 2019; see also, Introduction). This theorization highlights that affect is not something that can be engineered or controlled; rather, it follows unpredictable trajectories (Morrow, 2019). A theorization of affect as the capacity to affect and be affected offers theoretical insights for a deeper understanding of how affect, power and fascism are connected. This is why the notion of biopower is fruitful for exploring how specific "technologies" are used to create and nurture fascist affects at the micropolitical level.

Foucault's (1980, 2003) concept of biopower refers to the specific techniques and technologies of power that attempt to control life. Biopower functions as an umbrella term combining two different yet overlapping forms of power: the discipline of the individual body so that it is integrated in the broader societal body; and biopolitics, which aims to regulate and control the population so that it is adjusted to social and economic processes (Schuller, 2018). As Schuller explains, biopower functions

> through the diagnosis, surveillance, and subjectivization of the docile body and the transformation of a multiplicity of individuals from a congregation of persons into a biological phenomenon [...] that could be measured, administered and regulated over generations through the same processes governing the natural world. (pp. 14–15)

On the one hand, then, discipline focuses on the body at the level of individual through normalization mechanisms; on the other hand, biopolitics focuses on the body at the level of the collective through regulatory mechanisms that attempt to control all of life by processes such as examination and classification (Rose, 2007).

In relation to affect, discipline works in two ways, according to Anderson (2012): In the first way, discipline acts on the individual "as an affective being who can 'control' unruly passions"; in the second way, discipline "extends to emotions as the physiological and biological basis of what a body can do" so "the body's reactions and actions are automated" (p. 31). Fascist affects, for example, are developed through a desire for more organization and management, for more order and control, for rules to be followed, enforced and even loved (Mohammed, 2020). What is crucial to note, explains Mohammed, is how the emotions we feel (e.g., anger, outrage) reflect that "we not only want to 'follow the rules' which come to be taken for granted as a part of the social order, but we want others to demonstrate the same discipline and conformity" (2020, p. 203); thus we feel anger or outrage when others fail *"to want to follow the rules"* (2020, p. 203, original emphasis).

At the same time, Foucault's second form of power, biopolitics, works to make collective affective life the "object-target" (Anderson, 2012, p. 32), such as, for example, when the population is segmented into a set of differentiated affective publics through tests and surveys that track how populations "feel" so that any "abnormal" actions can be detected, corrected or regulated (Anderson, 2014). On this perspective, it can be argued that microfascism works as a foundational technology of biopolitics. For example, when it comes to ultranationalism, the population is covered by fostering the vitality of those who are considered members of the nation, while designating others for exclusion, dispossession and even death. This affective modulation is a collective phenomenon; the modulation becomes, then, a collective and political force. Historically, fascist leaders have been able to mobilize these affects and emotions to give the feeling of superiority to the population. For instance, Foucault (2003) views Nazism as an expression of biopower, because of their politics of eugenics: "controlling the random element inherent in biological processes was one of the regime's immediate objectives" (p. 259). Therefore, it is crucial to observe how biopolitics (e.g., the politics of eugenics or ultranationalism) is not only intimately related to the practices of everyday micropolitical fascisms but also related to the larger, macropolitical movement.

Once we (e.g., researchers, educators, policymakers, students) begin to identify how apparatuses of discipline and biopolitics act on the body and population to normalize and control the affective lives of individuals and collectives, then the entanglement of affect and biopower with practices of microfascism is made more visible. In other words, microfascism can be understood as a form of discipline and an intensification of biopolitics. The "object-targets" of microfascism are practices that emerge to shape and condition capacities to affect and be affected. At the same time, however, as Foucault (1980, 2003) reminds us, power is not only repressive but also productive, which means that affective life as a whole exceeds attempts to make it into an object-target for forms of power (Anderson, 2014). Affective life can be patterned and organized at the micropolitical level, yet in ways that exceed biopolitical techniques, without being entirely separate from them (Anderson, 2012). This implies that there is always some possibility for "resistance" that could unmake microfascist subjectivities (I come back to this later).

The entanglement of affect and biopower in microfascism raises fruitful questions for exploration and analysis in democratic education: How do we identify and trace the ways in which bodies experience microfascism within schools and classrooms? How do school practices and institutions create affective spaces in which microfascism is allowed to be cultivated? When such practices are enabled, how can educators and students disentangle themselves from the cultural and political scripts and power structures to unmake microfascism? What are the risks involved when educators and students use affective techniques to unmake microfascist discourses and practices? How do certain affects (e.g., solidarity, empathy) become part of affective responses to counter microfascist discourses and practices?

These questions challenge our understandings of just what manifestations agency may take in relation to the affective infrastructures of microfascist practices in schools (see also Zembylas, 2020a). Furthermore, these questions open up new ways of understanding affect and biopower in ways that disrupt and rupture practices and spaces of microfascism. Attending, therefore, to the affective life of microfascism in schools may constitute an important political intervention, because it enables the subversion and reversal of the mechanisms and techniques of discipline and biopolitics (Anderson, 2012). Hence, paying attention to the affective complexities of microfascism, as those are entangled with biopower in schools and classrooms, is likely to challenge the "invisible affective infrastructures" (Zembylas, 2020a) of microfascist processes. The next section will look at two examples from school life to show how the concepts of microfascism, affect and biopower could shed light in understanding how curriculum and pedagogical practices can become manifestations of microfascism.

Microfascism in Schools and Classrooms: Two Examples

The first example focuses on what Fitzpatrick and Tinning (2014) call "health education's fascist tendencies," namely, how health education practices become a means of discipline and control of the body that "may equate to a form of fascism" (p. 132). In this regard, suggest Fitzpatrick and Tinning, "health fascism can be seen as a form of micropolitics of health and the body which is taken up by individuals at the personal level" (2014, p. 134). Issues of concern in health education range from alcohol and drug use, teenage sexual behavior and pregnancy, to obesity and poor nutrition. Health education becomes a form of health microfascism, argue Fitzpatrick and Tinning, when it is framed within a discourse of moral panic by which students are compelled to self-monitor, regulate and control their bodies in the name of health.

While the goal of health education is to promote the "making" of healthier citizens, there is a clear distinction between health promotion and health fascism. In light of what Lupton (1995) has called "new prudentialism," that is, the valorization of physical activity among youth for "good health," the student is compelled to "choose" this behavior through a set of techniques for self-management and autonomy. This new prudentialism, according to Lupton, produces a different kind of acting on the self that also includes emotional management and regulation (Lupton, 1998), inciting subjects to shape themselves bodily and emotionally for the sake of "happiness" and "healthiness." Health education, then, can become a site in which this process "has the potential to become a form of health fascism" (Fitzpatrick & Tinning, 2014, p. 135), if it creates pedagogical spaces in which the student is enabled to find "salvation" and "prudence" through means of behavioral control rather than critical thinking and empowerment.

The changing political context, especially the rise of neoliberalism, has been a key influence on health education as a means of behavioral change and individual responsibility in the school curricula of many countries (Fitzpatrick & Tinning, 2014). Neoliberalism, argue Fitzpatrick and Tinning, provides the perfect context "for the propagation of microfascisms that regulate the body in particular ways and thus the perfect space for a form of health fascism" (2014, p. 137). As noted earlier, Deleuze and Guattari (1983, 1987) remind us that the desire for control resides within each of us; there is always a fascist in us, as they point out, despite our proclamations that we are anti-fascist on the molar level. Similarly, health education has the potential to become a site of microfascisms, when it harbors norms of bodily appearance and emotional life that become fixed and regulate students.

A relevant example is the fascist formation of the "ideal" body of the Nazis grounded in stereotypes of the perfect bodily form and shape – a muscled, fit, healthy and aesthetic body – a normative ideal that was promoted both in schools and the society during National Socialism (Mosse, 1996). The obese body in contemporary times is a counterexample, indicative of illness and ugliness, signifying the risks of not engaging in certain activities such as exercising and eating healthy foods (Fitzpatrick & Tinning, 2014). The desire, then, for the "ideal" kind of body (the lean "healthy" body), for the aesthetic body, which is used as means of "marginalization and persecution" of the nonaesthetic body (e.g., the obese body), can become a fascist tool in health education, according to Fitzpatrick and Tinning, if it reinforces this marginalization through "the fascist learning aesthetic of the cult of the body" (Fitzpatrick & Tinning, 2014, p. 139).

The second example I discuss here is citizenship education's goal in many countries to create a "good citizen" and how this goal can also be used as a means of social and behavioral control that may equate to a form of fascism. As Westheimer (2008) suggests, "good citizenship" to many educators means obeying the law, respecting authority and being nice to compatriots – precisely the kind of acts that many Germans did during National Socialism but failed to question critically the consequences. As Paz (2020) writes,

> One does not have to be a monster, a sadist, or a vicious person in order to commit horrendously evil deeds. Normal people in their everyday lives, "decent citizens," victims and even respectable political leaders, who are convinced of the righteousness of their cause, can commit monstrous actions. (p. 371)

A citizen who obeys the law, respects authority or votes regularly is not necessarily someone who would challenge an "act of citizenship" (Fortier, 2016) that desires to order, control, repress and impose limits as a form of fascism. In this regard, citizenship education can become a site that nurtures microfascism, if it promotes technologies of governmentality that prescribe what it means to be a good citizen through what Fortier (2010) refers to as forms of "governing through affect."

Fortier (2016) uses "acts of citizenship" to refer to "both institutional and individual practices of making citizens or citizenship, including practices that seek to redefine, decenter or even refuse citizenship" (p. 1039). As she explains, acts of citizenship are performative instances of making or un/remaking citizenship that can come from a range of institutional, collective or individual actors. Acts of citizenship, then, are affective acts in the sense that they are bound up with disciplinary power relations involving emotions, feelings and bodies. In particular, Fortier (2010) uses the term "governing through affect" to indicate the management of affect for the purpose of community cohesion, namely, how the state or other sites of disciplinary power (e.g., fellow citizens; social and political organizations; schools) stipulate what it means to be a good or ideal citizen.

Governing-through-affect has two important components (Fortier, 2010) that deserve a careful consideration, when it comes to gaining a fuller grasp of the ways in which microfascisms work through affect in the context of citizenship education (see also Zembylas, 2015b, 2018f). First, governing-through-affect refers to how students are affectively governed by others (e.g., the school as an institution, teachers, fellow students, etc.) through the creation of particular affective relations. For example, students may be encouraged to draw boundaries of their bodily existence and feel proximity with those having the "same" ethnic or cultural origin, while they may learn to be suspicious or even feel superiority toward "illegal immigrants," "irregular migrants," refugees or other "foreigners." Schools and classrooms are sites of micropolitics in that they are spaces where particular forms of knowledge and ways of understanding citizenship are formally legitimated. In this case, microfascism is disguised as governing-through-affect within a veil of self-determination, self-identity and self-discovery (see Mohammed, 2020).

The second component of governing-through-affect is how students as "affective subjects" (Fortier, 2010) learn to govern themselves by expressing "appropriate" emotions of "good citizenship" such as pride, patriotism and loyalty (Zembylas, 2018f). Johnson (2010) considers how "citizens are expected to demonstrate that they feel loyal, patriotic and integrated" (p. 501). Learning to express feelings of belonging or rightful place (Fortier, 2016) in schools and classrooms – and how citizenship itself can bring up certain feelings such as feelings of safety – becomes a process of policing the affective boundaries of the school community. For example, students who wear a veil or even prefer to speak a foreign language are suspected of not having the appropriate feelings of belonging and thus might be identified as legitimate subjects for critique, fear or suspicion (see Johnson, 2010). These practices provide the perfect affective space for the circulation of microfascisms that regulate students' bodies in particular ways and thus become the perfect means for a form of *citizenship fascism*. These perspectives draw attention to how curriculum and pedagogy may be used to teach students how to attach particular feelings to certain aspects of citizenship (e.g., national pride, etc.), while excluding other feelings such as solidarity and empathy for noncitizens, migrants and refugees (e.g., see Pomante, 2017).

All in all, the two examples discussed here – health fascism and citizenship fascism at the micropolitical level of everyday life in schools and classrooms – are entangled with and inform macropolitical fascist formations or, what Evans and Reid (2013) call, "liberal fascism" – the "inherently fascist character of liberal modernity itself" (p. 3). This is of key importance to keep in mind in contemporary discussions about populist, right-wing extremist and neo-fascist ideas and how they emerge in schools as well as the rest of the society. As Evans and Reid remind us,

> We say fascism is in us, in a way to indicate that not only do we make fascism come about every bit as much as fascism makes us come about, nor that we all contain a potential to become fascist or behave fascistically, but that we exist and act politically only through practices that are themselves already fascist, with little potential to be otherwise. Politics demands of us that we not only desire but love power. Such a love cannot be acclaimed non-fascistically. (2013, pp. 3–4)

Following Deleuze and Guattari (1983, 1987), Evans and Reid may express the idea of fascism being "in us" in rather strong terms; however, a key point for educators to take away is that everyone is more or less complicit in the desire for control and order (see Chapter 11). Understanding the consequences of this desire is of crucial importance in educational efforts to unmake, to the degree that is possible, microfascist subjectivities in schools and classrooms.

Unmaking Microfascist Subjectivities in Schools and Classrooms

What I wish to emphasize in the last part of this chapter is that understanding how microfascism emerges in schools and classrooms can help educators develop pedagogical strategies for responding to fascist tendencies. The question that drives my analysis here, then, is, what can educators do pragmatically to make a meaningful intervention and combat a body that is cancerous (Deleuze & Guattari, 1987), namely, to challenge and even root out the "fascist within" (jagodzinski, 2019)? Needless to say education cannot stop fascism; however, it can make a contribution at the micropolitical level to cultivate an "affirmative critique" (Braidotti, 2013) toward microfascism; namely, a critique that is not simply limited to identifying the negative consequences of microfascisms in everyday school life but also highlights "positive" and hopeful stories of "alternative" affective relations and embodiments – e.g., relations that appeal to solidarity, critical empathy and collective action against any form of social exclusion and marginalization (Zembylas, 2019).

Before outlining some ideas how education may contribute toward the cultivation of affirmative critique and relations and combat microfascisms in schools and classrooms, there is an important point that needs to be emphasized. It is not this chapter's intention to advocate that pedagogical discourses and practices ought to declare themselves to be "anti-fascist" in order to effectively address the creation or propagation of microfascist subjectivities in schools and classrooms. Rather, I share Evans and Reid's argument that "nothing seems [...] more degraded, more banal, than the laying claim to being 'anti-fascist' for the same reasons that nothing seems more undignified than the desire to speak on behalf of 'victims'" (2013, p. 4). In the context of democratic education, then, with all its political, ethical and affective complexities, this claim suggests that the pedagogical goal is not to "make" students anti-fascists "because to believe in the integrity of such a moral claim is to be wilfully blind to the fascism that, necessarily, underwrites one's own political subjectivity" (2013, p. 4). There is no position "with less integrity and compromise with that which it seeks to combat," add Evans and Reid, "than the card-carrying 'anti-fascist'" (2013, p.4). Hence, I do not wish to claim that pedagogical strategies ought to be anti-fascist, if they are going to be productive and effective in identifying and challenging microfascist subjectivities in schools and classrooms. Rather, what is important is for pedagogical strategies to identify and then challenge "fascism in all its forms" (Evans & Reid, 2013, p. 2), as those forms are manifested in schools and classrooms. This is more than enough work for educators to accomplish – compared to making big proclamations and attaching moral labels to what they do as being "anti-fascist."

The first step in pedagogical efforts to unmake microfascist subjectivities is identifying the ways in which desire is mobilized in educational settings to control, repress, order and impose rules as a form of fascism. If educators are attentive to their own microfascisms and those elicited by their students, then it will become clearer to understand how and why the desire to follow rules and see others conform to them is central to formulating pedagogies that problematize the consequences of this desire. It is crucial, then, for educators to understand how the diverse range of students' as well as their own affective responses to rules and control constantly run up against social- and political-wide ways of knowing and feeling about the self and others. Therefore, a point of departure for educators is to examine how affective dynamics work micropolitically to organize students' affective responses (e.g., to racism, nationalism, extremism, sexism and ableism) and under which circumstances there can be an antidote to the microfascist practices in everyday life (Zembylas, 2019). A key pedagogical question then is, how and with which pedagogical resources can educators and students first of all identify forms of fascism and its damage micropolitically?

What is needed are pedagogical strategies that render the burdens of microfascism unbearable, namely, strategies that show to students how they are prevented from reimagining reality and opening new potentials in their lives, if they are trapped into fixed desires and anxieties about themselves and their relations to others. In other words, educators need to cultivate spaces of resistance micropolitically through the "diligent unmaking of the various subordinated subjectivities" (Mohammed, 2020, p. 208) that students develop in schools and classrooms. Students often learn in schools to submit to an order and a set of rules, and they become attached to the idea that if their bodies, health or citizenship were "properly ordered" then everything would be fine; thus they take such ordering as desirable and treat every complexity encountered as distraction (Fitzpatrick & Tinning, 2014). A valuable pedagogical strategy, therefore, would be to create opportunities for students to "refuse to allow any fascist formula to slip by, on whatver scale it may manifest itself, including within the scale of the family [and I could add the school as well] or even within the scale of our own personal economy" (Guattari, 2009, p. 166). This implies that students need to be given opportunities to understand that the reduction of the complexity of each subjectivity into a fascist formula forecloses countless other ways to apprehend and negotiate relations with others.

Deleuze and Guattari (1983, 1987) suggest that to challenge microfascisms in everyday life we need to find ways of developing an active practice of resistance to microfascist impulses (Mohammed, 2020). As Mohammed suggests, gaining a deeper understanding of the ways in which one's desires to cultivate fascist behaviors are coded by the social, the unconscious and other things "is a long and draw-out labor that involves the development of a reflexive practice of self-scrutiny" (2020, p. 208). This labor entails, among other things, a pedagogical effort to teach students how to acknowledge their complicity in microfascisms – something that turns out to be a deeply affective and political process (Zembylas, 2020a). However, attempts to instill guilt and moral taint in students for their microfascist behavior as much as to pamper them under the disguise that "everyone is fascist" after all will most likely fail, because they psychologize a challenge that is deeply political; therefore, the "solution" that is offered is stuck in dealing with the emotional aftermath of microfascisms rather than with the making of microfascism and how educators can contribute to unmake it.

As noted earlier, to suggest that educators and students need to examine their mobilizations against microfascist undertakings is not to imply that the goal is for students to become anti-fascists. Rather, to combat microfascism requires a critical understanding of how affect and biopower are distributed throughout the school fabric and have consequences on what is collectively legitimated and accepted. Yet, to avoid fixation on the negative aspects of these consequences, it is valuable for educators and students to reorientate knowledge practices in order to invent and circulate new modes of relation and belonging – that are more inclusive and hopeful for all, not only for some – in replacement of the affective dynamics of microfascism. What this brings to the discussion of pedagogical strategies against microfascisms in schools and classrooms is that to escape the threads of fascism, pedagogic work has to take the form of creating spaces and practices that attempt to invent new social imaginaries, relationalities and embodiments. Pedagogical strategies that bluntly reject microfascist discourses and practices are counterproductive and may lead to a moralizing approach that fails to give cognizance to the affective, political and other factors that contribute to the complex process of naturalizing microfascisms in everyday life.

For example, as noted in Chapter 1, pedagogies that are "reparative" (Sedgwick-Kosofsky, 2003) – that is, pedagogies that attempt to address microfascisms within a frame that takes into consideration histories of violence, trauma, oppression and social injustice, without falling into the trap of sentimentality – might be valuable (see also Zembylas, 2018a, 2020b). Reparative pedagogies are those pedagogies that aim at developing and sustaining reparative relations and transformative actions as "responses" to microfascist practices. Reparative pedagogies are affective practices that critique liberal discourses (e.g., tolerance, diversity and multiculturalism) because they find them inadequate, or too conveniently packaged, to the difficult legacies of fascism in all of its forms. These pedagogies ask from educators and students to engage in alternative ways of relating to others – not in order to make themselves or others feel "good" but rather to seek a deeper understanding of the affective complexities of microfascism, and particularly the complexity of complicity in racism, nationalism, extremism, sexism and ableism. The goal of pedagogies of reparation, then, is not to offer any consolation, as a result of the microfascist practices in which all of us more or less engage; to understand our complicity requires a great deal of work to identify the moments of entanglement among affect, biopower and fascism. At the same time, as also noted in previous chapters, this process requires a strategic approach to empathizing with those who engage in microfascism, not in the sense of offering them a solace or sentimental refuge but rather of acknowledging how microfascism affects us all with the aim to produce new vocabularies of hope and forms of living within a community in which everyone is truly included.

As one might surmise from this analysis, engaging pedagogically with microfascism in schools and classrooms is a calculated risk that can threaten to reduce this work into a superficial and sentimental discussion of students' feelings; avoiding this pitfall requires pedagogical practices that are attuned to the pedagogical, affective and political complexities involved in developing a nuanced language for identifying and challenging the visible and invisible affective infrastructures of microfascism in everyday life.

Concluding Remarks

This chapter has attempted to demonstrate how Deleuze and Guattari's notion of "microfascism" is of crucial importance to an understanding of the complexities of contemporary pedagogical efforts to combat right-wing populism, extremism and fascism. I have tried to illustrate this through discussing two examples – one in health education and another in citizenship education – highlighting how affect and biopower are intimately linked to microfascist practices in schools and classrooms. Finally, I have suggested pedagogical strategies that could challenge and unmake microfascist subjectivities, emphasizing that there are many complexities involved since fascism is easily disguised in many forms that are often aligned with (neo)liberal values. Educators and students must be vigilant about fascism; it is something that arises in their everyday lives with grave consequences individually and collectively. They (and we) may believe that these consequences are beyond our reckoning (May, 2013). However, the consequences are very much relevant; the moment we believe they are not, it is precisely that moment we embrace fascism.

PART II

Renewing Democratic Education

CHAPTER 5

Affirmative Critique as a Response to Post-truth Claims

While Part I of the book "scanned" the political landscape of right-wing populism and interrelated phenomena (i.e., post-truth, microfascism) and discussed how affectivity plays a crucial role in their circulation, Part II (Chapters 5–7) focuses on how specific theoretical ideas (i.e., affirmative critique, agonistic emotions/affects, affective atmospheres) can be the point of departure for the renewal of democratic education. Clearly, these ideas are meant to serve as illustrations of the possibilities that can be created to rethink democratic education with new theoretical lenses; these ideas are not exhaustive in any way of these possibilities, but rather they demonstrate that the project of renewing democratic education has to draw theoretical inspiration from every possible source that is available, when it comes to acknowledging affectivity and its consequences. The present chapter begins with exploring the notion of "affirmative critique" – an idea that has already come up in several chapters of Part I – because it highlights that it is important to shift the negative tone that prevails in critiques of post-truth and populist claims toward an affirmative politics. Needless to say, this shift from negative to affirmative politics has crucial pedagogical implications that I sketch partly in this and the next two chapters but discuss more extensively in Part III of the book.

My point of departure in this chapter is Bruno Latour's question, "What has become of the critical spirit? Has it run out of steam?" (2004, p. 225) in a provocative essay published more than fifteen years ago. Latour argued that *critique* – understood as a specific set of methods expressing doubts and challenging implicit assumptions in texts such as deconstruction and new historicism – eventually boomeranged, because it had gone too far. Challenging scientifically established facts (e.g., climate change) had gone too far, suggested Latour, especially by social scientists who tried "to detect the real prejudices behind the appearance of objective statements," eventually concluding that "there is no such thing as natural, unmediated, unbiased access to truth" (2014, p. 227). In his analysis,

Latour argued that such claims are grounded in a debunking critical spirit; their tools are distrust and doubt rather than the creation of a hopeful future. Therefore, he suggested a position that aims at instilling optimism into a renewed critical spirit, focusing on how things can be constructed rather than de(co)structed. In his own words:

> The critic is not the one who debunks, but the one who assembles. The critic is not the one who lifts the rugs from under the feet of the naive believers, but the one who offers the participants arenas in which to gather. The critic is not the one who alternates haphazardly between antifetishism and positivism like the drunk iconoclast drawn by Goya, but the one for whom, if something is constructed, then it means it is fragile and thus in great need of care and caution. (Latour, 2004, p. 246)

The key point here is that, for Latour, a new mode of critique is needed, grounded in a positive and constructive thinking, because critique based on negation or opposition cannot serve reality anymore.

In his push against critique as negation or opposition, Latour has not been alone. Several philosophers have suggested positions on critique that are devoid of negativity (Bargués-Pedreny, 2019). For example, Badiou (2013) discusses the new possibilities emerging from an affirmative logic and suggests that "the affirmation, or the positive proposition, comes before the negation instead of after it" (p. 3). Similarly, Braidotti (2013) suggests affirmative critique as a response to the fatigue and negativity of deconstruction. Two philosophers who have made notable contributions toward the critique of negative critique over the years have been Michel Foucault and Judith Butler. Foucault – especially in his "What is critique?" talk (Foucault, 1997b) but also throughout his lectures after the 1970s – proposes that critique should be thought of as a "critical attitude," a virtue, and the "art of not being governed like that." Butler – who has been building over the years on Foucault's analysis, especially in her "What is critique? An essay on Foucault's virtue" (2004b) and "Critique, dissent, disciplinary" (2009), and generally her works on Foucault's later work on ethics – elaborates on critique as a certain kind of *practice* or *action* that takes place in certain historical conditions and resists the norms that are being formulated. The notion of (affirmative) critique as a practice and action, rather than a theory to be applied, is crucial in my efforts in this book to invent pedagogies of affect that highlight democratic education as an affective practice that has the potential to renew democracy and democratic participation in educational settings.

Negative account no longer serves reality, suggest Mejia, Beckermann and Sullivan (2018), especially in the current political climate of post-truth in which negativity and deconstruction prevail, particularly by those who advocate nihilism and hatred of the "other." As noted in Chapter 3, "post-truth" is understood as "relating to or denoting circumstances in which objective facts are less influential in shaping public opinion than appeals to emotion and personal belief" (Oxford Dictionaries, n.d.a). Blunt denials of social and scientific facts or conspiracy theories abound, especially among conservative and right-wing groups around the globe, and "fake news" or "alternative facts" have become their favored mottos whenever they dislike objective facts. In discussions about post-truths, which play out differently of course in different contexts, one major characteristic is the "Us-versus-Them" dichotomy that is often drawn between those who claim to know the truth and others who consider this to be fake. A characteristic example of the us/them dichotomy is found in the rhetoric of Donald Trump and his supporters as well as other populist leaders around the world (see Chapters 1 and 2). The challenge is that negative critique and post-truth politics create an impasse in public discourse and political life. If negative critique does not serve us any more, then, how might positive thinking or *affirmative critique* – that is, critique that is devoid of negativity (Bargués-Pedreny, 2019) – release us from this impasse, and particularly what would be the pedagogical implications of this idea?

This chapter seeks to explore how, why and under which conditions a move away from critique as a negative practice toward an – educationally more valuable – affirmative notion of critique is important in formulating pedagogies that might respond more productively to the challenges of the post-truth era. Post-truths may take different shapes in schools ranging from arguments against climate change to positions grounded in misinformation (e.g., how much the United Kingdom pays in health costs to the European Union). My concern here is not so much with the extent to which schools are responsible for post-truths, but rather with equipping students to be able to not only dismantle post-truths but also orient themselves otherwise in relation to them in the future. As Latour seems to be suggesting, when the tools of analyzing reality in schools are predominantly distrust, doubt and the relativization of everything, then the "ethos" that is cultivated is most likely that of negativity and post-truth politics. Therefore, it would be worthwhile to explore the following question: What does it mean politically and pedagogically to adopt an affirmative rather than a negative critique in education? For example, what does this imply pedagogically in schools, especially at the secondary school level, in which discussions of "fake news" and "post-truths" are more likely to arise? How might adopting an affirmative critique and ethos in pedagogy help educators address these challenges more productively?

In the first section of the chapter, I engage in a brief historicization of the notion of "critique," clarifying the meanings of negative and positive critique in the context of broader theoretical and political discussions of critique. In the next two sections, I engage with Foucault's and Butler's analysis of critique to show how a combined Foucauldian–Butlerian framework reconceptualizes criticality as an affirmative practice. I choose to build on Foucault's and Butler's analysis of critique precisely because it elaborates on critique as a certain kind of *practice* or *action* that is "response-able" toward post-truths. The ontological perspective of critique-as-practice, I will argue, reformulates pedagogy's orientation along the lines of what Hodgson, Vlieghe and Zamojski (2017) call *a post-critical* philosophy, that is, "a post-critical orientation to education that gains purchase on our current conditions and that is focused in a hope for what is still to come" (p. 15). In the last section, I discuss the pedagogical implications of suggesting an affirmative notion of critique as a practice and an ethos that can be enacted in addressing the challenges emerging from post-truths in educational institutions.

Negative and Affirmative Critique

My point of departure, as noted earlier, is Latour's view that scholars' continued use of critique as a method of unmasking hidden assumptions is no longer useful and may even add to the "ruins" and "destruction" (2004, p. 225) left by various conflicts such as the culture and science wars. Latour argues that critical methods grounded in negative critique are outdated – they are remnants of "the last war" (2004, p. 225), he says – so they cannot respond effectively any more to their rapid mimicry by conservative groups who use such methods to relativize facts. Thus, he suggests that critique – as negation and opposition – cannot serve reality anymore, because it has become obsessed with the deconstruction of facts. This method has been co-opted by right wing groups, as this is evident in the blur between left-wing and right-wing rhetoric:

> [C]onspiracy theories are an absurd deformation of our own arguments, but, like weapons smuggled through a fuzzy border to the wrong party, these are our weapons nonetheless. In spite of all the deformations, it is easy to recognize, still burnt in the steel, our trademark: Made in Criticalland. (p. 230)

Latour is alarmed that both conspiracists and social critics "share the same skeptical perspective of the world" (Fassin, 2017, p. 6). Critical methods, in other words, have turned against the scholars who developed them and right-wing groups have taken over the critical enterprise by using these methods to question well-accepted facts (e.g., climate change). As a way out of the dark situation that (negative) critique finds itself, Latour (2004) suggests that we need to shift our attention from "matters of fact" to "matters of concern," where the issue is not going to be whether a fact is true or not but of what it is capable. To do so, Latour proposes a "stubbornly realist attitude" (p. 245) that focuses on matters of concern. As he asks, "Can we devise another powerful descriptive tool that deals this time with matters of concern and whose import then will no longer be to debunk but to protect and to care [. . .]?" (2004, p. 232). Latour's position seeks to turn negative forms of critique toward more affirmative modes (Bargués-Pedreny, 2019) that are intended to "detect how many participants are gathered in a thing to make it exist and to maintain its existence" (Latour, 2004, p. 246).

Historically speaking, there have been both "negative" and "affirmative" positions of critique (Rebughini, 2018) – positions that are undoubtedly affective, taking different trajectories of affect, of course. Negative critique is "focused on the 'negation' of reality, conceived as a field of potential relations of domination, false consciousness, reification that have to be rejected and unmasked" (Rebughini, 2018, p. 5). Critique as negative has mostly identified with Hegelian–Marxian thought because of its emphasis on the negation of what already exists, and a rational and foundational standpoint from which critique is launched. In this respect, "critique is a self-reflexive continuous search for possible complicities with power, common sense, self-evidence or status quo interests" (Rebughini, 2018, p. 8). In social theory, this sort of critique has been associated with critical theory and the Frankfurt School (e.g., Theodor Adorno, Max Horkheimer); in education, it has been exemplified in approaches such as neo-Marxist, feminist, post-colonialist and anti-racist traditions as well as (Freirean-based) critical pedagogy through which the critical potential of education is explored to interrupt the reproduction of the conditions of oppression and exclusion. In other words, in the transition from political philosophy or political critique to specifically pedagogical concerns – as this is exemplified, for example, in the work of Freire and critical pedagogy – what is common is their focus on the negative and oppositional aspects of critique.

It has been argued, however, that debates on critique have a blind spot, because they often focus on the negative aspects of critique and fail to consider its productive and affirmative force: "Surely suspicion can also be pedagogical, protective, enabling and caring," notes Barnwell (2015, p. 923), yet negation is often unproductive, as "there is only critique and the criticised status quo – nothing else is possible" (Hodgson, Vlieghe & Zamojski, 2018, p. 10). I am not suggesting here that critique is always driven by suspicion or that negative critique is always "bad" and ought to be rejected. Rather, my concern is to turn attention to the neglected force of affirmative critique and its pedagogical implications. Importantly, there has recently been a growing interest in affirmation in the humanities and social sciences, including education (e.g., Gunnarsson & Hohti, 2018; Hodgson et al., 2017; Staunæs, 2016, 2018). This shift has been characterized as the "current affirmative turn" (Alt, 2019, p. 140), emphasizing "the need to do something *other* than critique or something *more* than critique" (2019, p. 137, original emphasis), which is manifested as negation and opposition. In this sense, affirmative critique is "more centered on the search for an alternative to such reality that needs a capacity to imagine and project the new" (Rebughini, 2018, p. 5). As Rebughini clarifies further, "While the emphasis on negation seeks to establish why critique could lead to an emancipatory reality, the emphasis on affirmation endeavors to demonstrate how the complexity and unpredictability of reality engages imagination to offer new solutions to common needs" (2018, p. 5). Affirmative critique emphasizes imagination and emotions for which experience and contingency constitute a moving and temporary standpoint for critical agency (Rebughini, 2018, p. 6). In this case, critique is about the production of innovative actions and embodied practices with the purpose of enacting what "it could be." As Staunæs (2016) explains:

> An affirmative critique reflects an ambition of transcending the idea of analysis as reflections of reality and instead analyzing tendencies with the purpose of reconfiguring the world. However, the direction for change or not-change is not pre-ordained. An affirmative critique unfolds like a curious form of critique, defending itself from moralism. That means scientifically reconfiguring what we think we know with certainty by pointing out what could be different, while simultaneously consulting common concerns and hopes for what the future may bring whom. (pp. 66–67)

Affirmative critique, notes Staunæs, is related to work conducted by Foucault, Barad, Haraway and Braidotti, and focuses more on producing possible alternatives by transforming critique into a set of embodied practices, in material and situated dimensions, for changing the world. In relation to post-/anti-truth tendencies that might appear in classroom discussions, for example, critique is no longer about who is manipulated or not, and whether some groups have a privileged access to truth. To engage in affirmative critique is not limited to resistance against an argument or a position but rather pays attention to the "not-yet," namely, to what could be different and transcend the present (Rebughini, 2018, p. 10) – e.g., what could be done differently in the fight to save the environment from human-made destruction? What would it take for us, humans, to *become* otherwise in efforts to confront climate change? Thus, it is through becoming something else, says Rebughini, rather than through mere resistance to and negation of "what is" that new, creative possibilities emerge in a situation.

The rejection of a negative critique in favor of a more affirmative one, involving matter, body and affect as elements of change calls for an idea of the "critical" in the social sciences and humanities that recognizes the importance and complexity of the connections that compose a situation. In this perspective, argues Rebughini, "what eventually counts is *how critique works*, rather than who critiques, what is critiqued, or why critique exists" (2018, p. 14, added emphasis). Hence, the "critical" is no longer based on judgment (e.g., the judgment of the self-reflecting subject) but rather on the ways that subjects and objects come together, relate in the world, and connect or disconnect. As Thiele also emphasizes, "Affirmative critique initiates transformation in the here and the now, without the messianic promise or need for a 'beyond'– another world supposedly escaping 'this mess' we are in 'all together'" (2017, p. 27). In this sense, it is argued that critique is a matter of *virtue* rather than of judgment, which brings me to Foucault's perspective of critique.

Foucault's Perspective of Critique

First of all it is important to emphasize that Foucault is interested in examining how critique works, how it is performed and how the practice of critique is understood historically (Ball, 2017; Lemke, 2011). Lemke explains that Foucault breaks with the "juridico-discursive" (Foucault, 1980, p. 82) style of thought that focuses on critique as judging and condemning, a predominantly negative practice; rather, he seeks to give critique a more positive content (see Foucault, 1984). This would mean creating and assembling rather than debunking and judging things, as it is usually done when we engage in negative critique (Alt, 2019). As Foucault puts it in his landmark essay on critique, "There is something in critique which is akin to virtue" (Foucault, 1997b, p. 25). Critique, then, is marked by an *ethos* that makes it a transformative force of experience as opposed to the application of preexisting categories as negative critique (see Alt, 2019). What is being affirmed, as Alt points out, is not necessarily the truth of this or that thing (e.g., democracy; equality) but rather the interrelatedness and messiness of the contemporary reality – e.g., how the affirmation of our interrelatedness in the world has different political and ethical effects such as practicing social equality in everyday life (e.g., see Ranciére, 1991).

In general, Foucault views critique as a "critical attitude" (1997b, p. 24), a form of engagement and practice that problematizes the ways that power and knowledge work to govern individuals. In other words, to engage in critique means to consider how current structures and conditions construct and constrain our possible modes of action and being in the world (Ball, 2017; Olssen, 2003). For example, to engage in critique of post-truths in the classroom does not imply to simply identify how post-truths are "wrong" – ethically or politically – but rather to construct possible actions of being in the world that go beyond the us/them dichotomy invoked by post-truth claims. At the heart of Foucault's understanding of critique, then, is the "art of not being governed like that" (Foucault, 1997b, p. 29), namely, the possibilities of resistance and innovation in relations to self (Osborne, 2009). Importantly, as Ball (2017) explains, Foucault's project of critique does not include a set of particular actions that someone should do to escape or oppose the phenomena of being governed, but rather it includes a permanent attitude of skepticism. Ultimately, then, critique for Foucault is "the movement by which the subject gives himself the right to question truth on its effects of power and question power on its discourses of truth" (Foucault, 1997b, p. 32).

Foucault locates the emergence of critique earlier than the Enlightenment in the fifteenth and sixteenth centuries as an attempt to read scripture differently from pastoral powers (Ball, 2017; Boland, 2014). In this context, critique appears as a practice of freedom in which individuals engage in self-reflection without direction from others, thus making an ethical and political stand of "not being governed like that." To explain this notion, Foucault (2009) talks more broadly about "counter-conduct," by which he refers to the struggles and forms of resistance against the processes implemented for governing subjectivities in "the everyday." Historically speaking, counter-conduct was manifested "as a questioning, reworking and elaboration of pastoral power, which at times eroded but also at other times reinforced, redirected or improved the mechanisms ... of conducting power" (Odysseos, 2016, pp. 183–184).

In other words, Foucault understands critique as a *practice* that is inextricably linked to the issue of how *not* to be governed in particular ways (Odysseos, Death & Malmvig, 2016). Through his account of critique, Foucault attempts "to conceptualize the multiple dimensions and inter-relationalities of both practices of resistance and practices of governance" (Rossdale & Stierl, 2016, p. 159). Foucault's analysis focuses on the practices – rather than the ideologies – through which counter-conducts are enacted. For him, Rossdale and Stierl point out, the processes of counter-conducts involve concrete enactments, that is, specific tactical displacements that "enable a critical alternative to become new form of power" (Larsen, 2011, p. 43). It is this movement toward practice that makes Davidson (2011, p. 28) suggest that Foucault's notion of counter-conduct "adds an explicitly ethical component to the notion of resistance [...] [and] allows one to move easily between the ethical and the political, letting us see their many points of contact and intersection."

Importantly, Foucault's understanding of critique goes beyond the conceptualization of critique by critical theory, such as the Frankfurt School, by viewing critique *as* genealogy (Boland, 2014; Fassin, 2017; Folkers, 2016; Olssen, 2003; Saar, 2002, 2008; Vlieghe, 2014). Foucault (1984) describes genealogy as a particular investigation that examines how the subject is a historically situated construction rather than as a "transhistorical subject" being assumed in terms of a universal moral or ideological framework. The focus of genealogy is not essence, that is, "what is," but *becoming*, that is, how things have come into being and how they can become otherwise. As Foucault explains, "And this critique will be genealogical in the sense that it will [...] separate out, from the contingency that has made us what we are, the possibility of no longer being, doing, or thinking what we are, do, or think" (1984, p. 46). A major difference, then, between critical theory and genealogy is that

> critical theory considers it possible to separate what is true from what is false (ideology being precisely what deceives human beings by blurring this separation and thus allowing the reproduction of domination), while genealogy is interested in identifying what counts for true and false in a given world at a given moment [...]. Emancipation therefore consists, for critical theorists, in removing the ideological veil imposed on people so as to allow them to realize the deception that renders their domination possible, and for genealogists, in contesting the self-evident representations of the world they hold true while acknowledging the possibility of other representations. (Fassin, 2017, p. 14)

Advocating the importance of adopting a critical attitude that works genealogically, Foucault reframes critique as thinking critically within a framework that no longer operates through the movement from falsehood to truth but rather assumes an "experimental attitude" (Foucault, 1984, p. 46), namely, "at every moment, step by step, one must confront what one is thinking" (p. 46).

In sum, it may be argued that in the current post-truth context, Foucault's concept of critique-as-practice makes an invaluable contribution in reconsidering how to respond to post-truths. There is no innocent escape from the problematic foundations and effects of negative critique toward post-truths. The affirmative difference that Foucault makes with his notion of critique-as-practice lies in paying attention not to espousing a view of an ideal (truthful) situation but affirming the caring of the present – e.g., democracy, equality – through one's actions.[1] To further unpack this idea, I turn now to Judith Butler's analysis of critique in Foucault's work.

Butler's Analysis of Critique in Foucault's Work

In her famous essay, "What is Critique?," Butler (2004b) provides her most explicit meditation on Foucault's talk of the same title, focusing on the connection between critique and virtue (Vogelmann, 2017). On Butler's reading, at the heart of Foucault's notion of critique is that critique requires virtue rather than judgment:

> [I]f that self-forming is done in disobedience to the principles by which one is formed, then virtue becomes the practice by which the self forms itself in desubjugation, which is to say [. . .] that we break the habits of judgment in favor of a riskier practice that seeks to yield artistry from constraint. (Butler, 2004b, p. 321)

According to Butler, Foucault's notion of critique has to be understood as an ethical practice, because it focuses not on prescriptions and moral imperatives but on the "aesthetics of existence" (Foucault, 1980), that is, how to live one's life in a particular way according to the "art of not being governed like that" (Butler, 2004b; Foucault, 1997b, p. 29). As Butler (2004b) emphasizes, critique as virtue "is not only a *way* of complying with or conforming with pre-established norms. It is, more radically, a critical

---

[1] Foucault's (2001) concept of *parrhesia* – namely, the activity of saying the truth, especially dangerous truths that challenge the status quo – is a powerful practice for creating an affirmative culture of critique in the context of the post-truth present. For example, education scholars (Ball, 2016) discuss how the (pre)conditions for parrhesia lie both within and outside teachers' practices simultaneously. It is beyond the scope of this chapter (which focuses on critique) to discuss this aspect, but it is worth exploring in the future the courage both to speak truth and listen to the truths of others as manifestations of a more affirmative critical culture in education and society.

relation to those norms" (p. 305, original emphasis). Engaging in critique, according to Butler's interpretation of Foucault, "is working on oneself to become a different subject; critique means becoming critical, becoming disobedient – and thus becoming virtuous" (Vogelmann, 2017, p. 198).

Therefore, critique in Butler's account is related to subject formation: "To be critical of an authority that poses as absolute requires a critical practice that has self-transformation at its core" (2004b, p. 311). Associating critique with self-transformation makes critique as desubjugation central in Butler's work: Critique features as a source of resistance that is not grounded in any foundational moral work, but rather on the risk of one's very formation as a subject. This is why critique *should not* be a matter of judgment, suggests Vlieghe (2014, p. 1029), but rather a matter of virtue, because critique in Butler's account is a practice based on the suspension of judgment. Boland (2007) also observes that Butler's analysis of Foucault's critique as a practice of virtue based on the suspension of judgment helps us rethink critique as a *performative* enactment of critical subjectivity: "Critique is performative not just in the sense that it is an act, but in the sense that it continuously 'acts out' the irrevocable, traumatic inauguration of the subject" (p. 109). In this sense, criticality in the social arena, including education, is seen as a constant process of desubjectivation (Youdell, 2006).

In "Critique, Dissent, Disciplinarily," Butler (2009) emphasizes that critique as a social and ethical practice is inevitably embedded in particular changing historical conditions and practices that make certain things "speakable" and "thinkable" (p. 777). As she argues, "[Critique] follows, rather, from a distinct and largely contingent historical accumulation and formation of conventions that produce subjects who, in turn, open up a set of possibilities within that historical horizon" (p. 788). The subject, then, who engages in critique is not external to the norms she or he criticizes, hence there are no transhistorical norms or normative practices of critique. At the same time, the subject who engages in practices of critique, points out Butler, becomes self-forming through the very process of formation. As Butler also points out elsewhere, the subject who practices critique is inevitably involved in a reworking of the norms and conventions of one's formation, and therefore, he or she can participate "in the remaking of social conditions" (2005, p. 135).

In *Giving an Account of Oneself*, Butler (2005) theorizes the process of subjectivation, emphasizing that this process is always relational and, therefore, it has important ethical and political implications concerning the self and others. Butler challenges a fundamental humanist assumption that is often taken for granted, namely, that self-reflection and, therefore, self-knowledge, is a prerequisite for critique. As she argues, "an account of oneself is always given to another, whether conjured or existing, and this other establishes the scene of address as a more primary ethical relationship than a reflexive effort to give an account of oneself" (Butler, 2005, p. 21). In other words, the claims made about a coherent set of self-knowledge as a result of a reflexive effort are ungrounded, because any account of oneself always takes place as a relational process; this process highlights that the subject always participates in the remaking of social conditions, interrupting essentialist claims about oneself or others.

In sum, Butler distinguishes two interrelated dimensions in Foucault's notion of critique (Karhu, 2017): First, critique as a form of disobedience understood as a way of resisting subordination; and, second, critique as an ethical obligation to produce a self. Taken together, these two aspects, suggests Karhu, highlight the possibility of inventing a new self who practices resistance against norms and conventions. Butler's interpretation of Foucault's critique emphasizes his critical attitude as a virtuous ethos, conceptualizing critique as an ethical practice of self-transformation (Vogelmann, 2017). However, as Vlieghe (2014) rightly points out, Butler's interpretation of Foucault "should not be understood as a plea for anarchism or as an expression of the utopian yearning that we might actually escape power" (p. 1030); as Foucault has taught us, power relations are inescapable. Rather, the aim is to be willing to put at risk our "self" and what we think we know about truth; subject formation can be resisted and reclaimed through an aesthetics of existence.

All in all, Vlieghe (2014) identifies two important contributions from a combined Foucauldian-Butlerian framework, when it comes to the possibility of critique. First, "these thinkers argue for a possibility to distance oneself from and to resist current orderings of social life" (p. 1021). For example, when it comes to post-truth claims, it might be suggested that a Foucauldian–Butlerian framework can help us resist such claims, not by falling into endless debates on what is true or false but by focusing on *how* truth and the systems of post-truth themselves come to count as (post)-truths. Second, critical distance is, according to these thinkers, realized when one is willing to go through experiences that challenge what is taken-for-granted. For example, if educators want to challenge post-truth claims, this will not happen (merely) at a discursive level; it has to happen at the level of *practice*, such as, for instance, through bodily and affective experiences that create new relationalities and challenge the norms implied by post-truths. In other words, the world is to be affirmed as its modes of being. Conceptualizing critique within a combined Foucauldian–Butlerian framework opens up modes of being that are transformative but not premised on the "must-be"; rather, they are premised on the need for action-oriented critique. If (post)-truth is a system that is exercised not only through discourses but through a whole series of other practices, as Foucault emphasizes in his later work on ethics, then post-truth claims need to be challenged at a whole set of different practices, including the affective, the bodily, the material and the social.

Pedagogical Implications

As the discussion of Foucault and Butler shows, affirmative critique has existed for some time. It hasn't, however, taken that form predominantly in education and the social sciences. What I am arguing here is that the post-truth context requires something different that makes affirmative critique more urgent in our pedagogies. In the last section of the chapter, I take up the Foucauldian–Butlerian framework that has been outlined so far to articulate an educational philosophy and pedagogy that posits critique as an affirmative practice in the current post-truth context. It is important to clarify from the beginning that affirmative critique is not a "tool" that can be applied to educational practice. Foucauldian–Butlerian conceptualization of critique as practice and ethos implies that there is something inherently educational in critique. Therefore, an educational philosophy and pedagogy of affirmative critique is an approach that aims to enact possibilities of speaking, thinking, acting together, by going against the grain in order to bring something new and unexpected, e.g., to (re)establish relations in/with the world in ways that care for the present and protect that which we value and wish to pass on (Hodgson et al., 2017).[2]

In what follows, I discuss what may be entailed in a pedagogical approach in schools and universities in which the ethos of affirmative critique may be enacted as a productive response to post-truths. As Peters (2017) points out, "it is not enough to revisit notions or theories of truth, accounts of 'evidence', and forms of epistemic justification as a guide to truth," in education, but rather "we need to understand the broader epistemological and Orwellian implications of post-truth politics [...]. More importantly [...] we need to combat 'government by lying'"

---

[2] See also Pinar (2006) for a discussion of the need to establish a new pedagogical model of the public sphere based on similar ethics as those analyzed in this chapter.

(p. 565). I would argue that we need to move a step further than that. Hodgson et al.'s (2017) notion of "post-critical pedagogy" can be valuable here in making the shift from critical pedagogy as combative – which has been the dominant Western mode of educational thought and practice grounded – to pedagogical approaches that cultivate an affirmative attitude to what is "good" in the "here and now." What is being affirmed as "good," for example, is "love for the world," which "is not an acceptance of how things are, but an affirmation of the value of what we do in the present and thus of things that we value as worth passing on" (2017, p. 18); the things we value differ from context to context, yet there might be some commonalities (e.g., love, interrelatedness).

Post-critical pedagogy is situated against critical pedagogy that is grounded in an inherent negative critique toward the world in expectation of a utopia that is never to come (Hodgson et al., 2017), a form of critique that has run out of steam, as Latour (2004) said. Post-critical educational philosophy, according to Hodgson et al., starts from the assumption that the negative emphasis of critical pedagogy is anti-educational and might actually work against the possibility of educational transformation. Post-critical pedagogy is articulated on the basis of principles that relate to affirmative ideas such as love and caring and to the positive role of teacher as initiating the new generation into a common world. As Hodgson et al. (2017) explain, "This is not an acceptance of how things are, but an affirmation of the value of what we do in the present and thus of things that we value as worth passing on. But not as they are: educational hope is about the possibility of a renewal of our common world" (p. 18).

I would like to complement the idea of post-critical pedagogy with the notion of "response-able pedagogy" (Bozalek & Zembylas, 2017) that has been recently suggested as an approach that cultivates in students "response-ability" (Barad, 2007; Haraway, 2016). Generally speaking, response-ability refers to the ability or capacity to respond. This term has been described by Barad as "differential responsiveness (as performatively articulated and accountable) to what matters" (p. 380), and by Haraway (2016) as "cultivating collective knowing and doing" (p. 34). Response-able pedagogy, then, is not simply an example of the type of learning that can take place when power relations, materiality and entanglement are acknowledged in critical ways; response-able pedagogy also constitutes an ethico-political practice that incorporates relationality into teaching and learning activities (Bozalek & Zembylas, 2017).

Response-able pedagogy, therefore, offers a pedagogical principle not found in critical pedagogy, namely, an affirmative critique that addresses

Pedagogical Implications

the post-truth/negative critique/us–them impasse. For example, bringing together Foucault's and Butler's notions of critique with the ideas of post-critical and response-able pedagogies implies that it is not enough for the educator to offer media literacy lessons grounded within a critical pedagogy framework – one which would teach students how to distinguish between news and "fake news" or post-truth claims. Rather, it would be of the utmost importance for the educator to provide students sustained opportunities to realize their entanglement in social and political conditions (structural inequalities, material conditions, etc.) that give rise to suffering and inequality. But even this is not sufficient for educators to make students aware of how they are complicit in power relations or how social and political conditions are associated with the production and circulation of post-truths (see Chapter 11). Beyond this, an affirmative critique means that students are encouraged to historicize the trajectories of post-/anti-truth tendencies with the purpose of taking responsibility and action that bring something new to alleviate suffering in the world.

In putting ideas on post-critical and response-able pedagogies in conversation with Foucault's and Butler's notions of critique, then, I want to suggest three general pedagogical principles (along with a few examples of classroom practices) that could cultivate response-ability in students, when they address post-truths in schools and universities: striving to diagnose the "good" in the present (rather than opposing the wrong of a post-truth); appreciating the new possibilities opened by unwieldy knowledge to focus on what we have in common; and, adhering to a principled practice of desubjectivation. These three principles partly address the three risks emerging from attempts to counter post-truth claims in educational settings, as those are discussed in Chapter 3 (i.e., the backfire effect; the ignorance explanation; and, sympathy fatigue). Although there is no one-to-one correspondence between these principles and the risks discussed earlier in the book, my goal here is to articulate an affirmative attitude and ethos of engaging students with post-truths that takes into account these risks. Needless to say, how post-truth plays out in educational contexts will differ.

The point of departure for an affirmative critical activity in the classroom is a kind of diagnosis of what is "good" in the present (Hodgson et al., 2017). In other words, dealing with post-truths in the classroom is not about debunking these statements and how wrong they are but about paying attention to the conditions (e.g., marginalization, suffering, injustice) that give rise to post-truths. In particular, students may be encouraged to engage in actions of solidarity and strategic empathy to those who suffer, regardless of whether they agree politically with them or not. For example, as discussed in previous chapters, Hochschild (2016) offers a compelling example of how and why (white) Tea Party Republican voters in the American South feel anger, bitterness and resentment for people of color, immigrants and refugees. Post-truths, then, may be produced and circulated by those who may believe that they receive no sympathy from anyone for their own suffering. Therefore, the pedagogical challenge for educators and students is how to create spaces in the classroom so that engagement with post-truths does not merely constitute a negative critique but rather how to take responsibility for the good in the world by showing strategic empathy toward others' beliefs (Zembylas, 2012, 2013a, 2018d; see also Chapter 3). Strategic empathy can open up affective spaces that might eventually go beyond post-truth claims and connect people on the basis of goods we care for.

The second principle of a pedagogical engagement with post-truths has to do with appreciating the new possibilities opened by unwieldy knowledge to focus on what we have in common. Instead of adopting an oppositional stance toward post-truths, in other words, the emphasis is on cultivation of an affirmative attitude in students that consists of open-mindedness, humility and relationality with others. For example, as Hodgson et al. (2018) write in their attempt to articulate a post-critical pedagogy, "we don't simply rethink the notion of citizenship education for a 'post-truth' politics. [...] we focus instead on what takes place in the present, on what we do have in common" (p. 16). This entails focusing on the values that are important to pass on rather than getting immersed in debunking the intellectual vices of those who have different values; the goal is to achieve commonality as basis of transformative action rather than as an educational problem, suggest Hodgson et al. (2018). Hence, teachers can create opportunities in the classroom to show students that we do not become better alone but through interactive and collective effort that emphasizes what unites us rather than what divides us.

Finally, the last principle of pedagogical engagement with post-truths is adhering to a principled practice of desubjectivation. Desubjectivation, suggests Vogelmann (2017), becomes possible when individuals are encouraged to change their perspectives on how they establish their relation with their selves and others to the point they counter norms, conventions and post-truths. For example, "un-learning" (Foucault, 1997b) is an important task of the self; to un-learn who students are seems to be an important experience that they are deprived of in schools. "Isn't this, after all, what we want when we are teaching students to be critical," ask Harwood and Rasmussen (2013, p. 882), that is, to be able to practice critique as an ethical practice of the self through which students reinvent themselves and relate to others differently? This affirmative ethos is completely opposite to that of debunking post-truths and claiming that students are emancipated and empowered from negative critiques. Furthermore, the desubjectivation of the educators includes their own regimes of verification that have been established in institutions (schools and teacher education) through audit culture (see Shore & Wright, 2015; Taubman, 2009). Educators will have to engage in various productive counter-conducts to reconfigure institutions enthralled to increasingly reductive notions of "learning" as the replication of predetermined, quantifiable performance outcomes. For instance, educators need to take responsibility to show that there are inventive potentials in learning when institutions pay attention to relational affects and atmospheres in the classroom (Zembylas, 2018e). Hence, a pedagogical approach toward post-truths in schools that is inspired by affirmative critique creates pedagogical spaces in which educators and students can become response-able to each other and offer alternative options to us/them categorizations.

Conclusion

My effort in this chapter has been to move away from critique as a negative practice toward an (educationally more valuable) affirmative notion of critique and articulate the pedagogical implications in the context of post-truths. My position, joining others in the "affirmative turn" in the social sciences and humanities, was that a Foucauldian–Butlerian framework could help educators formulate an affirmative and productive response toward post-truths. Critique is inherent to the project of education, especially in relation to societal transformation (Ball, 2017), yet it is important to problematize negative forms of critique in dealing with post-truths and articulate educational philosophies and practices that invoke an affirmative attitude.

A Foucauldian–Butlerian framework of critique-as-practice is important for educators and pedagogies at all levels of education, because it *does* what it says, namely, it not only enables us to walk important steps (e.g., diagnose the present; focus on what is "good" now rather than getting stuck to negativity) but rather "*is already* what makes us take these steps" (Vogelmann, 2017, p. 208, added emphasis). In other words, this framework is not trapped in negative critique but encourages educators and students in schools and universities to engage in affirmative practices that move beyond binaries of true/fake, us/them that perpetuate oppositions and animosities. Cultivating an affirmative attitude and ethos of critique in students constitutes a virtuous practice of self-transformation and a passionate pedagogical goal that educators cannot afford to ignore. At the same time, however, insofar as the turn to affirmation in pedagogy is not just about the mood with which an educator or a student conducts his or her teaching–learning praxis but also involves a more general conception of subjects' ways of relating to the world and to each other in formulating productive responses to post-truths, affirmation may also come with risks. The "affirmative ethos" in responding to post-truths can also be co-opted, if it loses sight of existing power relations and structures (Alt, 2019). This is not meant to diminish the importance of affirmation, as Alt points out. Rather it reminds us in democratic education that we need to pay attention to what values are affirmed each time in educational institutions and with what ethical and political implications.

CHAPTER 6

Agonistic Emotions/Affects to Counter Far Right Rhetoric

As previously noted in this book, there is presently a growing concern in Europe, the United States and many countries around the world about the resurgence of far right movements and political actors (Rydgren, 2018). The term "far right" – which is often interchangeable with the terms "extreme right," "radical right" and "right-wing populism" – refers to a range of ideological positions associated with political movements and parties of the far right (Mudde, 2000, 2007) that have enjoyed significant electoral success in recent years. The rhetoric of these far right ideologies is often populist, racist, xenophobic, anti-immigrant, anti-Semitic, homophobic, chauvinist, anti-globalist, Islamophobic and ethno-nationalist, and it is expressed through statements that are usually shocking and outrageous.

Although there has been significant academic attention in a variety of disciplines to explore the discursive and ideological structures on which far right rhetoric draws, a direct focus on the affective dimension of far right politics is still relatively rare (Kølvraa, 2015; Miller-Idriss & Pilkington, 2017) – a point that has been made throughout this book. A focus on the affective dimension of far right rhetoric and its pedagogical implications requires that we – educators, scholars, policymakers – need to pay explicit attention to the ways that political struggles are both discursively domesticated and affectively expressed in the classroom (and beyond). It is important, as Kølvraa points out, "to link a focus on affect to the analysis of textual statements, *without* reducing affect to a straightforward affect of (linguistic) signification" (2015, p. 184, original emphasis). In other words, far right politics needs to be explored within a theoretical lens that takes into careful consideration the affective complexities of conflicts and struggles over different political ideas.

This chapter draws on the concept of *agonistic* (from Greek αγών *agon* "struggle") emotions and affects to think with some of the arguments of Chantal Mouffe's (2000, 2005, 2013, 2014) political theory and discusses what this means pedagogically in handling far right rhetoric in the classroom. I make an argument that agonistic emotions and affects can be engaged with and channeled democratically in classroom debates. This attempt, then, makes a political and pedagogical intervention into the terrain of countering extremism in democratic education – an intervention that offers a theoretical and pedagogical way of addressing the tensions emerging from the affective dimension of far right rhetoric in classroom spaces. As I show, this intervention emphasizes the role of responsibility for democratic expressions of affect and emotion in the classroom (Zembylas, 2018c; see also Chapter 9).

I begin by reminding the reader of some important characteristics of far right rhetoric and how research in education has addressed far right ideologies so far; in this section, I also revisit some aspects of affect theory that are useful in appreciating the affective dimension of far-right rhetoric. The next part of the chapter draws on Mouffe's theory of agonistic pluralism as well as her reflections on the affective nature of the political, and discusses how these ideas, when put in conversation with affect theory, are useful in theorizing emotions and affects as agonistic. The last part of the chapter analyzes the pedagogical implications of an agonistic approach that handles productively the affective dimension of far right rhetoric in the classroom.

The Affective Dimension of Far Right Rhetoric and the Role of Education

According to Rydgren's (2018) recent definition, radical right parties and movements share an emphasis on ethno-nationalism that is rooted in myths about the glory of the past. Although right-wing groups are hostile to democratic governance, they are not necessarily actively opposed to democracy per se (see Mudde, 2000, 2007).[1] As Rydgren further explains, radical right parties and movements

> are directed toward strengthening the nation by making it more ethnically homogeneous and – for most radical right-wing parties and movements – by returning to traditional values. They also tend to be populists, accusing elites of putting internationalism ahead of the nation and of putting their own narrow self-interest and various special interests ahead of the interests of the people. (2018, p. 1)

---

[1] The most obvious examples could be drawn from forms of protests that exhibit, in some way, a nostalgia for the "glorious past" mixed with hostilities towards the actions of democratic governance – e.g., the 2017 "Unite the Right" rally in Charlottesville, Virginia.

Hence, one of the most distinctive ideological characteristic of radical right groups is their claim that they have the right to protect their national and cultural identity from threats, the most important of which is the alleged "invasion" of immigrants. As Bar-On (2018) further explains, those who advance liberal multicultural perspectives or internationalist ideas are seen as "traitors" to one's people.[2] Therefore, it is not only political elites but also cultural and educational elites that become the enemies of far right groups; cosmopolitan liberalism and the sociocultural left are seen as betraying the nation and corrupting the values of the nation-state (Rydgren, 2018).

One of the most powerful tools used by far right parties and movements in the social media, communication and public life in general is their provocative and shocking rhetoric.[3] In fact, this *affectively-based* rhetoric espoused by radical right movements and groups has been clearly linked in recent years to hate crimes and violence against migrants and religious, ethnic and racial minorities in several European countries (Miller-Idriss & Pilkington, 2017). Neither the content nor the provocative affective style of discourse adopted by radical right movements should come as surprise, because the so-called provocative politics of the far right is part of its strategy to inflame supporters to create unrest or commit violent crimes (Kølvraa, 2015, p. 186). Given that the radical right and populist ideas are found not at the pathological margins but among increasingly broad sections of society, especially among youth, it is of particular importance to study the intersection of radical right and education (Miller-Idriss, 2018).

In her work on the role of education in preventing violent extremism (PVE) and countering violent extremism (CVE), Davies (2008) argues that both formal educational work in schools and nonformal educational work in out-of-school settings (e.g., youth groups and sport clubs) can help through a number of measures such as building resilience and confidence among youth; enabling students to embrace value pluralism; gaining knowledge of rights; harnessing networks to counter extremism; and engaging youth in social action for change. Davies' (2018) recent review

---

[2] For example, in public discourses on Brexit in the UK, those who advanced a particular international vision for the UK within the EU were labeled as traitors, even if they advanced their voice through established democratic channels. In June 2016, Jo Cox, a British Labor Party Member of the Parliament was shot and stabbed by someone who believed that she was a traitor to the UK and that liberal and left-wing political viewpoints like hers were responsible for the world's problems.

[3] For example, in November 2017, US President Donald Trump retweeted videos posted by British First, an extreme right-wing anti-Muslim group. The tweets appear to show acts of violence carried out by Muslims, although doubt has been cast on the reliability of at least one of the videos. See www.youtube.com/watch?v=BxwDYrv32qI

of educational interventions in counter-extremism internationally reiterates that there is no robust evidence of a best way or sets of best ways for education to counter extremism; there is some promising evidence that equal educational access and quality education as well as broader support factors within schools (e.g., effective partnership with local agencies; links with the wider curriculum structures) may limit participation in extremism, but these results are mixed (Bonnell et al., 2011). Importantly, as Miller-Idriss and Pilkington (2017) suggest, "Assessing the state of the research on education and the radical right is further complicated by the fact that much of the work in this area is not specific to far or radical right populations per se, but rather targets areas such as prejudice reduction or the promotion of tolerance" (p. 136). Without *explicit* attention to the radical right through focused school-based interventions in schools, it will be difficult to address the multiple challenges of far right extremism and its infiltration among youth.[4]

An important challenge in designing educational interventions that address right-wing radical young people is the affective one. If intervention programs make far right young people feel ostracized and blamed rather than building trust and empathy, then it is likely that these programs will have the opposite effect (Cockburn in Miller-Idriss & Pilkington, 2017). Miller-Idriss's (2017) analysis shows that the appeal of far right and extremist movements to young people is often affective in nature and, therefore, this element is something that needs to be addressed by educators and policymakers. Hence, it is necessary to discuss what exactly defines the affective dimension of far right rhetoric and how this analysis may inform pedagogical strategies in productive ways, while minimizing the possibilities that these efforts will backfire. Kølvraa's advice is helpful:

> [O]ne needs to begin by not assuming that the content of the rhetoric is meant to be – *or to be received as being* – true in any kind of literal or "serious" sense. Indeed, if affect can never be fully captured in the signifying practice of language – because the attempt to speak the "truth" of affect catches only its domesticated and limited shadow (emotion) – then it might equally make sense that the only "language of affect" operating with any modicum of success is that which does not seek to speak any version of (literal) truth. (2015, p. 188, original emphasis)

---

[4] An interesting example of this point is the "fundamental British values" which are defined as part of the Prevent strategy: democracy, the rule of law, individual liberty, mutual respect for and tolerance of those with different faiths and beliefs and for those without faith. However, these values do not explicitly address the radical right, not to mention that these types of discussions include a notion of Britishness that may in fact provide coverage to radical right views.

Therefore, before we seek to devise any pedagogical approach to counter far right rhetoric in the classroom and beyond, it is crucial that we take into serious consideration the "affective investment" (Laclau, 2005a, p. 116) of young people in particular (political) ideas.

Building on the approach discussed in the Introduction, the reader is reminded that affect and politics are always intertwined, as affective dynamics can work to either reproduce or resist political relations galvanized by capital, the state or other systems of power (Massumi, 2002b; Pile, 2010; Thrift, 2008). The approach used in this book to investigate how affect and politics are intertwined pays attention to how larger-scale political praxis is connected to the micro-scale of bodies and the embodied meaning that is made out of the process through which a political space is affectively "charged." Affective contagion, as this process has been characterized (Erisen, Lodge & Taber, 2012; Kølvraa, 2015), refers to the process through which affective intensity is transferred in political space. As Kølvraa explains,

> Affective contagion is, then, not simply the mirroring of ideological dispositions between subjects, entailing a transfer of an already signified disposition in the domesticated sphere of emotion [...], but rather the circulation of affective intensity that might be signified differently at different positions in the political space. (2015, p. 195)

For example, to explore the affective contagion of far right political discourses and their pedagogical implications, one might be drawn to how the micro-level context (e.g., classroom) is affectively and emotionally charged by elements of far right rhetoric and how this rhetoric exerts *power* upon the actors and the audience at the micro-scale level *to* achieve desired ends (e.g., see Zembylas, 2011b). This *power-to* (Heaney, 2011, 2013) is a capacity that structures and is structured by both the macropolitical context and the micro-level of affective and emotional relations in classrooms and schools (Zembylas, 2013b).

Following Kølvraa (2015), the overarching point I want to make here is that the analysis of far right rhetoric in micro-level contexts (e.g., classrooms or schools) needs to avoid simplistic assumptions that followers of far right ideologies simply mirror the views of a charismatic leader because of an affective/emotional impact on them; rather, the focus should be on how affect and emotion "draw in" individuals and groups by transmitting affect and emotion "across an antagonized political space" in which meaning of ideological positions is not blindly copied but constituted through "the varying topography of how different issues enjoy different levels of affective investment ranging from indifference to 'popular hysteria'" (Kølvraa, 2015, p. 197). This brings me to the issue of (ant-)*agonism* in political spaces and the need to discuss the crucial role of emotions and affects in people's relations to the political dimension. These discussions are timely and important because the resurgence of radical right-wing parties and movements in various countries around the world demand a more sophisticated understanding of the affective complexities entangled in political struggles and conflicts. In the following section, I will discuss Mouffe's theory of agonistic pluralism, focusing in particular on her theorization of the affective dimension of collective identification.

Mouffe's Theory of Agonistic Pluralism: The Affective Dimension of Collective Identification

In their classic study of *The Authoritarian Personality*, Adorno et al. (1950) wondered about the appeal of fascist ideas: "Why is it that certain individuals accept these ideas while others do not?" (p. 3). Their response was that fascism was appealing "not to rational self-interest, but to emotional needs – often to the most primitive and irrational wishes and fears" (p. 10). The assumption that fascism – and, generally, extremist and far right ideas – and the emotions associated with such ideas are "irrational" is deeply problematic and is countered by growing research and theorizing in the social sciences and humanities in recent decades. This work suggests that not only is the reason/emotion split problematic but it also leads to other flawed assumptions – e.g., that people are ignorant and confused, and they blindly identify with leaders who remind them of themselves (Manning & Holmes, 2014). For this purpose, several scholars in the affective turn emphasize the need to pay explicit attention to and understand better the importance of affects and emotions in political life, arguing that emotions and affects are inextricable parts of what connects human beings to each other and how we make sense of the world around us (Clarke, Hoggett & Thompson, 2006; Demertzis, 2013; Ferry & Kingston, 2008; Goodwin, Jasper & Polletta, 2001; Hoggett & Thompson, 2012).

To discuss affects and emotions in political life, I turn to the Belgian philosopher Chantal Mouffe (2000, 2005, 2013), and especially her work on "agonistic pluralism" in democracy as well as her understanding of the crucial role of "passions" in people's relations to the political dimension. Mouffe's theory, which acknowledges the tensions within democratic deliberations, has hardly affected educational discourse so far (Snir,

2017); the few attempts by educational theorists to engage it (Biesta, 2011; Håkansson & Östman, 2019; McDonnell, 2014; Ruitenberg, 2009, 2010; Tryggvason, 2017, 2018; Zembylas, 2011a, 2018c) have focused on Mouffe's theorization of democracy and how it can be put in conversation with citizenship education discourses. Importantly, these attempts have also contributed to acknowledging Mouffe's ideas on the affective nature of the political. Here I build on these contributions, focusing in particular on how Mouffe's work in conjunction with affect theory can be valuable in theorizing agonistic emotions and affects.

Throughout her work, Mouffe has emphasized the importance of *passions* for political thinking and criticized rationalist accounts of politics (Mihai, 2014).[5] In particular, both deliberations and conflicts will and should involve people's passions, according to Mouffe (2005), because they provide indications that something is important or "at stake" in political issues or events. Following Lacan, Mouffe emphasizes that discussions about democracy cannot ignore the affective forces that fuel and make collective identifications – e.g., based on national identity or a particular political ideology – "stick" (see Stavrakakis, 1999). Mouffe's claim is that the nature of collective identification is psychoanalytic, namely, what moves peoples to identify with collectivities is their *lack* of identity in and of themselves (Ruitenberg, 2010). While in affect theory the nature of collective identification is not (exclusively) psychoanalytic, there is complementarity between Mouffe and the perspective of affective theory that recognizes the important role of affective forces in collective identification (see Thrift, 2008).

As Mouffe (2005) argues, the affective force of collective identification makes the rational basis of liberal and deliberative democracy untenable. In other words, the focus of liberal and deliberative theories of democracy on consensus is not only conceptually misguided but also politically dangerous (Mihai, 2014), precisely because it fails to take into consideration the affective dimension of we/they distinctions as much as it ignores the power relations involved in (supposedly) rationalist deliberations (Mouffe, 2000).

---

[5] As Mihai (2014) points out, Mouffe has resisted the use of the term "emotion" and preferred the term "passion." As she writes: "Mouffe seems unaware of the fact that the term 'passion' has been historically used to denigrate affect as irrational, disruptive and undesirable in the public sphere" (p. 36). Mihai argues that while this observation may be seen as a superficial terminological issue, it does reveal Mouffe's understanding of affect as cognitivist and psychoanalytic. This is why I also argue in this chapter (see next) that Mouffe's account of agonistic encounters needs to be read in conjunction with affect theory that moves beyond cognitivist and psychoanalytic accounts of affect and emotion.

For example, ignoring this affective dimension underestimates the powerful affective force of young people's identification with extremist groups providing a motivation for antagonism. Indeed, as Mouffe has argued, the overemphasis on consensus has contributed to the resurgence of far right extremism in Europe (2005, p. 3).[6] In particular, the lack of what she calls *agonistic* channels for the expression of conflicts creates the conditions for the emergence of ethnic, religious and other antagonisms that eventually lead to manifestations of far right extremism.[7]

In several of her writings, Mouffe (2000, 2005, 2013) posits an "agonistic pluralism" model of democracy to reframe antagonism and disagreement into productive forms of democratic engagement. Mouffe uses the term "agonism" to refer to relations that, while preserving the reality of conflict, do not eliminate passions from the public sphere in the name of consensus; rather, they mobilize passions for democratic ends. Too much emphasis on consensus and the refusal of conflict, says Mouffe, have led to disaffection with political participation; therefore, the public space is left widely open to extremist ideologies with platforms that give hope to many disenchanted people. For this purpose, to use Mouffe's terms, "enemies" must become "adversaries" and "antagonism" needs to turn into "agonism"; antagonism seeks to destroy its opponent, whereas agonism encompasses respect for the adversary to defend his or her position. Agonistic pluralism, then, is fundamental to the dynamics of the democratic process.

However, instead of moralizing the political discourse and call those who adhere to extremist ideologies "backward," "evil" or "irrational," Mouffe (2005) suggests that our conflict with such ideas should happen "in political and not in moral terms" (p. 120). In other words, the task of transforming antagonism into agonism will happen only if we do not see our adversaries in moral terms (good versus bad) but in political terms. Importantly, the moral assertion that good versus bad is limiting is shared by Deleuze and those that have drawn on this work since (Deleuze, 1988; Smith, 2012). To explain this assertion, Mouffe writes:

---

[6] For example, Mouffe (2005) criticizes Giddens and the third way "because it underlines the non-conflictual nature of his political project" and "erases the dimension of antagonism from the political" (p. 59). The belief that disagreements can be overcome through dialogue and education, explains further Mouffe, "is based on the idea that, with the passing of the bipolar era, states now face not enemies but dangers" (2005); however, such a consensual, post-political perspective fails to appreciate the fundamental conflicts and tensions embedded in modern capitalism.

[7] For example, in the UK media and ministers cite Prevent strategy data – e.g. see www.bbc.com/news/uk-46556447 – to argue that the number of people referred to the UK's terrorism-prevention program over concerns related to extreme right-wing activity jumped by 36 percent in 2017/2018, making it the fastest growing threat to national security.

When politics is played out in the register of morality, antagonisms cannot take an agonistic form. Indeed, when opponents are defined not in political, but in moral terms, they cannot be envisaged as an "adversary" but only as an "enemy." With the "evil them" no agonistic debate is possible, they must be eradicated. Moreover, as they are often considered as the expression of some kind of "moral disease," one should not even try to provide an explanation for their emergence and success. This is why, as we have seen in the case of right-wing populism, moral condemnation replaces a proper political analysis and the answer is limited to the building of a "cordon sanitaire" to quarantine the affected sectors. (2005, p. 76)

This means that when some demands are excluded (e.g., because they are racist), this is done so not because they are irrational or evil but because they challenge democratic institutions – without implying, of course, that these institutions are grounded in a superior rationality or are beyond any critique.

Faced with these tensions, then, we cannot ignore the affective dimension of collective identification in public life (Mihai, 2014). The goal, according to Mouffe (2005), is not to eliminate passions from public life but to "tame" (p. 149) them and foster forms of identification that are conducive to democratic agonistic practices. Taming the passions means expressing them in ways that treat others as adversaries rather than as enemies. As she explains,

> Emphasizing the role of passions is no doubt open to the objection that those passions can be mobilized in ways that will undermine democratic institutions. This is clearly the fear that leads many theorists to exclude them from democratic politics. But as I have argued, this is a very perilous viewpoint because refusing to provide democratic channels for the expression of collective affects lays the terrain for antagonistic forms of their mobilization. It is therefore vital for an agonistic politics, whose objective is the construction of we/they in terms of adversaries and not of enemies, to envisage the conditions under which adversarial common affects can be brought about. (Mouffe, 2005, p. 156)

Mouffe's idea that affects must support identification with democratic aims presupposes an understanding of affects "as malleable, transformable, sociable" (Mihai, 2014, p. 36), that is, as *educable*. Although Mouffe's early work is grounded in a social psychoanalytic understanding of affect (Stavrakakis, 1999), in her more recent work she finds insights in Spinoza's conception of affects and the notion that bodies have the capacity of being affected and affect others (Mouffe, 2014, p. 156). As she writes, "Like Freud, Spinoza believes that it is desire that moves human beings to act and he notes that what makes them act in one direction rather than in another are the affects" (Mouffe, 2014, p. 156). Mouffe points out that she finds Spinoza's ideas "helpful to envisage the process of production of common affects"; therefore, she proposes "to employ this dynamic to examine the modes of transformation of political identities, seeing 'affections' as the space where the discursive and the affective are articulated in specific practices" (Mouffe, 2014, p. 156). As she further explains,

> Those practices should aim at fostering common affects of an adversarial nature because, as Spinoza was keen to stress, an affect can only be displaced by an opposed affect, stronger than the one to be repressed. A counter-hegemonic politics necessitates the creation of a different regime of desires and affects so as to bring about a collective will sustained by common affects able to challenge the existing order. This is what I understand by the mobilization of passions and I am adamant that it would be tragic for the left, and for the future of democracy in our societies, to abandon this terrain to right-wing populist movements. (Mouffe, 2014, p.157)

Mihai (2014) argues that if we are to follow Mouffe's views on political affect and agonism, then the political goal of democracies will be to nurture "agonistic emotions," that is, affects and emotions that nourish the ethico-political principles that democracies are based on. Therefore, alongside Mouffe's social psychoanalytic understandings of collective identification, it is important to have an account that enables the theorization of *both* emotions *and* affects as agonistic. As Mouffe (2014) herself seems to recognize in her most recent writings, Spinoza's ideas can be valuable in this effort. Combining psychoanalytic theory and Spinozian ideas may raise some concerns about their compatibility. However, as I have shown earlier, there are complementary assertions between these perspectives; hence, I would argue that we can live with some theoretical mismatches, if our combined theoretical account takes into serious consideration the affective complexities involved in discussions of power, bodies and politics.

In the last part of the chapter, I put this theoretical proposal in conversation with pedagogical ideas, namely, I pay explicit attention to the affective dimension of far right rhetoric in the classroom through a lens that entails the *educability* of emotions and affects; without such a theorization it would be unclear how an affective identification with far right rhetoric will be challenged by an opposed affect/emotion.

Toward Agonistic Emotions and Affects in the Classroom?

Drawing on Mouffe's (2005) theory of agonistic pluralism, Ruitenberg (2009) has been the first educational theorist to propose an agonistic approach that highlights the role of political emotions. Political emotions are understood as those emotions and affects that are directed toward social and political issues – e.g., poverty, discrimination, racism, migration, suffering. For Ruitenberg, "educating political emotions would require that students learn to distinguish between emotions on behalf of themselves and emotions on behalf of a political collective" (p. 276). The first step in educating political emotions for an agonistic democracy, according to Ruitenberg, is to give the emotions a more legitimate place in education. But this is not enough, as she correctly points out, because educating political emotions should not be based on seeing emotions as a private site of control, but rather it should be based on understanding the cultural and political significance of emotions (see also, Ruitenberg, 2010).

Therefore, the purpose is to nurture not those emotions that are associated with an essentialist conception of identity "but rather emotions on behalf of a political collective, associated with views of particular hegemonic social relations" (Ruitenberg, 2009, p. 277). In particular, as Ruitenberg emphasizes, the focus should not be on "moral emotions" – that is, emotions that are directed toward a personal or interpersonal object – but rather on "political emotions" that "requires educating students about the power relations that structure societies as an *object of emotions*, for example through historical cases of political resistance to particular hegemonic arrangements" (Ruitenberg, 2009, p. 277, original emphasis). In other words, Ruitenberg highlights that the role of power in constituting our social and political emotions must be explicitly addressed in the curriculum.

Tryggvason (2018) has revisited Ruitenberg's (2009) work, emphasizing that a major contribution of her analysis is the destabilization of essentialist identities through the education of political emotions (see also, Tryggvason, 2017; Zembylas, 2011a). Therefore, an agonistic approach in educating political emotions recognizes the importance of sustaining "the political" in classroom discussions about emotions, conflicts and identities (Zembylas, 2018c). However, Tryggvason (2018) argues, this has to take place under certain conditions so that conflicts between political positions are not transformed into conflicts between individuals and identities. In other words, emotions in the classroom can become problematic, according to Tryggvason, if they are directed toward the personal lives of other students, or if their political content is antagonistic or anti-democratically oriented (see also, Mihai, 2014, p. 45).

A missing element from these agonistic accounts of political emotions in education – especially in relation to addressing the affective dimension of far right rhetoric – is precisely the need to take into consideration both emotions and affects as agonistic. In other words, it is crucial to develop pedagogical theories and approaches that recognize the affective complexities of young people's lives, "the contexts in which they live, as well as the [affective] appeal of the clarity which clear dualisms (good/evil, enemy/friend, etc.) provide to some far right communities" (Miller-Idriss & Pilkington, 2017, p. 142). The point of departure, then, ought to be the recognition of the affective dimension of far right rhetoric and its implications at all levels of life, beyond the simplistic version proposed by those who assume that far right ideologies can be eliminated altogether if an "appropriate" emotional/affective education is offered. This assumption poses the transparent self of liberal discourse, namely, that with enough rational reflexivity in the classroom, young people will be prevented from adopting far right ideologies.

This is, I think, precisely the problem with liberal accounts such as Nussbaum's book *Political Emotions* (2013), which advocates that liberal democracy requires nurturing political emotions such as sympathetic imagination, compassion and love. Nussbaum's assumption is that nurturing "noble" political emotions will eventually "exorcize" darker emotions such as fear, anxiety, anger, resentment, shame and guilt – namely, the emotional roots of right-wing ideologies (Salmela & von Scheve, 2017). Nussbaum's narrowly cognitivist framework underestimates people's affective investments and assumes a simplistic view of how negative emotions are converted into positive, into "appropriate" emotions, as she says (2013, p. 18) – a view that cannot properly grasp the affective complexities that are often involved in dealing with far right rhetoric (see also Miller-Idriss, 2017).

Furthermore, according to Davies (2008), when it comes to counter-extremism, pedagogical approaches that aim to "teach" people the "right" emotions and attitudes may not only be ineffective but can also backfire, leading individuals to retreat even further into narrow worldviews (Miller-Idriss & Pilkington, 2017). Hence, it is not enough to propose pedagogical approaches that teach "noble" political emotions in the hope that they will magically "convert" young people's darker emotions, as if this is merely a matter of human psychology. This assumption ignores that engagement with far right ideologies is driven not only by rationality but also by strong affectivity, wherein affective responses and linguistic expressions signal people's affective investments (Kølvraa, 2015). Therefore, it is the democratic duty of educational institutions – schools, universities and educational institutions in general – to provide arenas for "adversaries" (in Mouffe's sense) to give voice to their concerns.

For example, this idea would mean providing opportunities in the classroom to debate the politics of different ideologies, including far right ideologies, as long as this takes place within a democratic frame. It is easier said than done, of course; however, educators attempting to do this may need to employ a range of pedagogical strategies that skillfully navigate the dangers such as developing a supportive emotional atmosphere and a trusting, open relationship between educator and students; being sensitive to students' personal biographies; acknowledging how the educator and students feel about the issue at hand; emphasizing the importance of educators and students reflecting critically on their emotions and affects; recognizing and examining multiple perspectives and interpretations, yet identifying and taking a firm stance against racist views; and finally, using familiar active approaches such as discussion, small groups, and independent learning as shortcuts into controversy (Zembylas, 2015a).

Following Mouffe's agonistic approach, it is crucial that politically relevant emotions and affects between adversaries can find an outlet in the classroom, yet not within a moralizing frame. If engaging far right ideologies takes place within a moralizing frame – namely, framing the conversation according to simplistic and essentialist moral categories such as "good" versus "evil" – then, it is likely that this moralization will evoke pity or anger for those who espouse such ideologies rather than action that truly addresses the precarity of their lives and which possibly has attracted young people to far right rhetoric in the first place. The complexities related to the affective dimension of far right ideologies are not going to be resolved by seducing those who espouse such ideas in heated confrontations that antagonize them. Rather, agonistic pedagogical approaches need to engage with young people's political affects and emotions in ways that encourage expression of passionate commitments as long as they are compatible with the ethico-political ethos of democracy.

In other words, the pedagogical aim is to ensure that no one should be silenced insofar as the affects and emotions expressed are compatible with an agonistic democratic ethos. "This implies," Mihai (2014) argues, "that viewing those we disagree with as subhuman or evil and identifying ourselves with programs that seek their elimination violates the shared ethico-political principles underlying agonism" (Mihai, 2014, p. 44). Simplistic pedagogical strategies such as condemning or silencing distasteful views are often counterproductive (Miller-Idriss & Pilkington, 2017). Educators need to offer young people pedagogical opportunities that pay explicit attention to identifying and interrogating the transmission of the affective dimension of far right rhetoric within and beyond classroom spaces. However, the only rules "regulating" this deliberation "will get their content from the ethico-political principles that undergird democracy" (Mihai, 2014, p. 42).

Conclusion

Building on the arguments put forward by Mouffe in relation to agonistic pluralism and the role of political emotions and affects, it is possible to engage in a critical reconsideration of the affective dimension of far right rhetoric in education and counter it in productive ways. Countering far right ideologies pedagogically will not take place by eliminating those views from the classroom but rather by reassessing our approach to those ideologies, once we understand how sophisticated people's affective investments truly are. As Biesta (2010b) reminds us, democratic education is not about creating individual, democratic subjects that "have" a passion for democracy. This approach would be too "psychologized" as it would depoliticize democratic encounters and moralize them – which would eventually lead to a deterioration of classroom debates into inimical conversations (cf. Mihai, 2014). An agonistic pedagogical approach that pays explicit attention to the affective dimension of far right rhetoric means an approach that critically examines and challenges how far right ideologies are used to educate emotionally and affectively their own constituents and broader public.

Forming an agonistic pedagogical approach grounded in Mouffe's work helps educators gain a deeper appreciation of the mechanisms and processes through which young people move "toward" or "turn" away from far right ideologies. Hence, pedagogical explorations of far right rhetoric in curriculum and pedagogy can become strategic sites of ethical and political transformation that pay attention both to nonverbally articulated and embodied elements and to cultural norms that are perceived corporeally. In this manner, educators may generate pedagogical spaces for countering far right rhetoric – spaces that begin to move step-by-step young people from affective contagion of far right rhetoric to affective solidarity with those who suffer social injustices, without reinstating empty empathy, pity or sentimentalism. Needless to say, this process will be difficult, long and, at times, painful, but it is important to engage with the affective complexities of far right ideologies within a pedagogical frame that is agonistic rather than moralistic. The issue, then, is not about educating young people *for* a particular set of emotions and affects, no matter how "noble" these emotions are – as this would amount to a form of political indoctrination (see Chapter 8) – but rather to give pedagogical substance to the idea that the political emotions and affects expressed in the classroom will be constantly interrogated by the ethico-political principles of the democratic agon.

CHAPTER 7

Reinvigorating the Affective Atmospheres of Democratic Education

As noted in previous chapters, there is a growing concern that the rise of right-wing populism in recent years threatens liberal democracy (Galston, 2018; Mudde & Kaltwasser, 2012; Panizza, 2005). This concern is relevant to democratic education for two important reasons: First, democratic education can enrich understandings of the affective investments that drive people to populism; and second, democratic education can work to renew itself by taking into consideration the failures of current approaches such as intercultural and multicultural education to contribute more productively to stopping the tide of right-wing populism. In this last chapter of Part II, an attempt is made to put the conversation again in broader terms by asking what it might mean to think seriously about democracy, right-wing populism and democratic education as a set of feelings "circling in the air." How might thinking about democracy and democratic education as something that is *felt* and experienced *affectively* enable a richer understanding of the suspension of these feelings or the rise of populist affectivity?

My focus in this chapter, then, is on how democratic education may engage with its renewal by paying explicit attention to a neglected element in politics of affect: the role of *affective atmospheres*. The concept of "affective atmospheres" (Anderson, 2009) that is currently circulating in a growing number of academic disciplines explores issues ranging from public places and urban environments (Bissell, 2010; Gandy, 2017; McCormack, 2008) to conflict (Fregonese, 2017), security (Adey, 2014), surveillance (Ellis, Tucker & Harper, 2013), and national identity and nationalism (Closs Stephens, 2016; Closs Stephens et al., 2017; Sumartojo, 2016). These works emphasize that atmosphere constitutes a fundamental aspect of how we experience the world, and more specifically, how our activities and social relations are entangled with the spaces in which we act or dwell (Brown et al., 2019). Although there is ambiguity and multiplicity to the concept of atmospheres, it is generally understood in everyday language as "ambience," "sense of place" or the "feel" of a room, and more philosophically in terms such as "mood" or "attunement" (Bille, Bjerregaard & Sørensen, 2015; Riedel, 2019).

As Martin (2013) points out, democratic politics is an "emotional business" (p. 461); therefore, affects and emotions are inevitably part and parcel of political discussions in the classroom. I would argue, then, that democratic education has a lot to gain from examining the neglected dimension of affective atmospheres. Paying attention to the notion of affective atmospheres offers something new, because it helps us theorize how teachers and students come to feel, engage with and embody political concepts – such as democracy or populism – through a combination of "presence and absence, materiality and ideality, definite and indefinite, singularity and generality" (Anderson, 2009, p. 77). Approaching atmospheres as "something distributed yet palpable [...] that registers in and through sensing bodies whilst also remaining diffuse" (McCormack, 2008, p. 413) enables educators and researchers to explore the entanglement of historically structured social and affective relations with spatial and materialist elements in specific educational settings.

Taking feelings and spatialities of democratic education together, this chapter theorizes how democracy and democratic education take hold and circulate in classrooms and schools, and, therefore, asks under which circumstances inimical or threatening atmospheres are experienced, created or even "engineered," encompassing affective and material features that (de)legitimate democracy, democratic education and populism. My aim, then, is to render the concept of atmosphere tractable through a line of theorizing that recognizes the affective force of democracy and right-wing populism and asks how democratic education may respond by paying careful attention to democracy as affectively produced and transmitted in educational spaces. The chapter also examines what it would take to reinvigorate the affective atmospheres of democratic education in schools in light of the rise of populist affectivity in several societies.

The chapter proceeds in four steps. First, it elaborates on the concept of affective atmospheres and its relevance for understanding democracy, democratic education and right-wing populism within their spatio-affective unfolding. Second, it discusses some of the modes of engaging with atmosphere in the context of democratic education. Third, it focuses on what it means to stage or engineer atmospheres and how this applies to democratic education, highlighting both the risks and the possibilities. The chapter concludes with a discussion of the pedagogical and political implications of this analysis for strengthening democracy and challenging right-wing populism. The chapter can, therefore, be understood not only as an analysis of the usefulness of the concept of atmosphere in theorizing the affective in democratic education but also as a critical intervention to the challenge identified from the beginning of this book, namely, that of asking how the affective force of right-wing populism might be resisted or somehow transformed in the context of democratic education.

The Concept of Affective Atmospheres and Its Relevance

As noted in the Introduction, the so-called affective turn (Clough, 2007) in the humanities and social sciences has produced a series of contributions on the notion of affect (Ahmed, 2004; Anderson, 2014; Berlant, 2011; Cvetkovich, 2003, 2012; Massumi, 2002b, 2015a; Sedgwick-Kosofsky, 2003; Seigworth & Gregg, 2010; Thrift, 2008). As Anderson (2014) points out, "there is no such thing as affect 'itself'" (p. 13), but rather affect is understood as the capacity to affect and be affected (Massumi, 2002). In other words, affect is approached as an adjective or verb rather than as a noun or an inherent property of artifacts; this understanding of affect stresses its relationality (Bille & Simonsen, 2019). As Bille and Simonsen further argue, affect needs to be situated in practices that "are spatially embedded and felt phenomena" (2019, p. 2; see also Reckwitz, 2012; Wetherell, 2012).

As I have pointed out in previous chapters, this theoretical framing of affect provides an understanding of how we form relations and affective communities that share common ideals and values (e.g., democracy), how we become attached to certain political promises and programs and not others, and how we engage in collective action or refuse it (Vrasti & Dayal, 2016). The emotions of/about democracy are always practiced within a particular context; the context is "a vital element in the constitution of affect" (Thrift, 2004, p. 60). Hence the spaces of affect and feeling, including their material elements, are extremely important because they provide us with an understanding of emotions as embodied and (un)learned practices. In this sense, democracy or populism are (un)learned affectively; as affects, they are produced socially and spatially and they are distributed as economies (Ahmed, 2004). For instance, populist affective economies produce indignation, hate, fear and anger toward "others" (Gebhardt, 2019). In such discourses, writes Gebhardt, the other is constructed as threatening, creating a we-and-they categorization where space and feelings of belonging are demarcated. It is within this theoretical framing, then, that there is value to turn to affective atmospheres as felt spaces, because they unfold as relations, highlighting the attunement between affective practices and the social and material context (Bille & Simonsen, 2019).

The turn to atmospheres can be traced to the influence of German philosopher Gernot Böhme (1993) who is credited with drawing attention to the notion of atmospheres as "affective powers of feeling, spatial bearer of moods" (p. 119). In this line of thinking, the concept of atmospheres describes how people are affectively engaged with their social and material context. Importantly, as Bille et al. (2015) explain, the properties of atmosphere are found in the intersection of the objective and the subjective, that is, the *in-betweeness* of subject and object, of experiences and environments. In Böhme's (1993) words:

> Atmospheres are indeterminate above all as regards their ontological status. We are not sure whether we should attribute them to the objects or environments from which they proceed or to the subjects who experience them. We are also unsure where they are. They seem to fill the space with a certain tone of feeling like a haze. (p. 114)

Thus, for Böhme, atmosphere is not the subjective "feeling" of a room or a situation, nor is it an objectively observable state of the environment, but rather it is an intermediate position between subject and object (Bille et al., 2015). Atmospheres are not produced merely by objects or the persons that are present; they are characterized by the co-presence of subject and object (Böhme, 2017). Hence, there is always the possibility of *staging* and *engineering* an atmosphere (Bille et al., 2015; Philippopoulos-Mihalopoulos, 2016); thereby, atmospheres become central to pedagogical, social and political activities and experiences (I come back to this later in the chapter).

Drawing on this groundwork by Böhme, other scholars have further developed the notion of affective atmosphere. Whereas Böhme sees atmosphere as inherently spatialized, Anderson (2014) treats atmosphere as an "ensemble" of human and nonhuman bodies that come together and act in complex ways (Brown et al., 2019). As he explains, "Atmospheres are a kind of indeterminate affective excess through which intensive space-times are created and come to envelop specific bodies; sites, objects, people, and so on, all may be atmospheric or may feel and be moved by atmospheres" (Anderson, 2014, p. 160). In this sense, Anderson conceptualizes atmospheres as constantly evolving processes (see also, McCormack, 2008, 2018), thus emphasizing their emergent and unfinished quality: "atmospheres, emanating and enveloping particular things, sites or people, are endlessly being formed and reformed through encounters as they are attuned to and become part of life" (Anderson, 2014, p. 145). In this sense, Anderson (2014) points out, atmospheres are experienced through the changes in a body's affective capacities as it moves in and out of various relations.

In a similar vein, Ahmed (2014) describes atmosphere as "a feeling of what is around," "a surrounding influence," and "a way of receiving an impression, whether or not conscious." Thus, affective encounters cannot be traced back to the feelings of an individual but are rather shaped by the attunement between human and nonhuman bodies. As she writes, "the atmosphere is not simply 'out there' before it gets 'in': how we arrive, how we enter this room or that room, will affect what impressions we receive." In particular, Ahmed uses the term "atmospheric walls" to describe how spaces are "available to some more than to others." An atmospheric wall is "a way of preventing some from staying. [...] A wall is a technique: a way of stopping something from happening or stopping someone from progressing without appearing to stop this or stop them." What is remarkable about atmospheric walls, according to Ahmed, is that they are both invisible and selective: They are visible by those who are meant to be kept out, and invisible by those who have the right to pass through. Ahmed (2014) uses the concept of atmospheric walls to talk about racial exclusion:

> I think whiteness is often experienced as an atmosphere. You walk into a room and you encounter it like a wall that is at once palpable and tangible but also hard to grasp or to reach. It is something, it is quite something, but it is difficult to put your finger on it. When you walk into the room, it can be like a door slams in your face. The tightening of bodies: the sealing of space. The discomfort when you encounter something that does not receive you.

Summarizing the shift from affect to affective atmospheres, this rich and diverse body of work highlights three core themes (Brown et al., 2019, p. 10; see also Michels & Steyaert, 2017, p. 85): (1) Atmospheres exist between subjects and objects – they combine both affective and spatio-material elements but cannot be reduced to either; (2) Atmospheres are produced through a process of "attunement" between affective practices and the social and material context, so they are relational, namely, they cannot be attributed to a specific agent or entity; (3) Atmospheres occur through the entanglement of human and nonhuman bodies and forces, but they are not "in" space or time, but rather this entanglement constitutes its own "space-time." Taken together, these themes help us pay attention to atmospheres as processes in which "historically structured socio-cultural activity becomes folded together with more elemental forces" (Brown et al., 2019, p. 10). The next part of the chapter turns toward discussing some of the modes of engaging with atmosphere in the context of democratic education. My interest is focused on what atmosphere *does* and how it operates (see Riedel, 2019) through different modes of engagement; this analysis foregrounds the pedagogical and political implications of atmosphere that are further discussed in subsequent sections of the chapter.

Modes of Engaging with Atmospheres in Democratic Education

So far, my focus has been on describing what constitutes atmosphere and how it emerges. I now turn to the question of how to approach, understand and engage with atmospheres, particularly in the context of democratic education. As Bille et al. (2015) phrased this question in both methodological and ontological terms:

> Do we tease them [atmospheres] apart, separate out specific characteristics, categorize atmosphere as distinct from other terms such as ambiance, affect, mood, aura, feeling, presence, sense, experience and perception? Or do we seek to maintain the vagueness in the study of atmosphere, allowing the unclear to be taken at face-value as integral to its very nature? (p. 33)

For example, do we identify characteristics of affective atmospheres in a classroom or a school that cultivate democratic feelings and then argue that these characteristics need to be present in the construction of spaces for democratic education? Or does the indeterminacy and instability of atmospheres make such an endeavor meaningless?

Answering these questions is beyond the scope of this chapter – at least not without empirically grounded studies in various contexts where democratic education takes place – yet my sense is that studies of atmosphere in several disciplines so far have tended to seek for ways to bridge these questions (e.g., see Buser, 2014; Gandy, 2017; Michels & Steyaert, 2017). In particular, even though these studies recognize that atmospheres may be vague, they simultaneously attempt to engage with specific elements that make up an atmosphere – such as the spatio-material organization of a school and how it is entangled with the affective and emotional life of students giving rise to a particular affective atmosphere or altering an existing one (e.g., see Finn, 2016).

To go a step further though, atmospheres may be vague, but they are not neutral, as Brown et al. (2019) point out: "They attract and repel, amuse and horrify, enchant and become unbearable" (p. 13). To put this differently, atmospheres *afford* some events or experiences, while preventing others. An affordance "is a relational possibility between an organism and its environment that is perceived through its invariant features – water, for example, affords drinking" (Brown et al., 2019, p. 13). In other words, the relations between human and nonhuman bodies and forces within a particular context afford individuals to behave or feel in one way or another. The elements that make an atmosphere, therefore, can be identified in terms of their affordances.

For example, one can explore the affective atmospheres created in a classroom or school in which democratic education takes place. How do the curriculum, pedagogy, classroom organization and materials used afford the capacity of students and teachers to "feel" certain democratic values? In which ways are the atmospheres of democracy and democratic education *felt* by students and teachers? What are these atmospheres conducive for students to do or not to do in order to invoke experiences for/about democratic thinking and feeling? These questions draw our attention to the ways in which the singular and the collective, the subject and object, come together, enabling us to examine how the affective atmospheres created in classrooms and schools matter politically (cf. Closs Stephens, 2016).

What is significant here is that inspiring and enriching feelings for/about democratic values (e.g., liberty, the rule of law, etc.) in the context of democratic education cannot be traced back to the work of a single authority (e.g., the teacher who teaches about democracy or the curriculum that is taught) directing students' feelings nor is it necessarily the product of spontaneous events (e.g., the celebration of International Day of Democracy). As Ahmed (2014) explains, atmospheres "involve conscious decisions and collective will," and they can also be the product of habituation or institutional design (Vrasti & Dayal, 2016). A classroom atmosphere that legitimates democratic values, for example, generates distinct elements for what is appropriate and what is not when students engage in deliberations. To put this simply but certainly not simplistically, it is not enough to *talk about* democracy and its values in the classroom or school; democracy must be constantly practiced and *felt* in atmospheres that are created to orient students toward democratic values. To refer to atmospheres of democratic education in a classroom, then, is to touch upon the politics of distributing, organizing and making legitimate feelings for/about democracy, which invariably includes events and pedagogical practices that legitimate the importance of *living* democracy. In this way, an atmosphere of democracy is not only something students feel, but it also simultaneously positions the felt space as something students *do*.

In contrast to assumptions that democracy and democratic education simply entail particular images, texts, symbols or idea(l)s that are driven by reason and rationality, the provocation of affective atmospheres suggests paying attention to the ways in which key figures, images and sounds are circulated in classrooms and schools, (de)legitimating feelings for/about democracy. Rather than reading the emergence of democratic affects as traceable to an essence that comes from teaching about the values of democracy, we can read them "as a temporally and spatially specific encounter of swirling affects, memories, sounds, rhythms and images sticking to particular assemblages of bodies and materials" (Closs Stephens, 2016, p. 191). Similar to the cultivation of nationalistic affects that operate in specific affective atmospheres, as Closs Stephens points out, the manifestation of democratic affects does not take place in isolation, but rather these affects work as part of assemblages of different elements and assume different intensities at various space–time entanglements. This means, for example, that an image of an idea for/about democracy "does not assume the same political charge in each context and may not be charged at all" (Closs Stephens, 2016, p. 191). It also implies that feelings for/about democracy "can stick to many different kinds of objects, materials and bodies" (Closs Stephens, 2016, p. 191) – far beyond the familiar examples of images, texts and symbols that may celebrate democracy.

For example, writing about the atmospheres of progress in a data-based school, Finn (2016) lists numerous elements that are also relevant for the affective atmospheres of democracy and democratic education, such as the material appearances of democracy at a school "in speech and on walls, electronic whiteboards, computers, and classwork books and written books" (p. 33); pupils' bodily comportments such as how they stand, sit, move around and use their bodies in individual and group learning activities (p. 34); "signals of smiles or downcast eyes" and "the sounds of the classroom from the huffing, raised voices and throwing down of school bags in frustration and anger to the 'bright' tenor of many voices animatedly talking and reflecting together or the 'deep' silence of stilled bodies in thought" (p. 34). All of these constitute elements of atmospheres of democratic education in that they combine affective potentials and forces that are associated in *this* raced, gendered and classed context.

Dewalling classroom atmospheres that are *less* democratic, then, requires that educators become aware of the raced, gendered and classed dimensions of the taken-for-granted arrangements operative in many Western liberal societies and schools. At every step of the way, the affective atmosphere produced in the classroom "risks throwing up new walls in the face of undocumented, racialized, working class, queer, and differently abled bodies" (Vrasti & Dayal, 2016, p. 1004). The recognition, therefore, of "bad" or "undemocratic" atmospheres constitutes more than just an affective threat to students' well-being. As Gandy (2017) argues, "The presence of 'threatening atmospheres' connects with the affective potentialities of incipient violence. Certain hatreds such as racism or misogyny can lie dormant ready to reveal themselves in precise moments or situations" (pp. 364–365). By attending to atmospheres as practiced and felt in the classroom or school, it becomes possible to begin asking more challenging questions such as what sort of atmospheres are sought through everyday pedagogies in the context of democratic education? How do such pedagogical practices fail or succeed? How does that affect students in that space, when it comes to feeling and living democracy? What atmospheric norms require what types of pedagogies to cultivate democracy or distance students from populist affectivity within a particular space-time entanglement? Can there be classroom or school atmospheres that are staged, engineered or manipulated? The next part of the chapter turns specifically to the last question, focusing on how the notion of staging atmospheres applies to democratic education.

Staging Atmospheres in Democratic Education?

Despite the indeterminacy of atmospheres, there is growing attention to the *staging* and engineering of atmospheres (Bille et al., 2015; Buser, 2014; Marotta & Cummings, 2019; Philippopoulos-Mihalopoulos, 2016). The notion of staging an atmosphere, argue Bille et al. (2015), "is at first sight a paradox, since it can appear somewhat impossible to even try to stage a phenomenon as fleeting, ambiguous and vague as atmosphere" (p. 33). However, there are many examples of intentional efforts to shape the affective experiences of people in a particular space for utilitarian, commercial, aesthetic or political reasons. As Buser (2014) explains, "The practice of purposefully staging and manipulating atmospheres is pervasive, evident amongst the landscape of shopping malls, festival markets, sports and grant events, public spaces and other sites of managed social experience" (p. 235).

The rationale of staging atmospheres is grounded in the idea of manipulating spaces, objects and bodies in order to influence individual and collective behaviors and emotions (Böhme in Buser, 2014). An engineered atmosphere, writes Philippopoulos-Mihalopoulos (2016), provides a specific direction to affects and emotions through the design of space and activities so that different atmospheres might be produced and felt. In that sense, affects are "exploited and channeled to serve consumerist needs, capitalist abstractions, legal obedience and political placation" (Philippopoulos-Mihalopoulos, 2016, p. 158). Designing or staging atmospheres, explains Buser (2014), can range from the most extravagant (e.g., music festivals, sports events) to the everyday practice of human interaction (e.g., giving a lecture, teaching). What these efforts have in common – although manifested of course in different ways – is the configuration of spatio-material context to produce certain feelings and emotions or invoke particular action (or nonaction).

Needless to say, the issue of staging atmospheres raises the question whether and how this is relevant for democratic education, namely, to what extent the orchestrated – to the degree that is orchestrated – atmosphere in the context of teaching about/for democracy is actually shared by the students, "and to what degree the actions and moods encountered actually confer to the anticipations on which the place was staged" (Bille et al., 2015, p. 34). On the one hand, one may argue that such sort of staging of atmospheres should not even be taking place in any form of education, as this would amount to some form of manipulation. On the other hand, can we really ignore that some sort of staging already takes place, if we consider that there is some kind of planning involved in curriculum and instruction?

Looking more carefully at planning for instruction, for example, one realizes that it is fundamentally concerned with organizing pedagogical space in such a way that it aims at something; there is a teaching plan that attempts to move from something that is envisioned to implementation. This movement, explain Marotta and Cummings (2019), who refer to planning in general, "involves interactions between bodies in space, but also interactions between the present and the future," thus "planning plays a fundamental role in producing transitions, but then it needs to manage those transitions through implementation" (p. 196). The teacher, then, who teaches about democratic education, inevitably stages and orchestrates affective atmospheres, either this is done deliberately or not. A pedagogical space *could*, for example, feel safe, comfortable or exciting, but one may also argue that it *should* feel that way (cf. Bille et al., 2015).

Indeed, educators may realize or not that the affective atmospheres constructed in their classrooms shape students' experiences and moods for/about democracy through organizing objects, bodies and spaces. Realizing the pedagogical and political potential of this process may allow us to ask new questions concerning the role of atmospheres in pedagogical efforts toward democratic education: What are the effects of educators' attempts to teach for/about democracy through staging atmospheres that are conducive to democratic thinking and feeling? Is it better to leave this staging to chance? Will educators be accused for propaganda (even if it is for "noble" purposes), if they stage atmospheres that are designed (practically and politically) to purposely cultivate feelings for/about democracy? What are the consequences of these efforts for students? In a sense, according to Bille et al. (2015), whose analysis inspires these questions, "we may say that what we pursue [...] is the question [...]: what does an atmosphere make it possible to do, to perceive and to share?" (p. 33)

Perhaps more important for pedagogical purposes is also the idea that atmospheres change over time. As Buser (2014) writes, "The durability of any atmosphere is belied by an incessant potential for transformation through the introduction or realignment of objects, bodies and affects" (p. 235). Also, Bille et al. (2015) point out, "Not only does this testify to the historicity of atmospheres but, more importantly, to the fact that atmospheres emerge as multi-temporal tensions: they are at the same time a product of the past and the future" (p. 34). Inevitably, then, there is always some sort of transformation in atmospheres, either this is done intentionally or not. Therefore, atmospheres constitute a space of political formation, although they "cannot be completely controlled in any simple and unambiguous way by political agents" (p. 34). If power, then, is a constitutive element of affective atmospheres in any classroom setting that conditions how students feel for/about democracy (or other issues), then isn't it more productive to consider the quality of affective attachments designed for democratic education in a strategic manner? In other words, if democratic education is inevitably an intervention on an atmosphere that distinctly affects the conditions for students' attachments to particular ideas and actions, isn't it important that we discuss the extent to which educators should perhaps embrace staging atmospheres in their pedagogical practices? Needless to say, this proposition entails both risks and possibilities.

For example, it could be argued that by suggesting the staging of atmospheres of affects and emotions in the classroom, democratic education risks becoming a form of propaganda. However, such a risk is intrinsic to all forms of atmosphere *and* education, not only to democratic education as such. Therefore, the question is not *to stage or not to stage* atmospheres in the context of democratic education, but rather to what extent do educators need to pay attention to affective atmospheres in their classrooms so that the risks of propaganda and manipulation are averted?

At the same time, educators need to be conscious of the affective investments of right-wing populism (e.g., anger, fear) and invest in affective atmospheres that offer openings for affects and demands that are *not* oriented away from a democratic life or *toward* right-wing populism.

Focusing on how to design productive – in the Foucauldian sense, that is, generative, neither "good" or "bad" – affective atmospheres in the context of democratic education, then, means that educators need to pay attention to the complexity of atmospheres. The complexity of atmospheres and the extent to which they can be staged is not just a matter of scale, or of specific material or psychological manifestations that can be manipulated (Gandy, 2017) e.g., in the classroom, but also a unique opportunity to engage critically with the embodied and affective experience of democracy and (by extension, populism). Even if democratic education is opened up to the risk of staging atmospheres, there is no guarantee that the generated affects and emotions will indeed be directed toward democracy. Thus, the notion of staging atmospheres in democratic education, rather than being taken for granted or working as a proxy for propaganda, offers pedagogical and political openings for rethinking the implications of the affective investments that are promoted in democratic education. In the last part of the chapter, I will focus more specifically on the pedagogical and political implications of the notion of affective atmospheres for challenging right-wing populism.

Pedagogical and Political Implications for Challenging Right-Wing Populism

To reiterate my argument so far, I have suggested that the notion of affective atmospheres deserves more attention in democratic education, because it creates openings to address a key question: How can affective qualities create spaces of teaching and learning by highlighting how democracy (as well as right-wing populism) is embodied, affective, and (un)learned practice (cf. Anderson, 2014; Reckwitz, 2012; Wetherell, 2012)? Through focusing on how democratic education can be viewed as an *atmospheric intervention* (Marotta & Cummings, 2019; Michels & Steyaert, 2017), it is shown that the approach of affects as atmospheres points at the value of paying attention to the spatio-material and affective elements of democratic education. However, I neither want to overestimate nor want to underestimate the influence of affective atmospheres of democracy (or right-wing populism) and their socio-spatial capacities in the context of democratic education. Thus, this concluding discussion highlights some implications of adopting the notion of affective atmospheres to understand not only how the affective matters for strengthening democratic education (Sant, 2019) but also how it makes a difference for contesting right-wing populism. Given the complexity of this task, my aim here is not to provide a list of specific pedagogical actions but rather to sketch some ideas that could be useful in highlighting the capacity of students and teachers, individually and collectively, to affect and to be affected in the context of democratic education.

First, the shift from affect to affective atmospheres in exploring democratic education focuses on democracy as affective activity, that is, as a form of social practice rather than (only) as a set of theoretical ideas taught in the classroom, and highlights how students act as carriers of democratic practices (see also Chapter 5). This approach "brings the dramatic and the everyday back into social analysis" as Wetherell (2012, p. 2) writes. As she further argues,

> The unit of analysis for social and cultural research on affect, is not some kind of inarticulable, momentary, spurious, hard-to-detect, pre-conscious judder. It is affective-discursive practice, or that domain of social practice which bears on and formulates the conduct of activities we conventionally recognize as making psychological and emotional sense, and, in the process, making psychological subjects and emotional events. (Wetherell, 2015, p. 152)

This means that democratic education as an atmospheric intervention is inevitably a dramatic performance that comes with considerable affective considerations (cf. Michels & Steyaert, 2017). As Seigworth and Gregg (2010) also point out, affect can be approached "as an aesthetic or art of dosages: experiment and experience. Feel the angles and rhythms at the interface of bodies and worlds" (p. 16). Approaching democratic education as an atmospheric intervention, then, implies that affective atmospheres of democracy can be crafted intentionally by offering pedagogical opportunities to students not merely to articulate their emotions (Ruitenberg, 2009; Tryggvason, 2018; Zembylas, 2018c) but also to *experiment* with everyday practices that make students feel attached to democratic values. To fulfill the potential of democratic education as an affective practice, pedagogical practices need to provide spaces of attunement with democratic values, that is, spaces in which students actively practice feelings for/about democracy.

Given this point, then, the political task of democratic education lies in developing "alternative compelling forms of sociality" (Closs Stephens, 2017, p. 193), which can tempt students to take a chance on *living* in a democratic world beyond superficial or ideological proclamations about the value of democracy. This also implies providing opportunities to students to understand how affective dynamics work in various contexts to organize people's affective responses to right-wing populism and under which circumstances there can be an antidote to the affective regimes that are produced by right-wing populism in everyday life. For example, this means that democratic education invests in examining the negative and positive affects and emotions of those who feel attachment to populist politics, e.g., communities affected by economic decline or feel isolation for various reasons (see Chapters 1 and 2).

Focusing on the notion of affective atmospheres, then, raises the question of how this can influence a new politics of affect in the context of democratic education. The issue is, therefore, how different politics of affect create atmospheres that activate or cultivate certain affects and emotions. As Amin and Thrift (2013) suggest in their book on affect and politics, the affective turn in recent years has important political implications that call for the "active cultivation of alternative feelings so that new affective connections can be forged and a general desire for other ways of being in the world can emerge, and can be build into new political causes" (p. 158). But as Michels and Steyaert (2017) point out, "Anyone who composes affective atmospheres must accept that at any moment they can turn in another direction, in the same way that a change in the weather drowns one's hope of a cozy concert into a moment of existential fear that all this work has been for nothing" (p. 100). Therefore, it is important for educators and scholars in democratic education to understand that affects allow different ways of living and being in classroom and beyond, and that the politics of affect establishes possibilities that might create democratic or populist modes of engagement in or beyond classroom life (Mårdh & Tryggvason, 2017).

As empirical research on right-wing populism and its affective implications demonstrates in political life (e.g., see Hochschild, 2016), the appeal of any political message is always dependent on the articulation of "alternative" politics of belonging that offers hope to citizens for the future. This realization is politically *and* pedagogically significant for democratic education, because a solid analysis and understanding of the ways that various affective modes of democracy and populism circulate offers points of intervention to further the political and pedagogical spaces for democratic education. Hence, the implication of attending to the affective atmospheres of democratic education is to provide spaces for educators andstudents to engage critically and productively with their own and others' affects and emotions, in order to identify the consequences of different affective modes through which democracy and populism are articulated.

Paying attention to affective atmospheres in democratic education provides a chance to educators and scholars to ask pertinent questions, such as how do students' affective encounters with others draw them into democratic practices? Which affective conditions make students feel the risks of right-wing populism? How might students learn to challenge particular affective atmospheres or contribute to alternative structures of feeling that help brew more democratic kinds of political community in the classroom and beyond? How is it possible to break or interrupt populist affects in the context of democratic education? These are core questions for the future exploration of democratic education as affective atmosphere. These are the sort of questions that develop a new politics of affect in democratic education, because they allow educators and scholars to begin asking what new possibilities of feeling and acting are enabled in educational institutions.

Concluding Remarks

In conclusion, I have argued that the value of paying attention to affective atmospheres in democratic education makes it possible to trace the ways classroom and school atmospheres draw in spatial and affective forces as students become attuned and attached to democracy and/or right-wing populism. The implication of attending to affective atmospheres of democratic education, then, is to examine how students' and educators' bodies become attuned with specific affective potentials. "It is attending to the mundane as well as spectacular situations, collective or in solitude," write Bille and Simonsen (2019, p. 11) that have an impact on students' and educators' lives. Thus, the analysis in this chapter contributes to the conversation on how atmospheres are produced and shaped affectively in democratic education, and how these processes and affective attachments are tied to the construction of political belonging.

Future empirical exploration will specify the elements of staging atmospheres of democracy and/or right-wing populism by taking seriously the affective investments of the students and educators who engage with the atmosphere of democratic education in a classroom or school. Ultimately, it is the affective investments in democracy that make democracy worthwhile, as Mårdh and Tryggvason (2017) point out. Close attention to the affective practices of democratic education through which students and educators are moved by and act back upon these affective conditions will enrich present theoretical accounts.

PART III

Inventing Affective Pedagogies for Democratic Education

CHAPTER 8

Nurturing Political Emotions in the Classroom

As discussed in Parts I and II, there is a growing interest about the relevance of emotions and affects in political theory and practice, especially after the recent affective turn in the social sciences and humanities (Clarke, Hoggett & Thompson, 2006; Demertzis, 2013; Ferry & Kingston, 2008; Goodwin, Jasper & Polletta, 2001; Hoggett & Thompson, 2012). This work emphasizes that emotions and affects are fundamental to political life, especially to the formation of political community and identity. Although there are different theoretical understandings of emotion and affects in various disciplines, the academic study of politics for a long time has been firmly attached to a narrowly rationalist understanding of emotion as split from the head and mind (Clarke et al., 2006). However, in recent years, various theories emphasize that emotions are social and cultural constructs that have significant links to the body, social norms and values, and habituated action. At present, as Clarke and his colleagues point out, the dominant view holds that emotions are not subjective inner states but rather products of social relations. This understanding of emotions in political life creates conditions for increased political agency of individuals and groups whose participation has long been dismissed or undermined on the basis that they are overly emotional and irrational, including women, black people, and members of the working class (Degerman, 2019b).

In the area of democratic education (Gutmann, 1996; Sant, 2019), there has been a growing concern whether "political emotions" have or should have a place in the classroom (Ruitenberg, 2009; Tryggvason, 2017, 2018; Zembylas, 2009, 2014, 2018c; see also Chapter 6). According to Ruitenberg (2009), political emotions are those emotions that are directed toward social and political issues (e.g., poverty, homelessness, suffering). Such emotions (e.g., empathy, solidarity), she argues, should be given a legitimate place in education, because they are essential components of political and democratic life. Tryggvason (2017) suggests a broader definition of political emotions to include those emotions that revolve around one's existence, stemming from power relations embedded in the mere presence of the other. The more skeptical perspective does not reject the place of emotions in the classroom, yet it puts more emphasis on reason and rational argumentation, suggesting that emotions ought not to be trusted to have a legitimate place in political discussions in the classroom (Englund, 2016). The fear with bringing emotions into the classroom is that they may transform conversations into personal conflicts between individuals. Although this argument should not be interpreted as a total rejection of emotions in the classroom, it does challenge the extent to which democratic education ought to cultivate emotions such as empathy, solidarity or compassion (Tryggvason, 2018).

The question that I wish to explore in this and the remaining three chapters of the book is not whether or not political emotions and affects should have a place in the classroom; rather, I am asking, When political emotions and affects are invoked, can this be done without the process of democratic education degenerating into a form of emotional and/or political indoctrination? In other words, I am concerned that even when there are "good intentions," as discussed in Chapter 7, there is always a risk of forcibly or coercively causing students to act, think and feel on the basis of a certain ideology that promotes particular political emotions, regardless of how "noble" those emotions might be. Hence, Part III of the book focuses more explicitly on the issue of *inventing* (Deleuze & Guattari, 1994) affective pedagogies for democratic education, while avoiding the risks of indoctrination. How is this possible?

My source of inspiration in this chapter is Hannah Arendt's political thought on emotion and education. Arendt (1958/1998, 1963/1977, 1965/2006, 1978, 1979) claims that the emotions are apolitical and sees them through a lens of radical subjectivity (Degerman, 2019b; Heins, 2007; Nelson, 2004, 2006). As Degerman (2019b) explains, Arendt appears to blame the devastating effects of compassion and pity in political life, celebrating instead "heartlessness" and "toughness" because she believes that painful experiences can bring us closer to reality (Nelson, 2004, 2006, 2017). In regards to education, Arendt (1959, 1968) rejects the idea of politics having anything to do with education and suggests that political education is always tantamount to indoctrination. In other words, in her attempt to formulate a response on how to possibly prevent (moral) catastrophes such as those that happened in the twentieth century (notably in the Second World War), Arendt shows distrust both for emotions and political education. There seems to be a paradox though in Arendt's account of emotions, raising several critiques over the years; on one hand, she shows distrust for emotions, while on the other hand, she accuses the Nazis – especially Eichmann in her monumental essay on his trial (Arendt, 1963/1977) – of being "untouched" by the human suffering they caused. What I aim to show in this chapter is that despite the tensions and weaknesses that have been identified over the years about Arendt's views on both emotions and political education, she provides compelling insights against the possibilities of political education degenerating into moral-emotional rhetoric. Arendt highlights the dangers of constructing political emotions in the classroom as the foundation for political action, while acknowledging the constructive role for the emotions in the development of political agency.

I begin by outlining Arendt's critique of emotion and show how her skepticism is grounded in her broader political theory about the inner life of humans and the uncertain nature of emotions rather than a stance that devalues emotions. Next, I focus on compassion and pity as examples of emotions that show more forcefully Arendt's political thinking; my goal here is to demonstrate her view that modern democracy is threatened at its core by what she perceives as inflated moral emotions. In the third section of this chapter, I discuss Arendt's main views on political education and the dangers of moral and emotional indoctrination. Finally, I conclude by bringing everything together, emphasizing that Arendt's insights on emotions and political education can help educators avoid potential pitfalls in efforts that (re)consider the place of political emotions in the classroom.

Arendt's Critique of Emotion

Arendt's concerns about emotions in politics are rooted in her particular understanding of emotion "as a combination of wordless, visceral reactions and radically subjective experiences" (Degerman, 2019a, p. 826). These experiences are, according to Arendt (1958/1998), inherently hidden within the "darkness" of the human heart. The idea of heart as a place of darkness has been present in Arendt's work from the start of her scholarly career (Degerman, 2019b). Arendt's idea of the heart as a place of darkness has been interpreted by some scholars as a call for a distinction between the private and the public, or emotion and reason. However, as Degerman (2019b) suggests, Arendt's claim needs to be understood within her broader political theory as a deep skepticism in the ability of humans to grasp the contents of their own hearts; if we cannot truly know ourselves, we cannot fully trust ourselves. This is precisely what drives us toward the public sphere in the first place, as Arendt (1965/2006) suggests; sharing subjective feelings with others through words and actions alleviates this darkness.

Although by today's standards, Arendt's understanding of emotion as subjective feeling may seem rather limited, especially after the progress made in the affective turn in recent years, her insight that emotions and other subjective experiences are not inherently political is very important (Degerman, 2019a). In other words, Arendt argues that emotions are turned into something political, when they are shared and acted upon with others. As she writes,

> Compared with the reality which comes from being seen and heard, even the greatest forces of intimate life – the passions of the heart, the thoughts of the mind, the delights of the senses – lead an uncertain, shadowy kind of existence unless and until they are transformed, deprivatized and deindividualized, as it were, into a shape to fit them for public appearance. (Arendt, 1958/1998, p. 50)

Thus, sharing emotions in public enables the transformation of subjective experiences into a shape "fit for public appearance"; however, the political problem highlighted by Arendt is that the contents of the heart can never truly become public, no matter how much we discuss them (Degerman, 2019b). As Degerman (2019b) observes, Arendt "is right that no demonstration of emotion can prove what a person truly feels inside, something which the usual way we talk about emotions often obscures" (p. 160). Arendt is concerned that emotional experiences can be deceptive. More importantly, she questions whether we can really transcend the radical subjectivity of our emotional experiences and transform them into something else. Arendt's skepticism highlights that without the capacity to relate our emotional experiences to others, political action becomes impossible because it appears that there is nothing in common to act on together (Degerman, 2019a). As Degerman notes, Arendt's notion that political action entails a transformation of emotion "resonates with how other political thinkers and activists have described the experience of acting politically" (2019a, p. 828). Arendt's understanding of the "political," then, excludes emotion and so she argues that emotion has no place in politics; it seems circular, which is why she has been accused of making unclear arguments on this issue.

There is no question that Arendt (1978, 1979) is deeply concerned that the emotions can be used for indoctrination to serve the ends of totalitarianism, as shown in the history of the twentieth century. As she wrote, "The emotions are glorious when they stay in the depths, but not when they come forth into the day and wish to become of the essence and to rule" (Arendt, 1978, p. 35). As she had experienced firsthand the abuse of emotions in the hands of ideologues (especially in Hitler's Germany), Arendt is worried that emotions can be politically dangerous because they can be used to sentimentalize political issues and thereby seduce people into believing that they have particular emotional ties (e.g., of a particular race, nation or class) that can become the basis for exclusion and discrimination in political discourse and action. According to Arendt (1965/2006), public affairs cannot be truly democratic if governed by emotions and sentimentalism, no matter how "noble" the emotions may be – such as empathy, solidarity, compassion and so on (Heins, 2007).

Importantly, Arendt's concerns about the political abuses of emotion do not imply that she failed to identify a constructive role for at least some emotions (Degerman, 2019b). According to Nelson (2006), Arendt acknowledges that some emotional experiences help us become aware of and face reality, while others "anesthetize" us against reality through sentimentalism. The term "cheap sentimentality" is used by Arendt (1963/1977, p. 251) to refer to what she saw as misplaced expressions of guilt among German youth after the Second World War. Arendt was drawn to suffering "as a problem to be explored and yet remained deeply suspicious of its attractions" (Nelson, 2006, p. 88). Nelson (2017) calls Arendt's stance "tough" or "unsentimental" – not to be confused with indifference of callousness – because she sees the consolations of pain in intimacy, empathy and solidarity as politically dangerous. In other words, Arendt (1958/1998) believed that warm feelings of intimacy and solidarity – e.g., as those were exemplified among European Jews in their attempt to escape the hatred of Nazis and others – deprived individuals of their experience of reality by insulating them against its painful effects (Nelson, 2006). This "worldlessness" – that is, the escape from the world – and the emotions accompanying this experience have "disastrous" effects on politics and public discourse (Arendt, 1965/2006), because of "the failure of individuals to check vigilantly their impressions against others' and to amend and revise accordingly" (Nelson, 2006, p. 92). Suffering is a worldly experience, according to Arendt (1958/1998), and thus those emotions that serve to insulate or protect individuals from suffering actually prevent them from understanding the world.

Not surprisingly perhaps, Arendt's skepticism about the role of the "heart" in politics and the association of some emotions with alienation from the common world were considered by some as evidence of her "heartlessness." These accusations were particularly intense after the publication of *Eichmann in Jerusalem* (Arendt, 1963/1977), which was interpreted as a book that blamed the Jews for their suffering. In one of her interviews (with Gershom Scholem), she tried to address some of the angry reactions to her book by saying the following:

> Generally speaking, the role of the "heart" in politics seems to me altogether questionable. You know as well as I how often those who merely report certain unpleasant facts are accused of lack of soul, lack of heart, or lack of what you call *Herzenstakt*. We both know, in other words, how often these emotions are used in order to conceal factual truth. (Arendt in Nelson, 2004, pp. 224–225; see also Nelson, 2017, p. 74)

Arendt responds by embracing "heartlessness" as a necessary component of facing reality, and thus her repeated claim is that emotions lack the words to manifest themselves deliberately (Degerman, 2019b). Arendt's insistence not to pay attention to the emotions of suffering, as she was accused in *Eichmann in Jerusalem* – an approach that should not be interpreted as a denial or rejection of suffering and the emotions emerging from this experience – rests on her concern that there is always a risk when we shift emphasis from the event itself to the feelings about the event.

Overall, there are some paradoxes in Arendt's notions of emotions and her account is not as straightforward and clear. For example, her view that reason without emotion (even if that were possible) is what is appropriate to politics is in contrast with the view of her mentor and teacher Karl Jaspers (1961) who, like others, saw Nazi outrage as the result of technocratic reason being valorized at the expense of human emotion. Her account of Eichmann, in particular, represents a paradox. On the one hand, she suggests that Eichmann was a puppet or spoke the language of the state and was not "touched" by the mass suffering he caused; on the other hand, Arendt's championing of reason might be seen as a defense of scientific rationality and its dangers.

Despite the tensions and weaknesses in Arendt's celebration of the coldness of reason over emotion – especially in light of contemporary advancements in sociology and politics of emotion that hardly make a dichotomy between emotion and reason, but rather see them as entangled and intertwined (e.g., see Ahmed, 2004; Barbalet, 1998; Hoggett & Thompson, 2012) – her insights remain valuable because of her emphasis on the idea that the spectacle of suffering itself does not necessarily translate into emotions that are transformative. For a variety of reasons – such as "the capacity to be mesmerized by suffering or indifferent to it – the obscuring of fact by emotion, the corruption of motivation in the witness/reporter" (Nelson, 2006, p. 229) – Arendt reminds us time and again that transforming emotions into public issues should not be taken for granted. The examples of compassion and pity that are discussed next demonstrate this idea. Although the distinction between pity and compassion is not one of Arendt's most profound interventions, I use it here to show her contribution that tragedy is not automatically transformed into political emotions; my analysis in the latter part of the chapter will benefit from this idea in rethinking how democratic education could cultivate political emotions in critical yet not sentimental ways.

The Political Consequences of Cultivating Compassion and Pity

Arendt (1965/2006) discusses compassion and pity in the context of French Revolution. She argues that the French Revolution failed to establish political freedom because it was sidetracked by social concerns such as the growing misery and suffering of the masses. As she writes, "In times of growing misery and individual helplessness, it seems as difficult to resist pity when it grows into an all-devouring passion as it is not to resent its very boundlessness, which seems to kill human dignity with a more deadly certainty than misery itself" (Arendt, 1979, p. 27). Pity is "to be sorry without being touched in the flesh" (Arendt, 1965/2006, p. 75). For example, the French revolutionaries developed a repertoire of pity such as conspicuous crying at public events; their conception that pity was good derived from the perception that there was an inner goodness of pity, something of course that could not be confirmed (Degerman, 2019b). As Arendt suggests, "pity can be enjoyed for its own sake, and this will almost automatically lead to a glorification of its cause, which is the suffering of others" (Arendt, 1965/2006, p. 79). As such, pity is used by Arendt as the prime example for the subversion of politics and the corruption of solidarity and interpersonal compassion (Heins, 2007). As Heins explains Arendt's argument,

> The core of her argument [...] is that since the French Revolution an emotional change has taken place whereby the traditional emotions of charitable or caring compassion have been transformed into the more modern emotion of an eloquent, publicly generated pity. Compassion is an emotion that arises from the immediacy of the encounter between people in need of help and people willing to provide it. [...] By contrast, pity arises not from an immediate encounter but is the product of public speeches and public images that depict the misfortune of a great number of people that are "depersonalized" and "lumped together" as objects of public fantasy. (2007, p. 723)

In other words, compassion for Arendt means to suffer with another person as a result of witnessing firsthand the suffering of another person; when compassion is brought into the public sphere, it morphs into a perversion of itself, that is, pity (Degerman, 2019b). Although there is an important difference between compassion and pity, even compassion, in Arendt's view, is politically irrelevant and leads political projects astray, because the assumption is made that this emotion can be turned into a political virtue (Nelson, 2004). However, as noted earlier, Arendt emphasizes that emotion is, by definition, a radically subjective experience, therefore, emotion cannot be just turned into political action.

Importantly though, when Arendt concludes that compassion is politically irrelevant, she is not saying that compassion is bad for politics but rather that "we *cannot* base political action on compassion because politics requires plurality and dialogue, and compassion is singular and wordless" (Degerman, 2019b, p. 166, original emphasis). In other words, Arendt understands compassion as a subjective experience that remains as such, and therefore, does not lead to political action – even if it is publicly expressed. Given that politics requires dialogue rather than expression of subjective experiences, Arendt concludes that political capacity for action cannot be grounded in the production of any emotions, no matter how noble they may be. As she (1965/2006, p. 96) explains, "However deeply heartfelt a motive may be, once it is brought out and exposed for public inspection, it becomes an object of suspicion rather than insight." The medium of public speech is inappropriate for revealing someone's "true" motives or emotions, not only because words can be interpreted in many ways but also because moral emotions (e.g., pity and compassion) can be inflated with the illusion of being political virtues. This is why Arendt concludes that "pity, taken as the spring of virtue, has proved to possess a greater capacity for cruelty than cruelty itself" (1965/2006, p. 79).

Hence, Arendt is concerned that "modern democracy is threatened at its core by all too inflated moral emotions" (Heins, 2007, p. 724) as much as it is threatened by complete heartlessness. Regarding the former concern (i.e., inflated emotions), Arendt implicates pity as a "sponsor" of cruelty because of "pity's lack of objective substance and structural tendency towards discrimination [...] between those who are miserable and those who ought to pity them" (Degerman, 2019b, p. 168). Also, according to Degerman, for Arendt, "Solidarity provides a disinterested basis for recognizing the plight of a group of people, and responding to their unmet needs" (2019b, pp. 168–169). Thus it is possible that even "noble" moral emotions such as compassion and solidarity can be corrupted like pity, and therefore we must cultivate a suspicion of moral emotions in whatever forms we find them (Nelson, 2004). Regarding the latter concern (i.e., heartlessness), Arendt's point is that heartlessness is a serious political pathology that she identified among Germans after the Second World War as "the inability not only to feel guilt but also to yield to grief about the catastrophic destruction which came over Europe as a result of their action or inaction" (Heins, 2007, p. 725). In both instances, we notice Arendt's argument that inflated sentimentalism is equally problematic to heartlessness in that they both serve to shield people from facing reality.

What contributions do Arendt's political thought on emotion in general as well as on pity and compassion in particular make in contemporary discussions of emotions in politics? Here I want to briefly highlight two such contributions. First, compared to contemporary conceptions in sociological, cultural and political theories that emotions are not only subjective but also social, cultural and political experiences (Ahmed, 2004; Barbalet, 1998; Hoggett & Thompson, 2012), Arendt's conceptualization of emotion is admittedly narrow and reductionist. Yet, Arendt's insights about the role of emotions in politics are valuable because they reiterate that emotions cannot be reduced to words or automatically "translate" into actions (Degerman, 2019b). This contribution highlights, as Degerman points out, that words (language) and deeds (action) cannot prove the presence of "authentic" emotions in politics. For example, by teaching children or citizens that it is good to love freedom, democracy, equality and other "noble" values, they will not necessarily be led to express these emotions. But even if they do so, Arendt tells us, it does not mean we will create a better and more just society, as Nussbaum (2013) points out. This is the sort of idea that Arendt criticizes as politically naive and dangerous; that is, she emphasizes that we ought to be suspicious of the emotional grounding of political virtues – what Holmes (2010) would call the "emotionalization" of political values.

Second, in regard to pity and compassion more specifically, Arendt's contribution reminds us that there are serious political risks emerging from investing on feelings of pity and compassion. There is now a growing recognition in various disciplines about how narratives of suffering may lead to moralization by removing emotion from the call to political action and by framing the conversation according to sentimentalist moral categories such as that of "good" versus "evil" (Chouliaraki, 2012). This moralization takes place by resorting to a sentimental discourse of suffering that evokes pity for the sufferers rather than political action, leading to voyeurism and passivity (Zembylas, 2013a). Therefore, contemporary efforts to critique the moralization of pity and compassion reiterate Arendt's concerns about the dangers of pity and compassion and the political pathologies that are evoked. This contribution is important in contemporary theorists' attempts to enrich the (re)conceptualization of emotions and affects in politics. To situate these two contributions in the education sector, the next part of the chapter discusses some of Arendt's ideas for education and their implications, and then concludes with revisiting the place of political emotions in democratic education in light of Arendt's insights.

Arendt's Ideas for Education and Their Implications

Over the last two decades, there has been growing work on Arendt's ideas for education and their implications, exploring issues ranging from democratic education, to diversity and inclusion in the classroom, to educational authority (e.g., see Biesta, 2010b, 2013, 2016; Korsgaard, 2016; Mönig, 2012; Schutz, 2002; Schutz & Sandy, 2015). It is beyond the scope of this chapter to provide a comprehensive review of this rich literature, yet it is sufficient to reiterate some of Arendt's insights about education in order to make connections to her political thinking on emotion. Although Arendt's own understanding of education may have been limited (Biesta, 2010b) – a similar point I have also tried to make earlier about her understanding of emotion – her insights into the relationship between politics and education as well as how education may degenerate into moral-emotional rhetoric threatening democracy have important implications for contemporary democratic education.

The educational thinking of Hannah Arendt is articulated in two controversial essays, "Reflections on Little Rock" (1959) and "The Crisis in Education" (1958). The former was actually written first (Elshtain, 1995), while "Crisis" was meant as an explication of "Little Rock" after the reactions it had caused (Arendt, 1959, 1968). The historical context of both pieces is the attempt to desegregate Southern schools in the United States during the civil rights movement. In "Little Rock," Arendt argued against placing children on the front of desegregating schooling in the South because she thought it was a form of forced politicization of children. Arendt's ideas were largely rooted in her experiences from Nazi Germany in which she saw firsthand the emotional and political indoctrination of children with the brainwashing of the Hitler Youth (Schutz & Sandy, 2015). Whether or not the analogy between the Hitler Youth of Nazi Germany and the Little Rock's participation of black students in the civil rights movement was correct, as Schutz and Sandy (2015) point out, it seems that Arendt's concern was to contest the forced politicization of students, and thus she insisted that the "political" should be excluded from education (Schutz, 2002).

It is from this perspective that Arendt wrote her essay "Crisis," emphasizing that "we must decisively divorce the realm of education from the others, most of all from the realm of public, political life" (1968, p. 177), because "the child requires special protection and care so that nothing destructive may happen to him from the world" (1968, p. 186). As she further explained,

> Education can play no part in politics, because in politics we always have to deal with those who are already educated. Whoever wants to educate adults really wants to act as their guardian and prevent them from political activity. Since one cannot educate adults, the word "education" has an evil sound in politics; there is a presence of education, when the real purpose is coercion without the use of force. (Arendt, 1968, p. 177)

In this emblematic and often-cited quote, Arendt makes a distinction between the realm of politics that involves adults who are equal citizens and the realm of education that involves relations between grown-ups and children. Arendt argues that any effort to "educate" adults is inherently paternalistic insofar as it violates the dignity of equal citizens. Equal citizens, according to Arendt, can legitimately attempt to *persuade* rather than "educate" one another; thus she appears to reject the very notion of "political education" – not only for adults but for children as well (Danoff, 2012). To treat adults like students, argues Arendt, threatened the political, raising the possibility of a political leader being conceived as a "teacher" who assumes an authority of absolute superiority that cannot and must not exist among adults. Needless to say, the above quote from Arendt is full of assertions that are contestable. In what sense can one not "educate" an adult? How does one deal with the case of a "mature student"? What does the whole field of community education and adult education involve, then? What is lifelong learning? Is "education" to be seen as a "thing," a possession, rather than a process or activity?

Arendt (1968) approached the issue of educating children quite differently, arguing that, for the sake of the "world," teachers must have authority over them and help them navigate between the private sphere of the family and the public world (Schutz, 2002). Arendt insisted that the children have to be protected from the world until they are old enough to "bear" the political, because exposing them to the political when they are not ready to take on the role of public citizens jeopardizes not only them as individuals but also the political realm itself (Mönig, 2012). The crisis, then, that Arendt identified in "Crisis" was a lack of authority and responsibility for the world. Arendt responded with skepticism to the American progressive education movement that relinquished authority to the children. She considered this to be a dangerous fantasy that opened all kinds of problematic possibilities such as children growing up without a world at all. Thus, she argued that educators must assume their responsibility and introduce children to the world of history in which they have been born and prepare them for the time when they can act politically (Schutz & Sandy, 2015). As evident from the quote below, Arendt does not deny that her educational vision is conservative:

> conservatism in the sense of conservation is of the essence of the educational activity, whose task is always to cherish and protect something – the child against the world, the world against the child, the new against the old, the old against the new. (Arendt, 1968, p. 192)

Importantly though, for Arendt, the assumption of such authority and responsibility should not become an excuse for indoctrination, because then "we destroy everything if we so try to control the new that we, the old, can dictate how it will look" (Arendt, 1968, p. 192).

Over the years, education scholars have identified various tensions and weaknesses in Arendt's views such as the dichotomy she established between education and the public/political realm (Schutz, 2002; Schutz & Sandy, 2015), and Arendt's "developmentalist" perspective in which she maintained that the child is not yet ready for political life, so education has to be separated from politics and seen as a preparation for future participation in political life (Biesta, 2010b). However, despite these limitations, it is important to remember the context and background from which Arendt wrote. As Conovan (1992) reminds us, virtually all of Arendt's theorizing was a response to the problem of totalitarianism. Arendt's fear was that efforts to "educate" either children or adults are suspicious insofar as they may become efforts to indoctrinate them (Danoff, 2012).

While some scholars note that Arendt is wrong to reject the concept of political education as an oxymoron, and she makes a problematic distinction between education and politics (e.g., see Danoff, 2012), her ideas for education are valuable because they remind us that there is always the possibility that education may degenerate with great ease into moral-emotional rhetoric (Arendt, 1968). In this sense, she urges us to recognize that democratic education could end up becoming a form of moral education, coercion and indoctrination (Biesta, 2010b). It is important for educators, therefore, to acknowledge the political nature of democratic education and constantly interrogate those processes and practices in schools that seek to make children accept certain moral lessons or feel particular emotions about people or situations. Not all political education of children or adults is indoctrination, as Arendt would want us to believe, yet recognizing the limitations in educational efforts to resist oppressive indoctrination is extremely valuable. This idea implies that democratic education should focus on creating opportunities for political existence inside and outside schools (Biesta, 2010b), while encouraging vigilance toward the possibility that educational endeavors may fall into the trap of sentimental or moral-emotional rhetoric (Zembylas, 2014).

(Re)Considering the Place of Political Emotions in the Classroom

So far, I have sketched the conceptual framework through which Arendt understands emotions and political education. While critics point out that this framework is rather narrow – in regard to her understanding of both the emotions and political education – Arendt offers valuable insights to reconsider the place of political emotions in the classroom. The issue I discuss here, then, is not whether or not political emotions should be given a legitimate place in democratic education. This has been answered affirmatively by various education scholars (e.g., Ruitenberg, 2009; Tryggvason, 2017, 2018; Zembylas, 2009, 2014, 2018c) who argue that, one way or another, political emotions enter the classroom from the moment that emotions are bound up with power relations in a society and with a vision of a just and democratic society. Rather, the question should be whether or not democratic education can exist without any emotional or political indoctrination.

Thus, the issue I consider in this last part of the chapter has to do with the educational and political consequences of emotions in the classroom, that is, what happens when emotions are invoked in the classroom to achieve certain political aims rather than others. Who decides about these political aims and which emotions are invoked in discourses or practices? Is there a way to offer democratic education, while minimizing the possibilities of emotional and/or political indoctrination? How can political emotions be (re)considered to achieve a critical and multi-perspectival method for connecting thinking, emotion, and politics in the classroom? In order to address these questions, I will return one last time to another Arendtian idea, that of "enlarged thought." I argue that this concept creates openings that *suspend* one's own emotional interests and prejudices and focus instead on how students can operate collectively (i.e., politically) in a world with no fundamental agreements.

Simply put, enlarged thought is the ability to incorporate the perspectives of others into the thoughts, emotions and judgments one makes about the world. Arendt (1992) formulates this idea in the context of interpreting Kant's work on judgment as a point of departure to reframe the notion of political judgment in the wake of the horrors of the Second World War (Topolski, 2015). As Korsgaard (2016) rightly points out, this is not to be understood in the sense of having empathy for others; rather, it this should be understood as a way of thinking (and feeling) that is expanded precisely because it is not attached to one's own judgments but rather adopts "the standpoint of the world citizen" (Arendt, 1992, p. 44). In other words, enlarged thought involves bringing to one's mind the potential perspectives of all those who would have a claim and a judgment in a specific situation (Gillies, 2016). As Arendt argues,

> Political thought is representative. I form an opinion by considering a given issue from different viewpoints, by making present to my mind the standpoints of those who are absent; that is, I represent them. . . . The more people's standpoints I have present in my mind while I am pondering a given issue, and the better I can imagine how I would feel and think if I were in their place, the stronger will be my capacity for representative thinking and the more valid my final conclusions, my opinion. (Arendt, 2006, p. 237)

Enlarged thought, then, is the result of removing the limitations associated with our own judgments (e.g., subjective private conditions, feelings, self-interests) in order to train one's imaginations to *visit* the viewpoints of others (Arendt, 1992). By adopting this "visiting" stance, one is able to suspend his or her attachments to a particular identity or emotion and encourage multi-perspectivity that serves as the foundation for "being taught" by others (Biesta, 2013).

The implications of these ideas in relation to the conceptual framework sketched earlier about emotions and political education are twofold. First, it is important that educators provide contexts where students are exposed to a wide range of emotional, moral, cultural and social perspectives and viewpoints. The innovating character of "visiting" other perspectives lies in the fact that it provides an alternative to empathy (Biesta, 2010b) and other political emotions that are directed *only* toward one's own existence. The problem with empathy – as well as with compassion and pity, as discussed earlier – is that "it assumes that we can simply (and comfortably) take the position of the other, thereby denying both the situatedness of one's own seeing and thinking and that of the other" (Biesta, 2010b, p. 570). Political emotions in the classroom that fail to inspire this "visiting" are more likely to fall prey to the emotional and political indoctrination that Arendt is concerned about.

Hence, it is crucial for those involved in the education process to understand the dangers of "cheap sentimentality" in the context of Arendt's political philosophy and the matters which she brings to bare on facing the realities of suffering. For example, writing after the Second World War, Arendt (1979) argued that the "rights of man" proved to be illusory when the massive population displacements rendered millions of people "stateless." Arendt was disillusioned that stateless people found themselves in the difficult condition of rightlessness as they lost not only their citizenship rights but also their human rights (Zembylas, 2017b). Therefore, she argued that there is a right more fundamental than basic human rights as we know them: the "right to have rights," that is, the right to belong to a political community. Being "no-one" and not having the right to have rights is a useful addition to my analysis here on emotion and political education, because it describes the importance of being attentive to political realities. These realities are not resolved by sentimental means but rather by taking the individual person into the realm of political community, and considering the political consequences – e.g., of the condition of statelessness. A vision of democratic education or citizenship worth offering in the form Arendt might have imagined, then, entails creating opportunities for political community inside and outside school.

The second implication for democratic education of Arendt's ideas on emotions and political education is that in addition to providing opportunities for enlarged thought, students need affective and intellectual spaces that encourage them to practice making judgments and take political actions that expand inclusion, freedom and equality (Gillies, 2016; Korsgaard, 2016; Schutz & Sandy, 2015). This argument does not entail the cultivation of specific emotions such as empathy, tolerance or compassion – which would amount to a form of emotional and/or political indoctrination – but rather the creation of experiences that allow for the flourishing of an enlarged political existence. Political existence in the world as an embodied and embedded practice, argues Biesta (2010b), requires living with other people, strangers, in the world, while preserving the distance and strangeness that makes worldly ties possible. "Existing politically, to put it differently," explains further Biesta (2010b, p. 571), "is not about a common *ground* but about a common *world*" (original emphasis). To the extent that students are enabled to take political action that engages them with the different others, while recognizing the risks and dangers of excessive, abusive or otherwise normalized emotions, a renewed sense of democratic education may become possible.

Needless to say, we should not forget that Arendt is critical of the assumption that we can learn how to be democratic citizens in the classroom – an idea held by several liberal scholars in citizenship education (e.g., Gutmann, 1996; Kerr, 2005; Kymlicka & Norman, 1994). Whether there is, then, a way to offer democratic education, while eliminating completely the possibilities of emotional and/or political indoctrination seems to be untenable from an Arendtian perspective. For her, we – as educators, policymakers, school leaders – should be constantly vigilant of the dangers and risks of the rise of political emotions that reiterate the "darkness of the human heart." The acknowledgment, therefore, of the political dimension in emotions advocated by some theorists (e.g., Ruitenberg, 2009; Tryggvason, 2017, 2018) is merely the first step and it is certainly not enough. The problem of how to minimize the possibilities of emotional and/or political indoctrination is much more difficult to solve, but I would argue, against Arendt, that it is important that we work to find ways to address it so that students are enabled to enact enlarged thoughts and feelings inside and outside school.

It would seem all too easy to completely dismiss political emotions in the classroom out of fear of emotional and/or political indoctrination – especially, given the hardships currently facing so many people in exile and displaced by war and conflict. What these emotions at least tell us is what we ought *not* to do in political life, and if legal and state arenas – including education – are unable to tackle these issues, then exclusion is likely to remain a primary feature of state institutions. Sentimental kindness is not the answer; emotions need somehow to be "translated" into political communities that create strong individuals, collectives and institutions who can truly respond humanely to suffering.

Conclusion

To conclude, in this chapter, I argue that the issue of whether political emotions have any place in the classroom is not the most important one. Rather, what Arendt helps us understand is that if the heart is indeed a place of darkness – a metaphor for the uncertainty of emotions – then political education is inevitably a form of *emotional/affective education* that may degenerate into a form of indoctrination, regardless of the nobility of the values that are aimed to be "cultivated." This is inevitable, either we recognize it or not. The challenge is how to minimize this possibility by practicing the art of enlarged thoughts and emotions so that children are enabled to widen the scope of the differences they can live with and among others (Korsgaard, 2016), without sentimentalizing or moralizing this process. As Topolski (2008) writes, the crisis of education that Arendt addresses "is but a reminder of a greater crisis, that of the loss of the world that can only come into existence, and be preserved, through human interaction and plurality, the same conditions for 'healthy' citizenship" (p. 276).

Arendt's suspicion of political education should not distract us from the insight that the experience of democratic political participation in the classroom and beyond can help to inspire democratic practices. Her underlying concern that totalitarianism and indoctrination can always be around the corner, if we are not constantly vigilant, teaches us to reject the idealization of specific political emotions, no matter how noble they are, as politically dangerous. Thus, the desire on the part of liberal theorists in citizenship education who simply presume that citizenship education can be used to "cultivate" certain democratic values and skills seems to underestimate the potential of indoctrination. While it goes too far to say that all education is a form of indoctrination, I wish to suggest that what Arendt highlights, despite some limitations in her theorizing of emotions and political education, is that there is always one more step to take in efforts to create more opportunities for political action and resistance against emotional and political indoctrination.

CHAPTER 9

Toward Shared Responsibility without Invoking Collective Guilt

> It is a mistake to believe that making schoolchildren feel guilty in accord with the principle "your ancestors enslaved mine" will make them like the idea of human diversity any better or will seem to them anything more than a theatrical artifice.
>
> (Bruckner, 2010, p. 142)

In her landmark essay on the potential role of students' expressions of guilt in education, Todd (2003) suggested that guilt is a common response in classrooms dealing with portrayals of suffering and injustice – such as, the Holocaust, apartheid, gross violations of human rights and racial injustices. In general, students' responses come in two different types, according to Todd. On the one hand, they may take the form of feelings of guilt and responsibility for deeds students have not directly committed; guilt emerges as a result of feeling overwhelmed by stories of suffering. On the other hand, it is equally common, pointed out Todd, that students proclaim their innocence and anger at "being made to feel guilty" (2003, p. 93) for actions they have not themselves committed. Drawing on Melanie Klein and Emmanuel Levinas, Todd suggested that students' responses can be worked out in the classroom so that guilt is morally reframed as responsibility for the other.

This chapter joins this conversation and aims to explore two sets of questions that push further the idea that guilt has much educational value as much as it raises significant tensions and risks that need to be properly acknowledged and constructively addressed. The first set of questions is, how pedagogically productive is the idea of invoking in the classroom feelings of *collective guilt*? Is it pedagogically fruitful to teach students that they can learn about otherness from considering their own group guilt for crimes committed against others in its name? There are numerous examples of collective guilt, but perhaps the most prominent ones can be found in the cases of German people in the aftermath of Nazi rule and white

South Africans after the end of apartheid. Hence, one could ask, how ethically, politically and pedagogically viable is the idea of teaching contemporary students and youth in Germany or white South African youth and students that they ought to feel guilty for the suffering and injustice committed by their ancestors? How risky is this, if one really wants to encourage younger generations to take responsibility for changing their community and the world? These concerns lead to the second set of questions that is raised here: If there are significant moral, political and pedagogical risks and tensions from invoking feelings of collective guilt, how might educators reframe collective guilt as *shared responsibility*? What does this mean in educational theory and practice? In other words, how can students consider their responsibility in relation to suffering and injustice in the world without necessarily being branded collectively guilty?

Such questions arise at a historical juncture of widespread feelings that we are living in especially precarious times (Berlant, 2011; Butler, 2020), and hence there is an urgency for reframing experiences of shame, guilt and responsibility as productive orientations not only in the social and political arena (Ashenden, 2014; Lu, 2008; Young, 2011) but also in education (Applebaum, 2007, 2012; McLeod, 2017; Zembylas, 2018d). Although the role of students' expressions of guilt has been discussed as a pedagogical problem by Todd (2003) who suggested that Levinas's conception of ethical responsibility could be considered as a possible "solution," little attention has been paid to further theorizing the tensions and risks of invoking collective guilt as a means of encouraging mutual understanding, responsibility and reconciliation. The premise on which this chapter rests, then – i.e., that guilt is morally, politically and pedagogically productive – is not new; that premise is not the most important contribution of this chapter. The more important contribution is analyzing the moral, political and pedagogical implications of whether it is appropriate to invoke collective guilt and how such feelings can be transformed into shared responsibility in classrooms dealing with portrayals of suffering and injustice.

The chapter proceeds as follows. In the first section, I discuss the phenomenon of guilt as an issue of pedagogical tensions and risks, revisiting Todd's (2003) influential contribution and her reframing of guilt via Levinasian philosophy and psychoanalysis; this part also makes connections with recent theorizations of "white guilt" in relation to racial injustices. The second section of the chapter takes on the notion of "collective guilt" – the arguments for and against it – and discusses how and why it is relevant to education. In the third section, I juxtapose the notions of collective guilt and shared responsibility through a reading of Hannah Arendt's discussion of collective guilt and collective responsibility and Iris Marion Young's rearticulation of Arendtian views. The purpose of this juxtaposition is, in contrast to Levinasian and psychoanalytic views that draw attention to metaphysical or psychic aspects of guilt and susceptibility, to reposition responsibility as a shared, relational and political practice. The last section of the chapter discusses the moral, political and pedagogical implications of viewing the phenomena of collective guilt and shared responsibility through the lenses of Arendt and Young. I argue that a *pedagogy of shared responsibility* that aims at transforming declarations of guilt into practices of bearing responsibility offers an important intervention to efforts that seek to develop pedagogically productive ways of handling portrayals of suffering and social injustice in the classroom.

The Phenomenon of Guilt as an Issue of Pedagogical Tensions and Risks

The phenomenon of guilt emerges in education from the moment that educators bring stories of suffering in the classroom – e.g., newspaper articles and accounts of racism and racial injustice; biographical material on the Holocaust and other traumas experienced by others; artistic, literary and other portrayals of human suffering and injustice (Todd, 2003). When students confront such suffering, they frequently express feelings of guilt. Although there are potentially numerous ways of interpreting the meaning of guilt in these educational contexts, suggested Todd, there are in general two different types of students' guilty responses. These types are often entangled and so it is not always easy to draw clear boundaries between them.

The first type is feelings of guilt and responsibility although students have not been directly involved in the suffering of others. As Todd explained, "These students generally feel weighed down by the inadequacy of their position in the face of suffering they are witness to, and they express a sense of being overwhelmed by the enormity of it all, struggling to maintain a sense of hope when all they feel is despair" (Todd, 2003, p. 93). This type of guilt works as a sort of punishment directed toward themselves for being unable to act in a way as to prevent or ameliorate suffering. A slight variant of this type of response is the one by students who also feel overwhelmed by stories of injustice, "yet whose focus is less on what can be done for an other and more on trying to come to terms with one's own privilege" (2003, p. 93). In this case, the focus shifts from feelings of guilt associated with what actions could have been taken to prevent others' suffering to feelings of guilt that are linked to one's self and the recognition of one's complicity in others' suffering.

The second type of students' guilty responses takes a defensive orientation in which students attempt to negate the overwhelming effects of guilt by "proclaiming that they cannot be held responsible for actions that they have not themselves committed" (Todd, 2003, p. 94). In this case, there is a denial of one's complicity in others' suffering and a refusal to even recognize one's privilege; the focus of this type of response by students is on how they are not responsible for others' suffering, as they have personally done nothing wrong. "Their declarations of guilt and innocence," explained Todd, "appear less like guilt and more like externalized anger" (p. 94). However, it is important, according to Todd, that there is acknowledgment that some wrong has been committed, even if students deny their involvement. Pedagogically speaking, this acknowledgment may offer a point of departure to further explore how and why students feel compelled to distance themselves from that which is wrongful.

Often what unites both types of guilty responses, emphasized Todd (2003), is "liberal guilt," that is, "an individualistic response that detracts from marshalling the energy needed to recognize the larger, systemic factors that promote violence and maleficence toward others" (p. 95). Liberal guilt does not necessarily lead to taking social or political action to repair the harm committed but rather is limited in recognizing – in the best-case scenario – one's potential complicity in others' suffering. Liberal guilt, then, is self-absorbed guilt that centers on one's guilty feelings emerging from one's position of privilege, yet no action is taken to counteract the suffering one witnesses in the world. Liberal guilt is a major obstacle in progressive pedagogies, as Todd pointed out, and therefore an important pedagogical task is how to address and overcome this sort of guilt. Some provocative questions emerge in this effort:

> If guilt is such a relatively common response to others' suffering, pain, and discrimination, are we really doing it justice when we simply denigrate it or condemn it as being petty and sentimental under the rubric of liberal guilt? Can we recover an understanding of guilt that seeks not to deny or repudiate its affective power but instead considers the significance of such affect for moral action? (Todd, 2003, p. 97)

In response to these questions, Todd (2003) drew on Melanie Klein and Emmanuel Levinas to reframe guilt as a moral orientation that raises ethical and social responsibility to repair the harm done to others. Therefore, students' expressions of guilt may be approached productively as articulations of suffering in response to recognizing one's guilt and thus acting to repair such suffering. Todd suggested that expressions of guilt in the face of one's inadequate capacities to respond or repair such suffering can be understood through the lens of Levinasian ethics as a responsible response of a listener who acknowledges his/her guilt and suffers from this knowledge (Todd, 2003, pp. 110–113). In this frame, the role of the teacher is critical in evoking a sense of responsibility beyond the self and toward others. Thus, considering guilt as having a moral orientation offers pedagogical possibilities for cultivating in students a sense of responsibility.

Recent discussions of "white guilt" in the context of anti-racist education (Matias, 2016a; Taylor, 2011) and "white complicity" in social justice education (Applebaum, 2007, 2012) highlight the discomfort and resistance experienced by white students when issues of race, racism and whiteness are brought into the classroom (Zembylas, 2018d). White resistance, then, manifests itself in the form of white guilt or ambivalence (Leonardo, 2011) or white anger (Godfrey, 2004) – both forms of resistance are manifestations of liberal guilt, yet nuanced enough to think carefully about their differences since there are diverse ways through which "guilty utterances produce their own 'saying' and their own command" (Todd, 2003, p. 114). Hence, the pedagogical task of addressing white guilt in the classroom must include the identification of different manifestations of guilt, namely, the processes through which guilty responses "are expressed, repressed, and projected, [...] in regard to the power structure of race" (Matias, 2016b, p. 226). Applebaum's (2007, 2012) work, in particular, suggests that white complicity is not easily recognized, especially by those in dominant social positions; the invisibility of white complicity, she argues, is related to white-skin privilege that does not come from a particular individual act but is rather a product of social structures.

In general, what the pedagogical exploration of guilt in education teaches us is that the analysis of guilt should not be simply limited to the unconscious or innate feelings of discomfort, defensiveness or anger; rather, guilt takes on different declarations and manifestations that need to be understood as socially and politically produced within the affective, political and moral assemblages of structures of suffering and injustice. While Todd's reconceptualization of guilt highlights the psychoanalytic work that needs to be done in students' struggles to repair their relation to social violence and injustice and assume ethical responsibility – e.g., through different imagined relationships and modes of self-recognition in relations with others – there is still significant conceptual work to be done in exploring how to grapple with the political, moral and pedagogical implications of collective guilt. Following Todd's (2003) urge to refocus the exploration of the phenomenon of guilt in education on thinking more carefully how to respond to students' guilty declarations, I pay attention next to a deeper understanding of collective guilt and its implications in and beyond the classroom.

Understanding Collective Guilt

The dominant understanding of guilt is as an individual experience of (legal) liability, requiring some form of punishment that may lead to possible reform (Ashenden, 2014; Maddison, 2012). This conception of guilt, according to Maddison, has its roots in Christian theology and Roman law and later consolidated in the individualism of the Enlightenment. However, modern social theories (e.g., Durkheim, Freud), notes Ashenden, recognize that collective guilt may also be produced as a result of the coming together of individuals in society. Therefore, collective guilt is a concept that entails moral and psychological dimensions – an idea that transcends narrow legal individualism that rests on individual wrongdoing (Maddison, 2012). In this sense, collective guilt can be understood as a social phenomenon in which people claim to feel guilty for the harms committed by members of their group, thus recognizing their group as complicit in causing harm to others (Branscombe, Slogoski & Kappen, 2004).

A fundamental question that is raised in the wide-ranging literature addressing collective guilt – for example, in law, philosophy, anthropology, political science and psychology – is how it is possible that feelings of guilt can be shared among a collective, when the majority of individuals within that collective have not been directly involved in doing harm to others (Maddison, 2012). Much of this discussion emerged in the aftermath of Nazism in postwar Europe, but it is also animated by ongoing reflections on slavery, colonialism, structural racism, apartheid and other genocides (Ashenden, 2014). As Ashenden explains, while there is difficulty in accepting collective guilt within the terms of modern political culture, there is simultaneously recognition that collective guilt may be impossible of completely doing without. In fact, as it is argued, collective guilt can work to catalyze or paralyze discussions about "difficult" issues that have to do with recognizing how collectives are implicated in others' suffering (Curtis & Patrick, 2014).

It is worth mentioning here the key contributions made to this discussion by Karl Jaspers (1947/2000) and Hannah Arendt (1963/1977, 1987,

1994, 2003) in relation to Nazi Germany (see also Chapter 8). Both rejected the credibility of the idea of collective guilt and preferred the concept of responsibility. In particular, Jaspers (1947/2000) in *The Question of the German Guilt* used the term "metaphysical guilt" in reference to the feeling of intrinsic solidarity produced by the knowledge of crime. As he wrote, "There exists a solidarity among men as human beings that makes each co-responsible for every wrong and every injustice in the world, especially for crimes committed in his presence or with this knowledge" (p. 26). In this sense, responsibility has to do with our sense of who we are in the context of identities and relationships (Gordy, 2003). Hence, it can be argued that Germans are collectively responsible – rather than guilty – regardless of whether or not they supported the harm committed by Nazis.

Arendt also rejected the idea of collective guilt because for her, guilt could only be individual: "Where all are guilty, nobody is" (2003, p. 147), she wrote, adding that "guilt, unlike responsibility, always singles out; it is strictly personal. It refers to an act, not to intention or potentialities" (p. 147). Like Jaspers, Arendt draws a clear distinction between collective responsibility (which is always political) and personal responsibility (which is legal or moral). Therefore, she argues, one can be held responsible for things one had not done, but collective responsibility is political rather than legal or moral. As Schaap (2001) argues, whereas the idea of collective guilt is problematic because it attributes blame without regard to individual intentions and actions, Jaspers' and Arendt's understanding of collective responsibility is more appropriate because it refers to political liability based on association without attributing blame.

Analyzing the case of Germans in light of the legacy of Nazism, Schlink (2010) builds on Jaspers' and Arendt's views and suggests that collective guilt does not derive so much from a sense of responsibility for the harms committed by members of one's group but rather a feeling of responsibility for one's own solidarity with the perpetrators (e.g., Nazis or colonizers). As he explains,

> It is equally true today that one becomes entangled in another's guilt if one maintains or establishes solidarity with that person. The principle is as follows: to not renounce the other includes one in that person's guilt for past crimes, but so that a new sort of guilt is created. Those in the circle of solidarity who are themselves not guilty through actions of their own, bring about their own guilt when, in response to attendant accusations, they do not respond by dissociating themselves from those who are guilty. According to this principle it was possible for Germans, if not already guilty

as perpetrators and participants prior to 1945, to be implicated in guilt thereafter for not having separated themselves from the perpetrators and participants through renunciation. (Schlink, 2010, pp. 15–16)

National identification, according to Schlink, is one such form of solidarity that may contribute to what he calls a "community of responsibility" (Schlink, 2010, p. 14). It is evident, therefore, that social group or national identity seems to be a crucial component in understandings of collective guilt. Schlink's recommendation is to understand collective guilt in the very specific conditions in which it emerges and to render it subject to ethical recognition. This can be achieved by a conscious, systematic and perpetual vigilance of remembering the past and constantly raising ethical questions about each and every one's complicity in others' suffering. For as long as, for example, students in schools are taught uncritical histories of slavery, colonialism and genocide, or for as long as others' suffering remains unrecognized, the bonds of solidarity with perpetrators of historical injustices are maintained (Maddison, 2012).

In addition to Arendt's and other scholars' concerns about the notion of collective guilt, there are also those who find this notion morally flawed or irrational and conceptually impossible (Clark, 2008; Taylor, 1985; Wallace, 1994). As Clark (2008) argues, if we believe that an entire nation is collectively guilty, then the assumption is that this nation is fundamentally different from ourselves – an assumption that does not help us comprehend why the crimes were committed in the first place but rather conceptualizes a whole nation as a homogeneous entity comprised of people sharing the same views. Furthermore, Clark wonders how we would have behaved in similar circumstances if we were the ones directly involved (e.g., in Nazi Germany), as it is easy to come after the fact and accuse an entire nation of being collectively guilty. Therefore, she concludes that "collective guilt can be particularly objected to on moral grounds" as it is "unlikely to provoke moral outrage" (p. 674). Taylor (1985) and Wallace (1994) also criticize the idea of collective guilt by arguing that there are many questions of whether or not this form of guilt is appropriate either objectively or rationally. By that, they mean that if guilt is appropriate for personal culpability, then guilt is not something we could appropriately feel for others or render for groups. Hence, from a practical point of view, it may be more useful to speak of collective responsibility rather than collective guilt, as the latter does not really assist the process of dealing with responsibility (Gordy, 2003).

In light of the above metaphysical, political, moral and rational concerns raised about the notion of collective guilt and whether people can claim to feel guilty for the harms committed by one's group, many scholars seem to agree that perhaps the notion of *responsibility* is more appropriate, because it is a much more wide-ranging concept and, unlike guilt, it can be collective as well as individual (Ashenden, 2014). The distinction, then, between guilt and responsibility is important, although a clear separation of these two concepts would be problematic, according to Ashenden, because of their porosity to one another, especially at the collective level. Importantly, argues Striblen (2007), how one defines group responsibility determines what group members who did not directly perpetrate harm should feel. A useful distinction, therefore, especially for pedagogical purposes, as I will later argue, is that between "collective responsibility" – understood as non-distributive group responsibility applied only to the group considered as a single unit – and "shared responsibility" – defined as distributive and applied to each member of the group (Striblen, 2007). In the next section of the chapter, I clarify Arendt's conditions of collective and shared responsibility juxtaposing those with Iris Marion Young's reservations and thoughts on political responsibility. My ultimate goal is to highlight the importance of reframing collective guilt as shared responsibility and explore the pedagogical implications of this move.

Arendt and Young on Collective Responsibility

Iris Marion Young (2011) articulates a conception of collective responsibility that makes an important link between the individual and the social, that is, how the individual may be responsible for the harm committed by others. To do so, Young builds on Arendt's notion of collective responsibility to construct her social connection model of responsibility. In contrast to backward-looking models of standard liability that trace a direct relationship between a person or a group's action and the harm, Young seeks to create a forward-looking model in which responsibility is derived from our social connections with others, namely, from the ways we are interconnected with others in social and political processes. Young's model is forward-looking because it does not aim to go back to "isolate perpetrators" but "brings background conditions under evaluation" (2011, p. 105). In this sense, responsibility is shared among all those who contribute by their actions or inactions to the perpetuation of the harm committed by others; thus, everyone is involved, directly or directly, having a political responsibility in evaluating and changing the conditions that sustain harm.

Although Young criticizes Arendt's conditions for collective responsibility, which say that responsibility derives simply from common membership in a group, she grounds her social connection model in Arendt's important distinction between guilt and responsibility (Piliero, 2017). This distinction, suggests Young (2011), is important for political theory and practice, and I would also argue, it is equally important for educational theory and practice. In the following, I will turn to unpacking Arendt's understanding of collective responsibility and then explore how Young builds on this understanding to justify her own notion of political responsibility. This analysis is crucial for the last part of the chapter in which I suggest how a reframing of collective guilt into shared responsibility is helpful for teaching students about each and every one's complicity in others' suffering.

Central to Arendt's distinction between the individual character of guilt and collective political responsibility is her understanding of political responsibility as not a juridical notion but rather a belonging to and taking responsibility for the world. As she writes, "There is no such thing as collective guilt or collective innocence; guilt and innocence make sense only if applied to individuals" (Arendt, 2003, pp. 28–29). And she further elaborates, "As for the nation, it is obvious that every generation, by virtue of being born into a historical continuum, is burdened by the sins of the fathers as it is blessed with the deeds of the ancestors" (pp. 27–28). In other words, for Arendt, responsibility is linked to membership of a political community. One can escape this political responsibility only by leaving the community:

> [N]o moral, individual and personal, standards of conduct will ever be able to excuse us from collective responsibility. This vicarious responsibility for things we have not done, this taking upon ourselves the consequences for things we are entirely innocent of, is the price we pay for the fact that we live our lives not by ourselves but among our fellow men, and that the faculty of action, which, after all, is the political faculty par excellence, can be actualized only in one of the many and manifold forms of human community. (Arendt, 2003, p. 158)

Insofar, then, as political community has the character of fate (one can escape responsibility only by ceasing to be a citizen), we are, on Arendt's account, collectively responsible for wrongdoing done in our name (Ashenden, 2014). For example, German citizens who lived through the Third Reich were politically responsible for the crimes committed by the Nazis. The language of guilt is insufficient to get hold of the harm committed during the Nazi regime, according to Arendt, because to name "the criminality of the Nazi regime requires an account that recognizes the collective culpability of groups without rendering this in metaphysical terms" (Ashenden, 2014, p. 65). Furthermore, Arendt (1963/1977) is skeptical of Germans who express guilt because she sees this as an attempt to escape from the pressure of actual problems into what she calls a "cheap sentimentality."

Young (2011) adopts Arendt's distinction of guilt, which is personal from responsibility which is collective and political, but she finds unsatisfying the meaning Arendt gives to political responsibility based on membership alone. As she writes, "It is a mystification to say that people bear responsibility simply because they are members of a political community, and not because of anything at all that they have done or not done" (Young, 2011, p. 79). According to Young, Arendt leaves the meaning of collective political responsibility "too open" and that "simple membership in a nation [or group] is too static a meaning" (p. 87). Instead, Young argues that "to the extent that we participate in the ongoing operations of a society in which injustice occurs, we ought to be held responsible" (p. 104). In other words, she theorizes political responsibility by unpacking how people are engaged in public life that supports a regime that inflicts harm.

In particular, Young (2011) distinguishes four relationships that persons or agents have to the Holocaust's crimes against humanity based on her reading of Arendt's (1963/1977) *Eichmann in Jerusalem: A Report on the Banality of Evil*: (1) those who are directly guilty of crimes; (2) those who are not guilty of crimes, but who bear responsibility because they participated in the society and provided at least passive support that fueled the crimes committed; (3) those who took action to distance themselves from the wrongs either through preventing some or withdrawing; and (4) those who publicly opposed or resisted the wrongful actions (Young, 2011, pp. 81–91). These distinctions, argues Young, make possible a clearer elaboration of the complex relationships agents have to responsibility, because it goes beyond explanations based on membership alone: The first category concerns moral and legal matters; the second political; the third moral; and the fourth political.

Young suggests that the distinctions of responsibility she finds in *Eichmann in Jerusalem* go against Arendt's notion of collective responsibility because they indicate that responsibility can be distributed, namely, it is shared rather than collective (i.e., similar for everyone) (Piliero, 2017). Young (2004) argues that political responsibilities derive "not from the contingent fact of membership in common political institutions [but rather] from the social and economic structures in which they act and mutually affect one another" (p. 376). In other words, it is social connections that form responsibilities, not mere belonging or membership to a group (e.g., a nation). Mere belonging or membership to a group is a passive and apolitical act; belonging or membership to a group becomes active and political through public acts or failure to take action. Without a sense of collective responsibility, as both Arendt and Young emphasize, unimaginable violence becomes possible; therefore, both Young and Arendt advocate that it is right to hold people responsible for taking action or failing to do so in order to prevent harm (Piliero, 2017). As Young puts it very succinctly,

> One *has* the responsibility always *now*, in relation to current events and in relation to their future consequences. We are in a condition of having such political responsibility, and the fact of having it implies an imperative to *take* political responsibility. If we see injustices or crimes being committed by the institutions of which we are a part, or believe that such crimes are being committed, then we have the responsibility to try to speak out against them with the intention of mobilizing others to oppose them, and to act together to transform the institutions to promote better ends. (2011, p. 92, original emphasis)

Young's notion of political responsibility relates to Arendt's collective responsibility more than she thinks, argues Piliero (2017). Hence, the important point here is not to highlight Young's criticism of Arendt but rather to focus on how collective guilt can be reframed as shared responsibility. Reframing collective guilt as shared responsibility contributes to discussions in educational theory and practice on how to constantly rethink "what it is we are attempting to do in introducing stories of suffering into our classrooms" (Todd, 2003, p. 113).

Moral, Political and Pedagogical Implications: Toward a *Pedagogy of Shared Responsibility*

As noted earlier in the chapter, when students confront suffering, they express different types of guilty responses. Denial of collective guilt is a common response by students; feeling guilty and responsible, although students don't have a direct involvement in the suffering of others, is another common response. But are there any moral, political and pedagogical reasons for thinking that having guilty responses or cultivating guilty feelings in the classroom can be productive? Hannah Arendt and Iris Marion Young seem to suggest that collective guilt makes no sense within a frame that seeks to cultivate collective and shared responsibility. Their ideas shift attention away from the individualism of legalistic thinking and its emphasis on the causality of blame toward creating spaces that address how students can become responsible for others' suffering without being blamed for the harm inflicted by others. Following Arendt's and Young's analysis of shared responsibility, in this last part of the chapter, I will advocate for reframing collective guilt as shared responsibility in educational theory and practice by turning the question "Why do I have to feel guilt for my group and the harm others have committed?" into the following: "How am I co-responsible for the harm inflicted on my fellow human beings?" What I want to articulate here, then, is a pedagogical objective of shared responsibility in the classroom according to which students are prompt to recognize that all people are implicated in systems of oppression and injustice, yet it is important to delineate different degrees of culpability.

This transformative shift from collective guilt to shared responsibility is a double-edged sword – morally, politically and pedagogically. First, because it threatens "traditional" identities, values and beliefs (e.g., ethnic, religious, racial), and thus common guilty responses in the classroom may provoke defensive mechanisms that create major obstacles to this transformative shift (cf. Lu, 2008). As research on whiteness and emotionality in education shows, for example, Whites' feelings of guilt often create substantial difficulties for pedagogical efforts in the social justice classroom (Applebaum, 2007, 2012; Matias, 2016a). Arendt's and Young's notion of shared responsibility certainly encourages students and educators to interrogate the norms underlying social structures and the role of each and every one in these processes (cf. Applebaum, 2012), yet reactionary guilty responses constitute an ongoing challenge to transformative efforts. Second, the transformative shift from guilty feelings to shared responsibility will not automatically happen, but may in fact motivate attempts to alleviate the feelings of discomfort accompanying experiences of guilt through strategies such as scapegoating, paralysis and destructive quests for invulnerability (Lu, 2008). Once again, Arendt's and Young's notion of shared responsibility offers pedagogical opportunities not only to elucidate complicity in structures of oppression and injustice but also to diminish denials of complicity and promote more critical dialogues in the classroom. A relative "safe" pedagogical culture that helps students understand their complicity in critical but sensitive (yet not sentimental) ways is crucial in this effort (Zembylas, 2017c, 2018d; see also, Chapter 11).

In particular, transforming collective guilt into shared responsibility entails considerable moral and pedagogical landmines. Todd (2003) mentioned two that are worthwhile to recall. The first is an ethical question concerning how teaching about others' suffering should take place in the classroom (see Zembylas, 2015a). The suggestion here is to create opportunities for students to articulate the complexities of their declarations of guilt "through various forms of discussion, essay writing, or poetic expression" (Todd, 2003, p. 114). However, if this effort becomes an uncritical and moralistic lesson of "character education" that aims to invest on guilty feelings in order to invoke social responsibility, then I am afraid that moral prescription will close rather than open possibilities (Biesta, 2006; Fenwick, 2011). Therefore, it is important to conceptualize a pedagogical orientation that avoids both the pitfalls of a purely juridical or metaphysical address (i.e., the emphasis on the idea of guilt as individual or collective) and a "cheap sentimental" approach (i.e., the reading of sad and sentimental stories of horrendous suffering that move us to pity, patting ourselves on back, and then resuming our ordinary life) (Zembylas, 2016).

The second landmine is pedagogical and has to do with how educators need to think carefully about students' declarations of guilt in the classroom (Todd, 2003) and how each of those declarations needs to be responded with sensitivity, delineating different degrees of culpability. Applebaum's (2007, 2012) work deals specifically with the responsibility educators have to explore complicity and encourage a fuller engagement with social injustices in schools and the world. In particular, Applebaum (2007) suggests that Young's reframing of responsibility helps educators engage students in recognizing their complicity, while distinguishing "responsibility ... from guilt, fault, or blame" (p. 465). Applebaum refers to white complicity as the ways by which "white people perform and sustain whiteness continuously, often without conscious intent, often by doing nothing out of the ordinary" (p. 456). In this sense, white complicity is both a matter of doing and a matter of being. Arendt's and Young's notion of responsibility as shared, then, is helpful in addressing both of these dimensions, because it highlights the importance of acknowledging conscious and unconscious ways with which each and every one is differentially complicit in structures of injustice.

In other words, not everyone is complicit – and, therefore, responsible – in the same manner or to the same degree. In this sense, responsibility is not merely collective but rather shared. This distinction is crucial for pedagogical engagement with portrayals of suffering and injustice in the classroom, because by adopting Arendt's and Young's notion of shared responsibility, students are encouraged to understand that responsibility is not an all-or-nothing matter, but there are different degrees of culpability – e.g., there are differential ways of being complicit to oppression and to others' suffering. For example, accusing all white students as "racist" or all Germans as "Nazis" – that is, everyone as equally complicit – will provoke more defensive responses in an effort to exonerate themselves from these (totalizing, in their view) charges than productive engagement with *how* students are being complicit. What are the dynamics at play in acknowledging or denying shared responsibility? How do students become committed to learning shared responsibility practices or respond to differential ways of being complicit without feeling paralyzed from feelings of collective guilt or denial of complicity? In which ways do students learn to respond with shared responsibility in their lived everyday practices rather than seeing responsibility as an obligation? I would argue that these are the kinds of questions inspired by reframing collective guilt as shared responsibility grounded in Arendt's and Young's ideas.

Furthermore, there are some additional questions that have to do with how the idea of shared responsibility is related to context, when we are considering children and youth. If children and youth are not (as they are not) considered to be full members of the body politic, how does that affect how we think of Young's framework in relation to the evocation of collective responsibility in classrooms? Is collective responsibility different when considered in relation to the school community (of which children/youth are usually treated as citizens) compared to wider society (of which they are not)? These questions remind us of Young's admonition that mere belonging or membership to a group (e.g., being citizens or not) is inadequate as an indication of whether one has responsibility and which kind of responsibility. Even if, strictly speaking, children and youth are not treated as citizens in the wider society, what marks responsibility according to Young's framework, is political participation. In the case of children and youth, this means participation not only in matters of the school community but also in public matters beyond this community. If responsibility is shared, as Young tells us, then children and youth also have their own share of responsibility that needs to be critically explored on the basis of their actions or inactions in relation to the perpetuation of the harm committed by others. In the case of the school community, for example, this means exploring the responsibility children and youth might have for a classmate's bullying; beyond the school community, this might mean examining to what degree they are responsible for poor or homeless children/youth who live in their neighborhood or town.

All in all, the questions and concerns raised here allude to a conception of what may be called a *pedagogy of shared responsibility* that asks educators and students to explore "How do I bear responsibility for the oppressions and injustices in my community and the world?" This formulation does not seek to isolate those who are "guilty" from those who are not in order to differentiate the "good" from the "bad" people. Rather, the aim is to reframe pedagogical engagement from unchecked liberal guilt to an emphasis on the ways in which each of us bears responsibility to processes that produce unjust outcomes or suffering in the world. The notion of shared responsibility that I advocate here as part of a pedagogy of shared responsibility finds value in critical and decolonial pedagogical practices that challenge oppressive and colonial social structures (Zembylas, 2018d). It is important to reiterate that by exploring in the classroom the notion of shared responsibility grounded in Arendt's and Young's, we may be able to diminish denials of complicity by students (Applebaum, 2007). As Applebaum explains, this type of responsibility is important educationally, because it "can reduce defensiveness in which students look for others to blame instead of critically examining themselves" (2007, p. 465).

It is my contention, then, that a pedagogy of shared responsibility that aims at transforming declarations of guilt into practices of bearing responsibility offers an important intervention into discussions of oppression, suffering and social injustice in education. The role of educators is critical in evoking this sense of shared responsibility beyond feelings of collective guilt and bringing affective relations into the foreground (McLeod, 2017; Zembylas, 2017c). A pedagogy of shared responsibility can facilitate the decentering of guilty responses, can encourage students and educators to interrogate how all of us are (differentially) responsible to social injustices and suffering, and can enhance an "unrelenting vigilance" (Applebaum, 2007, p. 466) that locates ourselves and our everyday practices in structures of injustice. The transformation of collective guilt into responsibility that is shared is a relational and political practice, and therefore, not an easy task by any means. Yet, it is a pivotal task to the work of schools, implicated in the structures of violence and injustice that they (re)produce or can challenge.

Concluding Remarks

I began this chapter with questions prompted by how pedagogically productive is the idea of invoking in the classroom feelings of collective guilt, and I attempted to explore not only the persistence of collective guilt in students' responses but also the new possibilities that are opened with reframing collective guilt as shared responsibility. Arendt's and Young's accounts of shared responsibility offer opportunities that make educators and students aware of their responsibilities as members of certain social groups rather than being trapped in feelings of guilt. Feeling guilty about global poverty or ongoing discrimination against women and other social groups does not automatically generate moral and political actions for addressing suffering and injustice (Lu, 2008). Rather, refocusing on shared responsibility and what educators and students can do when they face stories of suffering and injustice asks them to examine the specific harms perpetrated by the communities to which they belong, and act accordingly (cf. Ashenden, 2014). The proposed pedagogy of shared responsibility, therefore, is not focused on blame, guilt or fault, but rather it has the potential to minimize denials of complicity and encourage students to interrogate the conditions under which they are responsive and responsible to others (Applebaum, 2007, 2012).

Perhaps the most important implications of pedagogy of shared responsibility, as it is suggested by this discussion, lie in reframing responsibility as a moral, political and pedagogical practice – a practice that is not grounded in a unitary moral framework of what responsibility looks like, but rather highlights the complexities and difficulties of working across the sufferings and injustices that often bind students and educators in guilty responses. As Biesta (2006) argues, a focus on action and practice turns students and educators toward the activity of coming into being. This activity "occurs through locating oneself alongside *different* others, in relations of responsibility" (Fenwick, 2011, p. 58, original emphasis). Thus, shared responsibility as a relational practice and disposition "is linked to democratic imaginaries, and has a collective remit, rather than a singular focus on personal responsibility" (McLeod, 2017, p. 53) or guilt.

When feelings of collective guilt are cultivated in the classroom to displace, comfort or alleviate the painful feelings accompanying stories of suffering and injustice, "they contribute to the distortion of moral judgment of culpable agents, and preclude the possibility of societal-wide self-examination, criticism and reform" (Lu, 2008, p. 375). There is urgency, then, for reframing collective guilt as shared responsibility through practices that distance students from feelings of guilt and encourage them to acknowledge their (differentiated) complicity to oppression and injustice. As Bruckner (2010) reminds us in the epigraph of this chapter, it is paralyzing to become trapped in the "tyranny of guilt," as guilt can congeal into an arrogant and dysfunctional masochism that leads to inaction. There are certainly pedagogical, political and moral risks in the effort to challenge guilty responses in the classroom, yet a critical engagement with shared responsibility offers new possibilities of cultivating responses that move *beyond* paralyzing feelings of guilt.

CHAPTER 10

Re-visioning the Sentimental in Pedagogical Discourse and Practice

The contemporary European refugee crisis, the rise of populism on a global scale, and state-sanctioned neocolonial, nationalist, sexist and racist practices are only a few of the crises that we face today and that mark "who may live and who may die" (Quinan & Thiele, 2020). For migrants and refugees who tragically perish in their attempt to make it to Europe or are met with a hopeless situation in borders, and for those subjugated groups who are targeted on the basis of gender, sexual, racial and ethnic differences, this is a form of "violence against those who are already not quite living, that is, living in a state of suspension between life and death" (Butler, 2004a, p. 36). The matters of life and death in the contemporary political climate raise urgent sociopolitical questions about how to make sense of the symbiotic co-presence of life and death – manifested ever more clearly in the growing disparities between rich and poor; citizens and noncitizens; culturally, morally and economically valuable and the pathological; and Whites and "others" – a sociopolitical situation in which some subjects are invited into life and others are marked for death (Haritaworn, Kuntsman & Posocco, 2014, p. 2).

My discussion in this chapter is inspired by Mbembe's (2003, 2019) concept of *necropolitics* – a concept that builds on Foucault's (2003, 2008) work on biopower, highlighting how power technologies are governing the regulation of populations and the management of life. Necropolitics explains how life in a biopolitical frame is always subjugated to and determined by the power of death, namely, the power to dictate who gets to live and who must die, or who must live and who is let die. The concept of necropolitics, then, can be used as a tool to understand the regularized death of subjugated groups (e.g., black people in the United States; migrants and refugees attempting to access Europe) in "zones of abandonment" (Povinelli, 2011), that is, sites that are not merely about exclusion but rather about death-making (Haritaworn et al., 2014).

Biopolitics and necropolitics have gained more and more scholarly attention in recent years in many disciplines as theoretical lenses through which to understand the governing processes, conditions and histories that underpin and sustain life/living and death/dying (Quinan & Thiele, 2020). Although biopolitical analyses of the potentialization of life have played a pivotal role in education (e.g., children's care, learning, well-being and development), necropolitical analyses of deciding who may live and who may die are rare – probably because contemporary education discourses are more attuned to the issue of life/living rather than death/dying (Staunæs & Conrad, 2020). Needless to say, testimonial narratives and images of death/dying are not absent from education – e.g., in social studies, most notably in teaching about the Holocaust. The problem is that these testimonies are often taught via a sentimental discourse that manipulates students into superficial sympathetic emotional responses that rarely lead to any action (Zembylas, 2008, 2013a, 2016). Hence, a fundamental question in theorizing the ethical, political and pedagogical implications of "making live and letting die" (Foucault, 2003, p. 247) is the following: How can the necropolitical be used in democratic education to make sense of death as a form of power against subjugated (e.g., Black, migrant, refugee) lives, without functioning as a form of sentimentality?

Sentimentality is typically understood as the excessive, self-indulgent and banal use of affect and emotion to manipulate audiences into sympathetic feelings (Robinson, 2012). Recent educational theorizing has already identified some of the dangers of sentimentalism in teaching and learning (e.g., see Carniel, 2018; Hållander, 2019; Zembylas, 2008, 2016). That sentimentalism functions as a "technology" of manipulating feelings in the classroom is not a new idea; what is new is the analysis and sorting through of various discourses about necropolitics and sentimentality, to figure out how those discourses operate in education to fabricate particular meanings for the compassionate recognition of the death of subjugated subjects. This chapter thus makes a contribution into contemporary discussions about the productive ways to handle pedagogically *whether* and especially *how* educators and students ought to view and mourn *which* testimonial images of dead bodies in the classroom.

To make this intervention, the chapter is divided into four sections. The first section discusses the notion of necropolitics and demonstrates how the circulation of necropolitical affects creates a sense of belonging through fear, trauma and racialized death. The second section focuses on sentimental biopower and theorizes how sentimentalism serves as a mechanism of connecting affectively and politically the individual and the social by cultivating an empty rhetoric through compassionate recognition that fails to interrogate racialized and gendered categories in political praxis. The third section discusses the ethical, political and pedagogical challenges of bringing into the classroom – I basically refer to secondary school and higher education classrooms – images of dead bodies; to illustrate these challenges I discuss the recent iconic example of the dead-body image of Syrian-Kurdish toddler Alan Kurdi, who drowned in the shores of Turkey in 2015. Finally, the last section of the chapter makes an attempt to reclaim the entangled meanings of necropolitics and sentimentality in pedagogical discourse and practice by re-visioning the sentimental as an ethical, political and pedagogical enterprise that interrogates the normalization of death-making in the current political climate.

Necropolitics

In his celebrated essay "Necropolitics" as well as his recent book with the same title, Mbembe (2003, 2019) argues that necropolitical analysis supplements Foucault's (2003, 2008) notion of "biopower." Biopower is identified by Foucault as a new technology of power that arises in the late eighteenth century and aims at governing populations through systematic monitoring and regulation of living organisms (e.g., demographics, health and hygiene, policing techniques). In particular, Foucault (2003) points out that there is a shift from a medieval system of sovereign power, which is characterized by the right to "take life or let live," to the emergence of biopower and biopolitical techniques of governance, which are characterized by the notion of "making live and letting die." The notion of biopolitics, then, is concerned with the bodies that live and describes those technologies of power that focus less on the disciplining and surveillance of individual bodies than on the crucial function of governing populations by creating categories of difference.

In his discussion of necropolitics, which situates biopower within global power relations and especially European colonial legacies, Mbembe (2003, 2019) explores how to account for death/dying and the power relations involved (i.e., necropower), namely, how subjugated people around the world are pushed into precarious living situations. As he wonders about biopower and necropower,

> Is the notion of biopower sufficient to account for the contemporary ways in which the political, under the guise of war, of resistance, or of the fight

against terror, makes the murder of the enemy its primary and absolute objective? ... What place is given to life, death, and the human body (in particular the wounded or slain body)? How are they inscribed in the order of power? (2003, p. 12; see also, 2019, p. 66)

Mbembe suggests that "the notion of biopower is insufficient to account for contemporary forms of the subjugation of life to the power of death" (2019, p. 92). He further argues that contemporary forms of subjugating life to the power of death "are deeply reconfiguring the relations between resistance, sacrifice, and terror" (p. 92), that is, they blur the lines between resistance (to hegemony) and suicide, sacrifice and martyrdom (Mbembe, 2003, pp. 39–40).

Necropower, then, creates what Mbembe (2003, 2019) calls "death-worlds" within which death is being deployed as a force, thus establishing boundaries between "legitimate" subjects, sanctioned for life, and "illegitimate" (or "illegal") subjects, sanctioned for death. However, Mbembe's analysis does not understand life and death as mere "forces" that exist autonomously, but rather as political tools through which power can circulate (Quinan & Thiele, 2020). In this manner, necropolitics uncovers the ways in which certain bodies in the contemporary world are marked for life, while others are subjected to living conditions that make them "living dead" (Mbembe, 2003, p. 40). In this manner, necropolitics highlights the asymmetrical conditioning of who gets to live and who must die, raising crucial questions about the conditions under which the power to kill and to let live is exercised, such as who are those subjects designated for death and who are those allowed to live in the contemporary world? Who makes these decisions and under which conditions? Who are complicit to these decisions and in which ways? Are *we* / am *I* complicit to this situation?

Mbembe (2003, 2019) identifies some of the spaces in which necropower has historically operated, namely, the plantation and the colonial world; he offers these examples in order to highlight the conditions (e.g., state of exception) under which technologies of death (e.g., racism) function. The examples of plantation and the colonial world show how the slave is a manifestation of "death-in-life" (Foucault, 2003, p. 21). In the contemporary world, Mbembe refers to two examples in which suffering and death are used as political technologies of domination and control: apartheid in South Africa and the occupation of Palestine. In the occupation of Palestine, for instance, Mbembe discusses how the lives of Jewish-Israeli citizens are enhanced by subjecting Palestinians to a death world or by inflicting suffering to Palestinians in ways that destabilize their daily life (see Bird & Lynch, 2019). Just as in the example of slaves in the plantation, Palestinians are being "kept alive but in a state of injury" (Mbembe, 2003, p. 21).

The examples mentioned by Mbembe (2003, 2019) show spaces that are "productive in an affective economy that circulates, multiplies, and invests in *death*" (Clough & Willse, 2011, pp. 17–18, added emphasis). Extending Mbembe's concept of necropolitics to bear upon the centrality of racialized death in contemporary times (e.g., the regularized death of black people in the United States), Bhanji (2019) argues that the circulation of necropolitical affects – what he calls *necrointimacies* – "coheres a morbid sense of belonging through fear, trauma, and the consumption of racialized death" (p. 115). To put this differently, there is a link between who is expressing intimacy toward whom and how intimacy is expressed; this link is always embedded within the logic of racialization (Povinelli, 2005). In other words, the distribution of intimacy – the feeling of intimate proximity toward some bodies and the distance from others (Ahmed, 2004) – is racialized. As Lowe (2015) also argues, the political economy of memorialization of racialized corpses must be understood in terms of colonial histories that govern the production and distribution of intimacy.

For example, the violated and injured body of color – as shown in images of lynchings of black people – is deemed as "killable," as racialized corpses have historically been relegated to the status of spectacular objects by white people (Bhanji, 2019). Bhanji further explains that images of brutalized bodies of color have historically circulated as fetishistic commodities: "The intimate spectacle of the dead or dying racialized body invites the witnessing white body into an affective citizenship that requires the Other be simultaneously possessed and repudiated" (2019, pp. 130–131). In other words, the spectacle of the dying/dead racialized body is inextricably linked with the affective economy of whiteness and its distribution of intimate proximity to or distance from "others." Thus the view of the abject body can be read as a testament of the deterioration and destruction of certain human populations – that is, as a form of "slow death" (Berlant, 2007) taking place through "slow violence" (Nixon, 2011).

Along similar lines, Puar (2007, 2017) has made an insightful elaboration of "queer necropolitics," which interrogates which queer lives are legitimated and which are left to die or are actively targeted for killing. Haritaworn et al. (2014) have also used the notion of queer necropolitics as a theoretical tool to bring into view everyday death-worlds "from the more expected sites of death making (such as war, torture or imperial invasion) to the ordinary and completely normalized violence of the market" (p. 2). Finally, Weheliye (2014) analyzes the racial dimensions of biopolitics and necropolitics by developing the concept of "racializing assemblages"; his theory understands race as a set of sociopolitical processes of racial differentiation that distinguish between those who are seen as fully human – e.g., white men – and the nonwhite, less-than human. All in all, these works on the necropolitical illuminate the ways in which normativity in death is linked to neo-colonial, neo-imperialist, neo-racist, and neo-liberal processes; in particular, this theorizing shows how the biopolitical and necropolitical – as "two sides of the same coin" (Braidotti, 2013, p. 122) – exert life- and death-giving forces that have gendered and racialized dimensions (Quinan & Thiele, 2020).

Sentimental Biopower

So far, I have focused on necropolitics as a tool to make sense of how the power of death establishes boundaries between subjects that are invited into life and those marked for death, and I have discussed how the differential distribution of necropolitical affects has crucial social and political consequences in terms of whose deaths are mourned or valued and whose lives have less value and are let die. A crucial question, then, with ethical, political and pedagogical implications, is the following: What "technologies" are used to align the "individual" with the "social," namely, how is the affective economy that circulates, multiplies and invests in death created?

Strick (2014) suggests that the answer to this question is found "between two crucial epistemic transformations that characterize modernity: sentimentalism and biopolitics" (p. 3). The "relay between the sentimental and the biopolitical circumscription of politics," he writes, "defines the meanings of suffering in different bodies and how these matter to the nation, science, and constructions of race and gender" (p. 4). In other words, necropolitical affects cannot be understood unless we acknowledge how sentimentalism and biopolitics are entangled in different public spheres, including education. Hence, in this part of the chapter, I shift my attention to how the entanglement of sentimentalism and biopolitics – what Schuller (2018) calls "sentimental biopower" – provides new theoretical openings to understand the racialized dimensions of necropolitics in public spheres. This theorization is crucial in understanding the effects of sentimentalism on pedagogy and education, an issue that I discuss in the next part of the chapter.

In general, sentimentality is understood as the use of excessive and self-indulgent affect to manipulate audiences (e.g., students) into sympathetic feelings (Robinson, 2012). It is associated with particular genres in the nineteenth and early twentieth centuries – initially the sentimental novel, and later, the melodrama – but now it is understood as a "mode" across genres such as literature, film and television (Williamson, Larson & Reed, 2014). Sentimentality works as a form of affective alignment between the individual body who constructs a set of emotions and the larger population in which the individual is enmeshed. As Berlant (2008) argues, the general organization of politics in the United States over the last 150 years depends on sentimental structures of attachment and identification in which the individual is directed toward particular affective attachments. As she explains,

> The political as a place of acts oriented toward publicness becomes replaced by a world of private thoughts, leanings, and gestures projected out as an intimate public of private individuals inhabiting their own affective changes. Suffering, in this personal/public context, becomes answered by sacrifice or survival, which is, then, recoded as the achievement of justice or liberty. (p. 41)

An important consequence of sentimentalism, then, is the depoliticization of issues and its replacement by a set of private sentiments. Sentimentalism, therefore, illuminates how affect, the relations between individual-social, and power go hand in hand, making sentimentalism an important instrument of governmentality.

In fact, Berlant (2008) suggests that sentimentality has emerged as a crucial biopolitical technology through which the emotional needs of the individuated subject (e.g., sense of belonging) are linked to those of a larger collectivity (e.g., nation, state). Berlant provides an important critique of the dominant liberal discourse of modernity that is grounded in what she calls "the unfinished business of sentimentality," that is, the way sentimentality is being used in public spheres simply to generate emotions that aim to touch audiences about pain and suffering; the unfinished business is that sentimentality in itself rarely leads to action for social change. As she writes,

> the unfinished business of sentimentality – that "tomorrow is another day" in which fantasies of the good life *can* be lived – collaborates with a sentimental account of the social world as an affective space where people ought to be legitimated because they have feelings and because there is an intelligence in what they feel that *knows* something about the world that, if it were listened to, could make things better. (Berlant, 2008, p. 2, original emphasis)

Similarly, Schuller (2018) critiques sentimentalism, connecting it to the biopolitical regimes that shape a culture's understanding of subjugated peoples' death, arguing that sentimentalism functions as a disciplinary mechanism through which the affective capacity of Whites or "civilized individuals" becomes a measure through which hierarchies of racial order are justified and normalized. As she explains,

> Sentimentalism stimulates the moral virtuosity and emotional release of the sympathizer and her affective attachment to the nation-state at the expense of the needs of the chosen targets of her sympathy, typically those barred from the status of the individuated Human: often the impoverished, the racialized, the conquered, the orphaned, and/or the animalized. (Schuller, 2018, p. 2)

In this sense, argues Schuller, sentimentalism "operates as a fundamental mechanism of biopower" (2018, p. 2), namely, it perpetuates the normalization of racialized intimacies by simply engaging in a superficial compassionate recognition of the sufferings of marginalized groups, while failing to offer a pragmatic affective inclusion of excluded and oppressed bodies into the national body (see also Strick, 2014).

Sentimentalism, then, is deployed as a biopolitical mechanism by invoking emotional reflection that is limited to expressions of sympathetic feelings rather than taking action to challenge the structural conditions of necropolitics. As Hartman (1997) suggests, sentimental techniques in narratives of race and racism are complicit with white hegemony, because they focus on feelings and the body thereby failing to pay attention to the importance of the political representation of marginalized subjectivities: "[S]entiment facilitated subjection, domination, and terror precisely by preying upon the flesh, the heart, the soul" (p. 5). In addition, Berlant (2008) argues that the sentimental evocation of "bodies in pain" is deeply problematic because it perpetuates the privileging of certain bodies and subjects, and the dismissal and pathologization of others:

> [Sentimentalism's] core pedagogy has been to develop a notion of social obligation based on the citizen's capacity for suffering and trauma. This structure has been deployed mainly among the culturally privileged to humanize those subjects who have been excluded [...]. But [...], the humanization strategies of sentimentality always traffic in cliché, the reproduction of a person as a thing, and thus indulge in the confirmation of the marginal subject's embodiment of *inhumanity* on the way to providing the privileged with heroic occasions of recognition, rescue, and inclusion. (p. 35, original emphasis)

In other words, as Strick (2014) also points out, sentimentalism reflects the norms of recognition (racial and gender differences), and hence it consolidates a mode of engagement with "others" that regulates the circulation of feelings so that the exclusionary and violent effects of these categories are not really challenged in structural ways.

A key strategy of biopower, therefore – a mode that Schuller (2018) calls the "sentimental politics of life" – takes shape as a technology to circulate and regulate feelings in a population so that hierarchies of race and gender are consolidated: "The sentimental politics of life helps illuminate how biopower is so effective at creating atmospheres in which people come to identify with the needs of the state and capitalism as their own best interests" (p. 19). Consequently, when individuals are urged to "empathize" with racialized and gendered "others" through sentimental processes, these sentiments and affects often become sites of imperial control (Stoler, 2002). As Stoler writes, one of sentimentalism's key victories was that children "became the subjects of legislative attention and were at the center of social policy as they had never been before" (2002, p. 120), thus justifying the removal of children from their homelands – one of the most cruel colonial practices in the nineteenth and early twentieth century in colonial territories such as Canada and Australia. Sentimentality, therefore, has long been "suspect" (Howard, 1999, p. 69) for being complicit to neo-imperial and neo-liberal projects. Hence, when sentimentality becomes an affective technology in pedagogy and education, it is important to examine more carefully its consequences, especially in relation to necropolitical affects.

Ethical, Political and Pedagogical Dilemmas of Showing Images of Dead Bodies in the Classroom: The Case of Alan Kurdi

This chapter so far has suggested that there is a crucial connection between necropolitical and sentimental discourses and techniques: Sentimentalism is used as a technology of power aimed at governing individuals' affective responses to necropolitical events. In the field of educational theory, the dangers of sentimentalism and more generally the "banality of empathy" (Serpell, 2019) in biopolitical analyses of teaching and learning are not new ideas (e.g., see Carniel, 2018; Hållander, 2019; Zembylas, 2008, 2013a, 2016). However, a dimension of these discussions that has not been adequately examined is how sentimentalism operates in the case of the compassionate recognition of the death of subjugated subjects. Hence, the key question that drives the remainder of my analysis is the following: Should educators and students – in secondary and higher education sectors – view and mourn images of death and dead bodies, if there are already serious concerns that these images may function as instruments of and targets for normalized necropolitical affects?

The obvious answer perhaps would be to say upfront that the use of *any* images of death and dead bodies in the classroom – for example, images of death associated with atrocities such as the Holocaust or other genocides – is unethical and inappropriate; doing so, of course, would end this discussion right here. However, if there is even the slightest possibility that images of death can indeed provide the point of departure for a transformative experience, when they do *not* become objects of voyeurism and sentimentalism, then it would be worthwhile, in my view, to further explore the ethical, political and pedagogical challenges involved in showing images of dead bodies in the classroom. To make this discussion more concrete, I will use a specific example, namely, the image of the dead body of Syrian-Kurdish toddler Alan Kurdi, who became an iconic symbol representing the trauma, fear and death associated with the contemporary European refugee crisis. I have chosen this example because it has received widespread attention both in the field of education (e.g., Carniel, 2018; Hållander, 2019) and beyond (e.g., Adler-Nissen, Andersen & Hansen, 2020; Papailias, 2019).

In September 2015, Alan Kurdi, a three-year-old Syrian-Kurdish boy, washed up on a Turkish beach after his family's failed attempt to reach Greece. The image of the child, dead on a beach, drew worldwide attention and sparked numerous memes in the social media as well as murals, graffiti and street-art around the world, showing the boy devoid of context, in the form of an angel or sleeping in a child's bedroom (Chouliaraki & Stolic, 2017; Olesen, 2018). An image of a dead person – let alone a child – is a taboo not only in media but also in education; this particular image was deeply emotional and moved people to tears (Adler-Nissen et al., 2020). In fact, this image was credited with causing a renewed attention to the European refugee crisis as well as a momentary surge in donations to charities that were engaged in helping Syrian migrants and refugees (Hållander, 2019).

World leaders and global citizens expressed their personal grief and determination to act; however, not only very little changed since then but also a year after Kurdi's death, policies adopted in Europe shifted from an open-door approach to attempts to stop refugees from arriving (Adler-Nissen et al., 2020). While the last few years saw a drop in migrant and refugee deaths, in part because fewer are attempting the dangerous journey and due to the growing anti-immigrant political climate in Europe, the death toll of those en route to Europe remains devastating: In 2016, there were 3,047 deaths; in 2017, the death toll amounted to 2,048 deaths; in 2018, there were 1,930 deaths; and over the first nine months of 2019, the death toll was 1,071 individuals (IOM, 2019; Quinan & Thiele, 2020).

Needless to say, there are many ethical concerns, namely, whether it is right to show images of refugees' dead bodies at border crossings (Lenette & Miskovic, 2016) and especially the image of a child such as Kurdi's dead body (Carniel, 2018; Papailias, 2019). Carniel (2018) discusses her ethical dilemma of whether to include the viral image of Kurdi's dead body in a class for humanities students; she eventually decides not to use it in the course, instead offering a blank slide with the word. Carniel encourages her students to make their own decisions about viewing the image, emphasizing that "media outlets did grapple with the dilemma of publishing the image of Alan Kurdi, fearing it was too graphic for western audiences who were unused to the circulation of images of dead bodies" (p. 152). Despite the political openings that could be created by showing this image, Carniel acknowledges the ethical and emotional risks "of being exploitative of the image, and more importantly, of its deceased subject" (2018, p. 152). At the same time, she expresses her ambivalence, pointing out that "no teacher seeks to traumatize their students, but similarly no teacher wishes to miss out on an enriching, albeit challenging, educational experience because of personal distaste" (p. 145).

Similarly, Hållander (2019) explores Kurdi's image in relation to the emotions evoked and their pedagogical potentialities to teach complex subjects such as injustice and historical wounds. As she writes, "I myself cried when I saw the image. I remember browsing for the visual when I first saw it on my phone. The second instant I saw the image, I stopped reading and found myself crying" (p. 468). In line with Carniel's (2018) decision, Hållander also decides not to use the image, explaining that "the choice on my part, as well as for Carniel, I read, was more about Alan Kurdi himself than the students' emotions or thoughts. Rather it was grounded in the idea that everyone has the right to be imaged in a dignified manner" (pp. 477–478). Hållander concludes that the pedagogical spaces of showing such images in the classroom are ambivalent; therefore, there are no a priori rules of whether or how to show testimonial images, but despite the risks, teaching and learning "difficult" material can become fruitful.

Finally, in my own work (Zembylas, 2008, 2013a, 2016) over the years, I have suggested that it is important for educators to confront the risks involved in teaching "difficult" material and reclaim sentimentality through a critical lens. "Critical sentimental education," the term I have used, can approach difficult testimonies (including images) of violence and trauma *both* with criticality *and* with affective engagement, highlighting critical consciousness about various forms of injustices and inspiring transformative action to address these injustices (see also Zembylas & Keet, 2019). As I have pointed out, critical sentimental education is an exploration that not only recognizes the role of emotions and affects in teaching difficult and complex subjects but also exposes the dangers and trappings of cheap sentimentality – such as, for example, the exploitation of images and testimonies of trauma and death to invoke excessive and self-indulgent emotions and affects for the manipulation of students into sympathetic feelings.

What previous work in educational theorizing has not done yet, however, is to bring together literatures applied only peripherally so far to ethics, politics and pedagogy: biopolitics/necropolitics, sentimentality and the ethical/political/pedagogical dimensions of images of "living death." Needless to reiterate once again, (uncritical) sentimentalism might function in the classroom as a superficial moralistic philosophy of sympathetic feeling that could further consolidate hierarchies of race and gender (see also Chapter 9). However, if the pedagogical sphere is defined a priori by prohibitions on viewing images of dead bodies, and therefore prevents grieving and mourning the "death of the other" – in the name of "protecting" students from material deemed "too graphic" for Western audiences or other ethical concerns – I would argue that this position reveals as much the *political* underpinnings of our pedagogical approach as our ethical reservations. In other words, the decision to avoid showing images of dead bodies is a political choice in the sense that it prevents the recognition of particular deaths; therefore, it may be said that a pedagogical approach grounded in this position is (unknowingly) complicit to colonial projects and the selective distribution of images of death. The last part of the chapter makes an attempt to reclaim the entangled meanings of necropolitics and sentimentality in pedagogical discourse and practice by re-visioning the sentimental as an ethical, political and pedagogical enterprise that interrogates the normalization of death-making in the current political climate.

Reclaiming Sentimentality, Making Visible Contemporary Necropower: Pedagogical Implications

To go back to the question driving my analysis in this chapter: What do we really hope to gain by viewing and mourning images of death and dead bodies in the classroom – such as the image of Alan Kurdi or images of death from the Holocaust and other atrocities? Clearly, providing trigger warnings is not the key issue here, as it does not really address this question (Papailias, 2019). Rather, this question forces educators to provide a deeper justification not only of whether but most importantly of *how* images of death could be used for pedagogical purposes. If the possibility of transforming something in the classroom through image testimonies is real and the ethical concerns can be fairly addressed (e.g., the right to image human beings in a dignified manner), then the pedagogical question about the potentialities of making visible contemporary necropower should, at least, be considered and explored.

If, for example, the pedagogical goal of showing images of death is to invoke empathy and highlight common human vulnerability by drawing attention to the materiality of (dead) human body, then I am afraid that neither sentimentality is really reclaimed nor the myths of "white innocence" about colonial histories, state racism and contemporary geopolitical complicities producing such deaths are challenged (Danewid, 2017). In fact, the uncritical and superficial use of death imagery sentimentalizes and infantilizes subjugated groups (e.g., refugees), placing one's self in the position of empathetic savior (Choulariaki & Stolic, 2017). In other words, it is more likely that showing death images under these pretensions will turn these images into objects of pity and philanthropy, reinforcing stereotypes of "saviors" and "victims" (Papailias, 2019).

Beholding the corpse of the "other," argues Papailias (2019), is undoubtedly full of ambivalences, yet this confronts us with our ethical and political responsibilities for the dead/dying "other." The ambivalences of showing images of dead bodies in teaching youth and adults should not negate attempts to engage with difficult questions invoked by such images regarding ethical obligations and political possibilities to speak and act in ways that interrogate normalized necropolitical affects. For example, showing death images in the classroom can be a point of departure to interrogate the relation between a colonial necropolitical engagement and violence or trauma – what Osuri (2009) calls "necropolitical complicity." Necropolitical complicity highlights the responsibility of both individuals and social groups in the death of "others," as a result of colonial histories, systemic racism and structural injustices.

In particular, educators and students may use death images to examine difficult and uncomfortable questions such as the following: How can educators and students in Western societies recognize their own necropolitical complicity and respond ethically and politically to its usual denial in colonial histories, systemic racism and structural injustices? What kind of pedagogical discourses and practices may counter the evasion of necropolitical complicity? How can death images contribute to begin the emotionally difficult process of recognizing the functions and consequences of necropolitical complicity? These are some of the questions that highlight the tensions of pedagogical efforts to address issues of (necropolitical) complicity within systems that perpetuate injustice and suffering in the current political climate (see also Chapter 11).

One of the biggest challenges in using death images in the classroom remains, of course, how to do so without invoking a self-indulgent, uncritical and superficial sentimentality. Much has been written about "moral spectatorship," that is, the distant suffering and politics of pity (Boltanski, 1999; Chouliaraki, 2008, 2012). Images as/and testimonies of suffering may lead to moralization by removing emotion from the call to action and by framing the conversation on the basis of simplistic and essentialist moral categories such as that of "good" versus "evil" (Chouliaraki, 2008, 2012). This moralization takes place by resorting to a sentimental discourse of suffering that evokes pity for the sufferers rather than compassionate action (Boltanski, 1999), leading students to voyeurism and passivity (Zembylas, 2008).

Reclaiming sentimentality in the classroom as an ethical, political and pedagogical enterprise that attempts to mold the values of social justice, decoloniality and solidarity has to make visible "the confluence of multiple toxic strands of contemporary necropower and biopower" such as Euro-American neo-imperial violence, human trafficking, the securitized/militarized European border regime and humanitarian governmentality (Papailias, 2019, p. 1053). For instance, this can be done through *both* acts of replication of images of dead bodies *and* the deletion of such images (p. 1053), depending on the contextual politics and ethics of showing images of death. In other words, the sentimental manipulation of death images and the moral dilemmas of commodifying the suffering of subjugated groups (e.g., migrants, refugees) can be avoided not by completely erasing the value of the sentimental but rather by reframing sentimentality through a historicization of necropolitical events and affects.

Building on Berlant's (2008) theorization about the construction of an intimate public that engages critically and sensitively with difficult issues, I am suggesting that sentimentality can be ethically, politically and pedagogically effective as an opportunity to make emerging emotions in the classroom the point of departure to recognize colonial histories, state racism and contemporary geopolitical complicities producing deaths. If we (e.g., educators) want to interrogate the trappings of sentimentality and especially narratives of pity, then it is crucial to use death images in order to challenge our own emotional investments and emotion-informed ideologies toward suffering, trauma and death, and seek to promote action and solidarity that make a concrete difference in the lives of subjugated groups (Zembylas, 2016).

Importantly, showing images of death should not invest in feelings of guilt to motivate sympathetic feelings for "others," as it is unlikely to establish any openings for action and solidarity against social structures of injustice. Feelings of guilt, as shown in Chapter 9, are deeply problematic because they are self-centered, apolitical and privilege issues of personal identity and difference (see also Zembylas, 2013a). If students are bombarded with death images of migrants and refugees telling them they should feel guilty for the suffering, trauma and death of "others," then it is likely that this approach will backfire and lead students instead to adopt an angry, reactionary attitude or an "empty viewing." It is important that death images provide students with opportunities to establish and maintain a critical attentiveness for "ethical seeing," that is, learning to interrogate and challenge positionalities and arguments that reiterate stereotypes based on colonial legacies or normalized necropolitical affects about who is grievable and who is not (Butler, 2004a; Zembylas, 2016).

Hence, it is problematic to close off the possibility opened by using dead-body images in the classroom to establish affective networks that elevate these images into a point of departure for action and scrutiny of necropower. As Papailias (2019) argues,

> [W]e cannot collapse an ethical argument regarding our historical and political responsibility for the harm befallen others onto a given political response. We need to be able to [...] consider how the dead bodies of missing and unidentified migrants and the "problems" their stubborn materiality poses (for identification, disposal, mourning) illuminate not only a necropolitical zone of dispossession and abandonment [...], but also the potential for "transgressive citizenship": as dead bodies acquire a posthumous legal subjectivity and identity, they also become the grounds for collective struggle against bordering practices. (pp. 1063–1064)

The decision, then, whether to use or not to use dead-body images in the classroom cannot become *only* an ethical issue, or *only* a political one, and certainly *not merely* a pedagogical problem. It is all of these simultaneously, and therefore, the decision whether or how to share death images has to be contextualized and historicized, not only for risk assessment purposes (e.g., protecting students from traumatization) but also for creating the ethical, political and pedagogical conditions that would enable the interrogation of colonial histories, state racism and contemporary geopolitical complicities producing such deaths in the first place.

Conclusion

My aim in this chapter has been to use necropolitics and sentimentality as theoretical entry points to broaden understandings of death as a form of power against subjugated (e.g., Black, migrant, refugee) lives in education. This theorizing has been approached through the dilemma of showing or not showing dead-body images in the classroom as an ethical, political and pedagogical intervention. This intervention entails numerous challenges such as the risk of traumatizing students; the danger of superficializing colonial histories, structural racism and contemporary geopolitical complicities producing such deaths; and, the challenge of finding productive ways to respond pedagogically to the emotionally difficult spaces of learning that are created, without sentimentalizing death.

One way to think critically and responsibly about necropolitics and sentimentality in education within the contemporary political climate is to refuse to banalize the death of "others" – "who for some of us indeed include our own" (Haritaworn et al., 2014, p. 20) – through *either* acts of replication *or* mere deletion of images of dead bodies. The ethical, political and pedagogical dilemmas of whether or not to use images of dead bodies in the classroom are not resolved by the decision to eventually use or not such images. Instead, the questions educators must ask are the following: What can be done in the classroom to attend to the forces that prepare subjugated bodies for premature death? What would a necropolitical and critical sentimental education that is serious about such a task look like? How can educators and students create "safe spaces" in the classroom to make sense of the entanglement of necropolitics and sentimentality, while also challenging and resisting neo-colonial logics? It is precisely these broader questions that need to be addressed, when we engage with the "biopolitical mess" (Bird & Lynch, 2019) that emerges from the dilemma of showing or not showing images of dead bodies in the classroom.

CHAPTER 11

For an Anti-complicity Pedagogy

The concept of complicity has become a recurring issue of concern throughout several chapters of this book (e.g., see Chapters 1, 4, 8 and 9). This concept has been making growing appearances in social science publications in recent years (see, e.g., Afxentiou, Dunford & Neu, 2017a; Applebaum, 2010; Firat, de Mul & Van Wichelen, 2009; Lepora & Goodin, 2013; Wächter & Wirth, 2019). While the definitions and scope of complicity vary widely in different fields, most scholars agree that complicity entails a (causal) contribution to wrongdoing (Lepora & Goodin, 2013). The emphasis here, notes Wächter (2019), who follows Lepora and Goodin, is on *contribution*, because complicity is not an act of wrongdoing perpetuated by a principal or several co-principals but a *secondary* act of wrongdoing. In other words, those who are complicit contribute to wrongdoing (knowingly or unknowingly) rather than fully participate in it (Lepora & Goodin, 2013, p. 80).

One of the challenges identified in contemporary work on complicity in the social sciences is the resistance of individuals and groups to acknowledge their contribution to wrongdoing, especially in contexts of difficult histories – that is, experiences and events of trauma, suffering, and violent oppression of groups of people such as racism, colonialism, the apartheid and the like (Peck & Epstein, 2017). For example, Applebaum's (2010) seminal work on white complicity in social justice education documents the pedagogical challenge of dealing with white students' denial and resistance in the classroom. Applebaum advocates for the need to develop what she calls "white complicity pedagogy" that encourages white students to acknowledge their complicity and unearned privilege as members of a group regardless of their personal circumstances or individual relationship to white privilege.

Crucial to emerging discussions about complicity and moral responsibility in democratic education is the notion of affect, as discussed throughout this book. A key feature of affect is that it cannot be reduced to a property of the subject, but it is felt as the capacity to affect and be affected (Deleuze, 1988). While discussions over the nature and scope of complicity in democratic education seem to recognize the involvement of specific emotions (e.g., guilt, shame) in students' resistance (e.g., see Applebaum, 2007, 2010, 2012, 2013, 2017), recent theoretical shifts on both affect (e.g., see Anderson, 2014; Anderson & Harrison, 2010; Thrift, 2008) and complicity (e.g., Afxentiou, Dunford & Neu, 2017b; McCarty, 2018; Reynolds, 2017; Wächter, 2019) extend our conceptualization of how affect and complicity are entangled in the classroom. The new openings emerging from these theoretical shifts create pedagogical spaces to inspire *anti-complicity* praxes – that is, actions that actively resist social harm in everyday life (Reynolds, 2017; Wächter, 2019).

In the last chapter of the book, I revisit the important role of affect in pedagogical efforts to engage students with complicity in democratic education so that anti-complicity is encouraged. In a sense, this chapter culminates my efforts to suggest affective pedagogies for democratic education that foreground how to deal with the fundamental issue of complicity, that is, what can be done pedagogically to minimize everyday complicity to acts of injustice, microfascism, and the perpetuation of far right rhetoric. Existing scholarship in social justice education identifies and problematizes the fact that students use "distancing strategies" to dissociate themselves from individual culpability (Applebaum, 2010, 2013, 2017). Hence, it is suggested that it is not sufficient for educators to simply make students aware of their potential complicity, but rather they should actively encourage students to take moral and epistemic responsibility for their learning (Whitt, 2016). However, I would argue that for this to happen, it is necessary that educators navigate students through the affective and political dynamics of complicity in *both* critical *and* strategic ways. In other words, a careful, thoughtful and incremental strategy is needed to move the focus away from what we do not want (i.e., more complicity) toward anti-complicity – what I call *anti-complicity pedagogy*.

It is with these ideas in mind that I, first, examine some of the ways in which social justice pedagogy has approached the question of complicity so far. This part of the chapter reviews pedagogical efforts and emerging challenges to help students recognize their complicity, especially in relation to structural injustice, racism and oppression – all phenomena that are directly or indirectly linked to right-wing populism and fascism. The next part of the chapter discusses some recent theoretical shifts in debates about complicity in the social sciences. This section invites us to reconsider the dominant moral philosophical account of complicity in favor of a conceptualization that pays attention to the entanglement among politics, history, ethics and one's positionality in exploring complicity. The third part of the chapter introduces how emerging theoretical discussions on affect, as presented throughout this book, contribute to a deeper analysis of complicity; in conjunction to theoretical shifts on complicity, theorizations on affect help develop a conceptual framework that allows both the affective and political dynamics of complicity to be recognized in democratic education. Finally, the last part of the chapter analyzes how educators could engage in, what Scott (1999, 2004) calls "strategic criticism", namely, a pedagogical approach that takes a critical stance toward situated complicity, yet in a strategic manner. This section addresses specifically how the notion of anti-complicity pedagogy may be "translated" into strategic moves in democratic education.

Complicity as a Pedagogical Challenge

There has been a growing literature around issues of complicity in the classroom, especially in relation to white denials of complicity and how social justice pedagogy could respond to diminish such denials. Applebaum (2007, 2010, 2012, 2013, 2017) has written extensively on white denials of complicity in relation to education, and therefore, her work will be featured more prominently here. First of all, Applebaum (2010, 2013) identifies several ways with which white students deny complicity, such as making claims of color-blindness, using distancing strategies, blaming the victim, and ignoring historical and institutional narratives that provide evidence for systemic racism. As she writes, "*Denials of complicity* are not understood by those who perform them to be 'denials' because white ignorance masquerades as white racial commonsense, logic, or good intentions" (Applebaum, 2013, p. 22, original emphasis). The invisibility of white complicity, argues Applebaum, is related to white-skin privilege that does not come from a particular individual act but is rather a product of social structures. White complicity, then, is a performative way of being in the sense that white people perform and sustain whiteness continuously, often unconsciously, or without doing anything out of the ordinary (Applebaum, 2013, p. 22).

Therefore, traditional notions of moral responsibility that ground complicity on causality and individual action "not only fail to expose White complicity but also contribute to the normalization of denials of complicity that protect systemic racism from being challenged" (Applebaum, 2010, p. 5). For this reason, Applebaum (2013) has turned to models of moral responsibility that reframe complicity as social rather than individual – e.g., Young's conception of a Social Connection Model of Responsibility, which helps articulate a notion of moral responsibility that recognizes all people as socially connected. Applebaum (2010) suggests that Young's reframing of responsibility helps educators engage students in recognizing their complicity, while distinguishing responsibility from guilt, shame, fault or blame. In other words, it is argued that each and every one is complicit in structures of injustice, and, therefore, morally responsible, yet not in the same manner or to the same degree; hence, it may be said that responsibility is not collective but rather shared (see Chapter 9).

Diminishing denials of white complicity in the classroom is clearly a challenging task for which education scholars have proposed various pedagogical strategies. For example, Applebaum (2007) has suggested that Young's model of responsibility can and should be taught in the classroom, so that white students are made accountable of their complicity in structural racism and injustice. As she has noted, this model "can facilitate the decentering of white emotions, can encourage uncertainty and a willingness to listen, and can enhance an unrelenting vigilance on the part of white students" (Applebaum, 2007, p. 466). Vigilance takes the form of critique as a practice that recognizes the suffering of others and the ways in which Whites are complicit in systemic racial injustice. Such a notion of vigilance, according to Applebaum (2013), encourages white students to interrogate their own self-conceptions as "good" (p. 32). In her more recent work, Applebaum (2017) argues that comforting the discomfort that emerges in the social justice classroom as result of addressing complicity is dangerous, not only because it constitutes a form of violence that allows for the suffering of students of color to go unnoticed but also because it allows white privilege to remain unchallenged. Hence, it is suggested that embracing the discomfort emerging from this process, while offering critical hope, is a type of support that can be offered to white students without comforting them.

Maudlin (2014), on the other hand, seems to be suggesting that an ideology of hope, even a radical one, might be equally problematic in confronting complicity because it operates to reinscribe white privilege. Although Maudlin cites Applebaum (2010), she calls for an abandonment of hope, because such a move does not only relinquish the possibility for white moral innocence but also challenges traditional notions of moral responsibility. Maudlin finds hope problematic – even those approaches that maintain a critical stance toward the past – because "it is grounded in a forward-looking progress narrative that obscures the material reality of the 'now' in favor of an anticipated future" (p. 146). The abandonment of hope is an ethical imperative, according to Maudlin, in critiquing white complicity; embracing suffering and the difficult now is what decenters white moral agency by shifting it toward the present. In other words, although Maudlin and Applebaum start from opposite points of departure regarding the role of hope, they both end up highlighting the recognition of vulnerability and suffering – albeit from different theoretical angles.

In her work on postcolonial engagements with questions of complicity in systemic harm, Andreotti (2014) has also called for an ethical response to denials of complicity, namely, approaches that expose the paradox of struggling for social transformation while being complicit to systemic harm that is perpetuated. Andreotti offers alternative ways to approach questions of justice and ethics such as the following: "How can we respond educationally and ethically to the collective phenomenon of denial of complicity in systemic harm, including its hegemonic and counter-hegemonic manifestations?" (p. 283) "What kind of education can counter the current trend of evasion of complicities in structural/material and cognitive/epistemic injustices?" (p. 387). These questions highlight the tensions of pedagogical efforts to handle issues of complicity within systems that perpetuate injustice and suffering.

Finally, Whitt (2016) takes on the students' use of "distancing strategies" to dissociate themselves from complicity and argues that such strategies perpetuate ignorance and unknowing, because they prevent students from understanding their own contribution to social injustices. In order to respond pedagogically to student distancing, Whitt argues that it is not sufficient for teachers to make students aware of their potential complicity. Beyond this, he writes, "teachers should cultivate epistemic virtue in the classroom and encourage students to take responsibility for better ways of knowing" (p. 427). Some epistemic virtues he suggests are humility, intellectual curiosity and open-mindedness. Whitt also outlines several classroom practices designed to help ameliorate students' resistance and ignorance (e.g., using films, engaging in metadialogue, recognizing the value of vulnerability and so on).

There are two areas that offer room for further development in this brief and certainly incomplete review of some of the scholarship on the pedagogical dimensions of addressing complicity in democratic education. The first concerns thinking about complicity and students' resistance within a continuum of positions individuals can occupy rather than as dichotomous ones (cf. Mihai, 2019). In other words, the issue should not be framed in binary terms, i.e., whether students are complicit *or* not, or whether students acknowledge their complicity *or* fail to do so. The issue is not *individual*, emphasizes Mihai, but rather *social* and *political*; hence, a more sophisticated understanding of subjectification is required to replace the highly individualized accounts of complicity that are often projected in discussions about complicity.

The second area for further development concerns how to address complicity pedagogy, when the complex affective dynamics of students' struggles and resistances are taken into serious consideration. Affectivity is deeply entangled with complicity through the interplay of hope, guilt, shame and other emotions that emerge within specific historical, cultural and political contexts and show students' emotional difficulties. Unless educators grapple with the affective dynamics of complicity as both an affective and political concept and act to draw out the complex interrelationships between historical pasts and present, I am afraid that our pedagogical interventions will be unable to challenge the deeply affective roots of complicity. In the next two sections of the chapter, then, I will attempt to analyze further these two areas taking into consideration some recent theoretical shifts in discussions about complicity and affect.

Complicity as a Political Concept and Act

My point of departure in discussing complicity is Afxentiou et al.'s (2017b) argument in their volume *Exploring Complicity: Concept, Case, and Critique* that "any attempt to establish, once and for all, the nature and scope of complicity, would do little more than shut down important avenues for critical analysis" (p. 1), and hence in doing so, "it would detract from our ability to imagine effective resistance against the causes of avoidable harms that can be elucidated through the lens of complicity" (p. 1). Therefore, my goal in this section is not to offer a definition of complicity that can be used in democratic education, once and for all, but rather to recognize the complexities of the concept of complicity and highlight some theoretical angles that have emerged recently in the literatures that make complicity their object of analysis.

As Mihai (2019) notes, there are two major theoretical accounts of complicity. On the one hand, there is the dominant moral-legal account that focuses on the different levels of *individual* complicity in wrongdoing; in other words, the emphasis is on legal reasoning and moral guilt, because familiar conceptions of responsibility have traditionally depended upon causality and intent (Kutz, 2000, 2007; Lepora & Goodin, 2013).

Complicity is understood in *atomistic* terms, based on the assumption that there are clearly and unambiguously morally right frameworks and that complicity entails violation of these frameworks (Afxentiou et al., 2017b). Such an atomistic understanding, however, according to Afxentiou et al., fails to acknowledge that moral wrongdoing lies in the social structures just as much as in individual moral agents (see also, Wächter, 2019).

The second theoretical perspective, then, has emerged as a critique to the atomistic understanding of complicity and focuses on the contextual and structural circumstances within which acts of complicity take place. Going beyond a simplistic notion of agency and subjectivity and acknowledging the role of power relations and social structures, this perspective understands complicity "as always enmeshed in complex social relations and influenced – though not fully determined – by one's location within those relations" (Mihai, 2019, p. 3). In other words, this perspective of complicity does not attribute moral responsibility to a single individual (or group or institution for that matter) but contextualizes and situates complicity within a broader social and political context (Afxentiou et al., 2017b; Wächter, 2019). As Afxentiou et al. (2017b) write, this perspective provides us with "a better understanding not only of complicit 'bad apples', but also of the rotten barrels which contain them" (p. 4).

In particular, Reynolds (2017) argues against the conceptualization of complicity as a disciplinary mechanism of assigning moral blame to individuals; rather, he views complicity as rhetoric device that raises critical sensitivity about our contribution to the perpetuation of social injustices. As he explains, "the power of complicity lies in the construction of a political narrative able to highlight the blurred lines of culpability, liability and responsibility in dealing with often-complex events and social practices" (p. 35). Reading complicity as a rhetoric device, adds Wächter (2019), highlights that it is helpful to consider complicity within the context of its formation, namely, "as embedded in *regimes of truth*" (p. 4, original emphasis). Conceptualizing complicity as a political concept, then, enables the recognition and problematization of the relational and affective dimensions of power relations involved in narratives about complicity in each context.

Furthermore, the political conceptualization of complicity moves us beyond the boundaries set by moral questions regarding individual's complicity with injustice, because this perspective considers subjective criteria (e.g., moral conscience) to be insufficient (McCarty, 2018). As McCarty explains,

> As a political concept, complicity serves a number of distinct, but interrelated, functions. It serves as a method of interacting with claims to justice and injustice, a basis for political status, a way of structuring our relationships to one another and to the state, a justification for seeking to exercise power over others, and a conceptual intervention into the logic of citizenship and tolerance that speaks directly to the terms of the social contract itself. (p. 3)

For example, the political meaning of complicity tells us what it means to have the status of a complicit citizen, what rights and responsibilities one has as a complicit citizen, and how to understand one's relationship to others (McCarty, 2018, p. 18). The problem though emerges, according to McCarty, when complicity becomes the main mechanism through which one engages injustice:

> Approaching injustice wholly – or in large part – through the lens of complicity shifts the focus away from the injustice itself or its victims and toward the complicit individual. [...] If we perceive the problem not as one of injustice, but one of having been made complicit with injustice, we run the risk of mistaking the comparatively minor harm of being made an unwitting co-conspirator for the real harm involved. (2018, p. 19)

Although the degree of harm may certainly be a matter of debate – as "complicity comes in different degrees and in different kinds," to quote Afxentiou et al. (2017b, p. 10) – McCarty's point is "to stop treating complicity as a problem to be solved and start treating it as a fact of our civic life to learn to live with" (2018, p. 19). This implies, for instance, that rather than structuring our lives in ways that focus on avoiding complicity altogether, we should recognize that this is an inevitable aspect of political life and we are all already complicit in all kinds of ways to unjust acts. Following Arendt (1963/1977), Sanders (2002) speaks of the necessity of acknowledging the "little perpetrator" in oneself and "the potential of evil is in each one of us" (p. 3) that makes us always already complicit in the wrongdoings of others. In this sense, complicity is "an ethico-political response available to anyone" (Sanders, 2002, p. 4) and hence "can serve as a catalyst for ethical and political action" (Sanyal, 2015, p. 13) that is anti-complicit (Reynolds, 2017).

All in all, the recently emerging theoretical perspectives that conceptualize complicity as a political concept and act offer two important contributions. First, the political conceptualization of complicity shows how complicity is mediated by power structures that normalize wrongdoing and render complicity invisible (Mihai, 2019). In other words, this understanding of complicity is "more sensitive to how power relations shape *both* the contexts *and* the agents of wrongdoing" (Mihai, 2019, p. 4, original emphasis). Against notions of complicity that individualize moral-legal responsibility, while ignoring each and every one's political responsibilities in social structures, a political conceptualization of complicity enables recognition of the historical, social and political conditions that render some sufferings and injustices permissible and habitual, or part of everyday repertoire and social interaction (Mihai, 2019). Any attempt, then, to redress wrongs and think politically (rather than merely legally), suggests Mihai, must rely on a critically reflexive account that recognizes the multiple complexities of complicity.

Second, a political conceptualization of complicity offers an understanding of resistance in a manner that transcends the binary model of agents as either complicit or resisting (Kurunczi et al., 2018). Given that it is difficult to define precisely what constitutes resistance (Hynes, 2013), Kurunczi et al. (2018) suggest that Reynolds' (2017) notion of anti-complicity "enables agents to contest the seemingly 'natural', conceivably 'real' limits of critique" (p. 2). In other words, if complicity is a matter of degree rather than a binary choice (see also, Mihai, 2019), then the potential of resistance as anti-complicity is also part of a continuum. Anti-complicity essentially means not only taking a critical stance toward complicity but also actively resisting doing social harm in everyday life. Needless to say, a critique of complicity is never free of complicities; we are implicated in the world that we critique, argues Ahmed (2013), and therefore, being critical does not suspend our complicity. In what follows, I focus on how the affective dimension of complicity makes our efforts to be critical even more challenging.

Complicity as Embodied and Affective Practice

My theoretical account of affect in this book has been described in the Introduction and outlined in previous chapters. Inasmuch as these theoretical perspectives pay explicit attention to affect as a body's capacity to affect and be affected, then I use this conception of affect to better understand bodily capacities to affect and to be affected as always collectively formed through relations that extend beyond them. In this chapter, I particularly emphasize non-representational theory (NRT) of affect, as this is exemplified by Thrift (2008) and Anderson (Anderson, 2014; Anderson & Harrison, 2010). As Lorimer (2005, p. 83) has put it, "non-representational theory is an umbrella term for diverse work that seeks to better cope with our self-evidently more-than-human, more-than-textual, multisensual worlds." NRT essentially constitutes a collection of approaches that locate meaning in the "manifold of actions and interactions" (Thrift, 1996, p. 6) rather than in discourse, ideology and *re*presentation. Thus, NRT moves the focus away from finding meaning in representations of the world, and onto what happens in the active world – the "bare bones" and "taking place" of occasions and the onflow of life (Thrift, 2008). One of the central tenets of NRT is that it stresses the importance of bodies and particularly affects in efforts "to apprehend and intervene in the non-representational powers of spaces of embodied movement and practices" (McCormack, 2003, p. 488).

As emphasized throughout this book, affects do not reside in an individual body or subject but rather emerge in encounters between bodies; hence, affects are not just feelings or emotions but forces influencing a body's modes of existence (Anderson, 2014). As Deleuze (1992) has put it, "you do not know beforehand what a body or a mind can do, in a given encounter, a given arrangement, a given combination" (p. 627). The view that affect is non-individuated and bodily potential that emerges from and express specific relational configurations has important ethical and political implications. As a reminder, here I highlight two such implications. First and foremost, my understanding of affect in this book pays attention to "affective events" rather than "emotional states." Deleuze (1988) argues that affect is more than the state produced when bodies are acted upon. From this point of view, there is always something excessive about affect that cannot be captured as an empirically observable state. Emphasizing the openness and potentiality of affect, as distinct from its actualization as emotion, highlights the transformative possibilities of forces that are not captured in individuated terms (Hynes, 2013). At the same time, it is important to remember that the relation between affect and discourse is not dichotomous but entangled (Wetherell, 2012). Wetherell refers to "affective-discursive practices" by which she highlights "the simultaneity of the embodied registration of an event and meaning making" (Wetherell et al., 2015, p. 59). For example, this would mean that any exploration of complicity must look at how individuals are embedded in specific affective-discursive entanglements within which they are inescapably complicit.

The insistence that affect is relational and embodied rather than individuated and/or constructed through language is reflected in Thrift's (2008) and Anderson's (Anderson, 2014; Anderson & Harrison, 2010) non-representational theoretical accounts that emphasize the body's productive capacity in a transpersonal space and its radical openness to others.

Both Thrift and Anderson theorize affect as a transpersonal capacity, that is, a capacity that transcends the individual, focusing instead on relations, events and entanglements with the nonhuman. Herein precisely lies the transformative potential of non-representational theory of affect, because by understanding affects as relations and practices, there are possibilities for new forms of politics that open up spaces of solidarity and social change.

In particular, Thrift's non-representational theory shows how the study of affect can enhance our understanding of politics. As he explains (Thrift, 2008, p. 182), citing Spinks:

> [T]he envelope of what we call the political must increasingly expand to take note of "the way that political attitudes and statements are partly conditioned by intense autonomic bodily reactions that do not simply reproduce the trace of a political intention and cannot wholly be recuperated within an ideological regime of truth" (Spinks, 2001, p. 24).

Non-representational theory, then, can be valuable in helping us pay attention to the idea that affective modes of being also constitute political practices. This implies that it is important to constantly examine the different ways that affective capacities of bodies are situated, providing openings for new modes of being in the world (Anderson, 2014; Anderson & Harrison, 2010).

I return now to the concept of complicity to illustrate how a differentiated conceptual vocabulary on affect might work to reconsider complicity. In pursuing the argument that the lens of affect contributes to the reconceptualization of complicity, I want to highlight two broad insights. First, affect renders visible the power of embodied complicities that serve to uphold social injustices. Second, affect enables an approach to complicity that views it as situated, relational and historicized, that is, as an enactment in contingent contexts; hence, if complicities are seen as events (rather than states), then new events can be brought forth that challenge social injustices. Each of these insights is briefly discussed below.

First, if the initial task for an analysis of affective life is to attend to differentiated capacities to affect and be affected (Anderson, 2014), then complicity is no exception. Rendering visible the often unconscious and embodied complicities that serve to uphold social injustices – be that by agents or by the practices they produce, be that by the oppressor or the oppressed (Wächter, 2019, p. 6) – seems to be an important task for social theorists and educators alike. This is a task that traces how complicities as affects emerge from and express specific relational formations that make up the practices of everyday life – e.g., the insidious practices of what Foucault and Deleuze called "little everyday fascisms" (Roudinesco, 2008; see Chapter 4), how they are embodied and percolate into structural violence and perpetuate complicities to social injustices and inequities. Such a consideration reorders our sense of how deeply embedded harm, inequality and injustice are in the fabric of everyday life (Thrift, 2008).

Second, an exploration of complicity through the lens of affect recognizes that bodies participate "in more or less complicit practices and patterns of behavior, in ways that can only be partially captured by the moral-legal paradigm" (Mihai, 2019, p. 5). Complicity, then, is to be conceived less in terms of willpower or cognitive deliberation and more via embodied and situated affordances, dispositions and habits (cf. Anderson & Harrison, 2010). This means that complicity is understood as a relational phenomenon "incessantly looping back and regulating itself through feedback phenomena" such as resistance and other affects (Anderson & Harrison, 2010, p. 7). This continuum of complicity and resistance implies that there is potential for the event of anti-complicity to be performed through everyday encounters and actions.

Both of these insights – namely, the recognition of complicities as affective and embodied practices, and the potential for anti-complicity – expand our educational theorizing of complicity in terms of making more capacious visions and acts of political responsibility become possible through pedagogic work. Recognizing the important role of affect in pedagogical interventions that address complicity opens the path for a more nuanced account of how to handle complicit students in the classroom in both critical and strategic ways.

Toward Anti-complicity Pedagogy

I have so far argued that, to appreciate the multiple complexities of complicity, it is valuable to take into consideration some recent theoretical shifts that highlight the political and affective conceptualization of complicity. I want to discuss now how this all bears on the issue of handling complicity pedagogically in the classroom. As noted earlier, students' denials of complicity can be motivated by various affects and emotions – e.g., shame, guilt, anger – that are inextricably linked to personal, political or ethical commitments as well as students' broader social, historical and political lifeworld. Handling students' denials of complicity, then, requires a strategic pedagogical approach that considers not only how to engage students critically with the affective and political complexities of complicity but also how to invent pedagogical spaces that inspire students to undertake anti-complicity praxes.

In effect, then, what starts out as a pedagogical effort to teach students how to acknowledge their complicity in social injustices turns out to be a deeply affective and political process that has *criticism* at its heart. In general, complicity tends to be treated as a disempowering imposition to individuals (McCarty, 2018), including classroom situations. In most cases, explains McCarty, "the individual did not actively choose to become complicit [...]. The complicit individual lacks power because they cannot wholly control – or sometimes even know about – the injustice for which they are being held responsible" (2018, p. 4). For this reason, we can reasonably expect some students in the classroom to perceive pedagogical efforts to make them admit their complicity as a form of criticism that creates moral and emotional distress to them. Hence, attempts to instill guilt and moral taint as much as to assuage such feelings of discomfort in students by pampering them (see Applebaum, 2017) will most likely fail, not only because students will be made to feel that the problem is personal, when it is actually a political one (see also, Chapter 9). Most importantly, these attempts will fail because they are often disguised as efforts to bring about real change in the world, when in fact they are stuck in a psychologized approach that simply tries to deal with the emotional aftermath of criticism (Bekerman & Zembylas, 2018; McCarty, 2018).

What is needed, then, is a form of criticism of complicity in the classroom that neither validates privilege nor attempts to assuage discomforting feelings of complicity. As educators, we do not want students too preoccupied with their personal moral status; rather, our insistence on complicity should be primarily concerned with the injustice at hand and how we can contribute both individually and collectively to address it (McCarty, 2018). Handling complicity in the classroom should not end up being a matter of moral narcissism but rather focused on achieving specific outcomes directed at opposing a perceived injustice. For example, if the issue is how to handle white students' denial of complicity, the pedagogical question at hand is not "What can I, as an educator, do to reaffirm students' moral agency so that they admit their complicity?" but rather "How can I, as an educator, move my students to take action in their everyday lives to refuse being complicit to social harm?" This, of course, does not imply that the moral or emotional experience of being complicit is undermined; on the contrary, as shown earlier, this would be impossible, given that complicity is deeply affective. However, handling complicity through the theoretical lens outlined here would not look to burden students with the moral weight of structural injustice or to have them share the guilt involved in the name of "a self-liberatory therapeutic confessionalism" (Pfister, 2006, p. 138). Rather, it would require from pedagogues to cultivate criticism of complicity in the classroom in a critical and strategic manner.

Scott (1999, 2004) proposes two critical concepts that I utilize here to develop a pedagogic response that takes into consideration the affective and political complexities of situated complicity: strategic criticism and strategic critical praxis. The notion of "strategic" means clarifying "what demand [criticism] has to meet, what its tasks are supposed to be, what target ought to make a claim on its attention, and what questions ought to constitute its apparatus and animate its preoccupations" (Scott, 1999, p. 5). This means that educators need to view complicity as part of an affective-political contingency that demands a practice of strategic criticism, yet in a manner that also inspires anti-complicity praxes. In the remaining chapter, I explain this idea and outline two strategic moves that would be important for inventing an anti-complicity pedagogy that engages students with complicity in a critical and strategic manner.

Scott (1999) suggests that our cognitive-political contingency – I prefer to call it "affective-political contingency" – demands a practice of strategic criticism that is based on the principle of "question and answer," namely, each position needs to be understood as an "answer" to a particular question within a particular affective-discursive domain. For example, an educator who faces white students' denial of complicity has to be concerned not only with whether or not students acknowledge their complicity but with how to make students understand complicity as situated – that is, how power relations and affective infrastructures in their specific setting constellate to formulate complicity. Some questions toward this direction would be, for instance, as follows: In which ways are we, students and educators in our community, complicit in the impoverishment of the poor and the vulnerable that follows from limited budgets or cuts in public spending? What specific actions can we take to relieve poverty in this community? How can we think and feel differently about those who suffer, without losing track of the origins of our own (undeserved) privilege?

In other words, complicity and its affective-political implications will be different in one context of coloniality (e.g., a rural high school in western Canada) compared to another context of coloniality, racism or sexism (e.g., an urban high school in Johannesburg, South Africa). Such an approach, suggests Andreotti (2014), can shed light on how issues of complicity emerge in response to contingent problems rather than being universal and canonical. If educators aim at teaching students to understand their complicity in specific rather than universal terms, the success of their approach will depend on their strategic understanding of how to enter this historically constituted field of ongoing moral argument in ways that calculate the stakes, namely,

> [...] (what might stand and what might fall as a result of a particular move), of ascertaining the potential allies and possible adversaries, of determining the lines and play of forces (what might count and what might not as a possible intervention), and so on. [...] It is only by understanding criticism in this way that we can determine the contingent *demand* of – and on – criticism in any conjecture. (Scott, 1999, p. 7)

These conjectures are in effect affective-political infrastructures that are generative of complicity as embedded in its temporally and structurally complex constellations. This is where strategy in our pedagogical approach becomes crucial.

In particular, I suggest that our pedagogical approach requires a strategic practice of criticism toward complicity that makes two important moves. First, it does not fall into the seductive trap of rationalism, namely, the assumption that if students acknowledge their (conscious or unconscious) complicity, then the "problem" is solved. In line with Applebaum (2013), I would argue that continuous attentiveness (vigilance) as a response to complicity is needed, but I would further expand this idea by suggesting that reinterrogating the affective-political contingency of complicity should also reorient students away from the assumption that the future can be guaranteed by the pasts accumulated in the present (cf. Scott, 2004). In other words, if complicity and resistance to it fall within a continuum, as noted earlier, then there is no progressive dialectical resolution in or beyond the classroom.

The second move I suggest has to do with how to engage students in actions that are anti-complicit, namely, actions that actively resist social harm. Scott (2004) proposes a form of strategic critical praxis that is conceptualized as a reading of the past, present and future imaginaries in ways that invent new vocabularies of transformative possibilities. If we are all acting-in-complicity in today's world and are therefore responsible in complicity (Sanders, 2002), then it follows that vigilance itself is not enough, as being critical does not suspend the fact that we are implicated in the world (Ahmed, 2013). From Scott's perspective, what needs to be emphasized is the "difference" that specific actions can make in reimagining and refashioning the future. The critical strategic praxis that Scott proposes can take the form of anti-complicity pedagogy, when students are actively engaged to be defiant in the face of structural injustice and resist social harm in their everyday lives.

It is therefore important that educators first identify the specific affective-political complexities around complicity, before encouraging students to engage in anti-complicity actions. Such a pedagogical approach involves espousing Scott's notions of strategic criticism and strategic critical praxis, namely, cultivating in students an anti-complicity attitude of one who interrogates whether or not the questions or concepts they are currently preoccupied with (e.g., moral responsibility, guilt) still have any purchase to address their present affective-political habitat. Educators can model their own engagements with strategic criticism by using conceptual tools that do not blame the individual for his/her complicity in social injustices but rather outline specific acts that show when and under what circumstances this becomes a process of refusing to allow ongoing systems of racist and/or colonial violence to continue harming other people.

Conclusion

Given the increasing attention that new theoretical ideas on affect and complicity are receiving in various fields in the social sciences, it seems an apt time in democratic education to analyze their potential impact on reconceptualizing complicity and how to address it in critical and strategic terms. I have argued that complicity is situated and embedded in specific affective-political infrastructures that operate between both the individual and the collective; hence, to frame the issue of complicity as merely atomistic misses the complexities involved. Certainly, questions of ethical and political agency remain important, but an attention to the affective and political dimensions of complicity adds to more conventional ways of viewing complicity.

As Macoun (2016) writes, "Framing critical encounters through a lens of complicity leaves us with both a political responsibility and a critical intellectual imperative to understand and contest systems of domination in which we are enmeshed" (p. 98) – through strategic pedagogical engagements that make contributions to resisting social harm. To fully enact an anti-complicity pedagogy means, therefore, abandoning the hope that one day we may be relieved from complicity to social injustice. However, it makes a difference how we engage strategically with complicity so that we stay with the trouble (Haraway, 2016). What I am advocating, then, is not only an awareness of complicity – or mere recognition of its affective and political complexities, for that matter – in democratic education, but above all the cultivation of anti-complicity praxes, which should not stop in the classroom.

Epilogue

As I am writing this epilogue, the world is struggling to recover from the terrible consequences of the COVID-19 pandemic. At the same time, people in the United States and several countries around the world are gathering for mass anti-racism demonstrations following the death of black man George Floyd in police custody in Minneapolis. Perhaps it is still inappropriate to speak about the post–COVID-19 era, just when the *dust* of suffering around the world has not settled yet, *if* it ever does. And yet, we must confront here and now a simple yet fundamental reality that has *re*-emerged in this era, as our quest for the role of democratic education continues: the long-lasting and intensifying precarity of humans on the basis of health, education, social, economic and racial inequalities (Butler, 2020). As Butler has written aptly, "The virus alone does not discriminate, but we humans surely do, formed and animated as we are by the interlocking powers of nationalism, racism, xenophobia, and capitalism." The pandemic as well as the massive anti-racism protests that have swept across the United States have exposed and reinscribed, according to Butler, "the spurious distinction between grievable and ungrievable lives, that is, those who should be protected against death at all costs and those whose lives are considered not worth safeguarding against illness and death." As this reality becomes more profound, one wonders whether there can be any viable education "response" that is able to stop the tide of bigotry, oppression and racism that are intertwined with the phenomenon of right-wing populism that has been the focus of this book. What if the theoretical ideas proposed in this book fail not because the theory is bad but because the "problem" has become so firmly rooted in the "heart" and "soul" of humanity (Lebron, 2013) that it cannot be uprooted anymore? Put another way, why would someone believe that a bunch of theories that take seriously the affective dynamics of right-wing populism in democratic education can offer a sufficient way forward to combat the bigotry that is so deeply embedded in the affective economies of everyday life?

In these last few pages, I want to directly confront these questions that perhaps have been – fairly so – lingering since the beginning of this book. I began by way of a set of commitments that fueled this book project as well as its limitations; I end by way of a major caveat that has emerged from them, regarding these limitations, as they become more and more obvious in the wake of the pandemic and the anti-racist movements since then. As I have alluded in the Introduction, no social or political problem – let alone a complex and evolving one such as right-wing populism – will ever be resolved by education or education alone. We cannot depend on modes of political or pedagogical engagement designed to persuade those in positions of relative advantage, especially when they are fueled by anger, fear and hatred, to do the right thing and change their hearts and minds just like that (Beausoleil, 2019). As Beausoleil explains,

> We cannot, in the face of widespread, highly invested and deeply entrenched practices, identities and systems, delude ourselves that transforming the perspectives, commitments, and actions of those in positions of power is either effective in itself or sufficient for structural change when taken as the sole strategy. Indeed, as transformative as any particular encounter might be, when these are unsupported by other measures the force of habit and institutionalized incentives for normalized behavior can still prove too strong a current to swim against. (p. 132)

Ever since Dewey (1916/1985) has inaugurated the discussion about the role of education in a thriving democracy, the struggle whether and how education can contribute to changing a society has been central to key approaches, pedagogies and philosophies of education (Gutmann, 1996; Sant, 2019). Therefore, I have to make clear that the pedagogical theories shared here, even if motivated by an admittedly mixed grain of idealism and pragmatism, ultimately express a sense of hope about the ability of educators and students to better themselves and the society they inhabit, and the theories offered in previous chapters are certainly no different (Lebron, 2013). Yet, as Lebron correctly points out, when it comes to difficult social and political problems such as racism and white supremacy, which are deeply associated with right-wing populism and fascism, "hope can be proven unfounded, misplaced, or simply naïve" (2013, p. 156). The ultimate test of these ideas, of course, is whether they can actually happen on the ground and have a positive effect, namely, whether they can change even a little bit how educators and their students think and feel about racism, white supremacy and their consequences in a democratic society, or even more importantly, whether they change the ways educators and their students *live* their everyday lives, renewing the democratic way of living in the world. But it is reasonable to wonder about these transformative possibilities until there is some kind of empirical evidence that educators can work out the mechanics of these pedagogical theories in practice.

However, I want to remind the reader of another dimension of pedagogy that has been present all along throughout this book. After Freire (2003), I reiterate the notion of pedagogy in a much broader sense than merely a teaching method. Freire emphasizes that pedagogy is the entanglement of philosophy, politics and practice that demands that educators engage themselves and their students in transforming oppressive social conditions. In this sense, all pedagogy is political and functions as "public pedagogy" (Sandlin, O'Malley & Burdick, 2011), that is, as a form that constantly involves pedagogical encounters with others. This broadened conception of pedagogy includes public sites of pedagogy, offering opportunities for educational researchers, practitioners and activists to mobilize alternative forms of counter-hegemonic learning (Burdick & Sandlin, 2013). I would like for the affective pedagogies offered in this book to be seen but most importantly to function as ways of engaging and living in the world rather than a collection of technical pedagogical practices (Salazar, 2013). What these pedagogies have in common is engagement that is affect-driven and that forms around affective economies that can be subversive or reproductive of the status quo. Hence, affective pedagogies are not specific to the classroom. While the affective modalities of democratic education and democratic engagement may invite different politics of affect (e.g., shame, anger, empathy), they should not be construed as classroom-bounded. The main point is that "affective attunement" (Papacharissi, 2015) with either right-wing populism or democratic ideas is "energized or powered" (Papacharissi, 2015, p. 134) by affective modalities that are always *public* in the broadest possible sense. Yet, once again, such political and pedagogic engagements must work in tandem with other forms of interventions in public life such as parallel initiatives that focus on policy or law changes rather than public opinion (Beausoleil, 2019).

To return once again to the question of pedagogic engagement, whether affective pedagogies – as public pedagogies – serve "public good" certainly adds another dimension to this conversation. Education in general is unavoidably entangled in debates concerning what counts as public good, because schools and educational institutions at all levels should (ideally) be defined and evaluated by their unique goal to *renew* the public by providing individuals with the skills, dispositions and perspectives required to engage with others about their shared interests and common fate

(Feinberg, 2012). Yet, what this implies for democratic education – without resorting to populist or sentimentalist tactics, as discussed extensively in Part III of the book – is not always clear or agreeable. My position, in a nutshell, is that good intentions, by themselves, are not enough to settle matters morally (Lepora & Goodin, 2013). As Lepora and Goodin argue,

> That you were only trying to do good is good, so far as it goes. But it does not go all the way. It matters morally whether you actually succeeded in realizing those intentions, in actually doing good rather than merely trying. Complicity is as complicity does: not as it wants or hopes or tries to do. (p. 170)

Anti-complicity pedagogy, as I have analyzed it in Chapter 11, is crucial as an affective pedagogy that aims to prevent the wrongdoing of another. But as I have also pointed out in other chapters, there should be no illusion that this or any other pedagogy suggested in this book – or any other book, for that matter – can provide a "formula" to be applied "mechanically to crank out some 'right answer'" (Lepora & Goodin, 2013, p. 171) – namely, the "right" pedagogical theory or practice that subverts right-wing populism, renews democratic education and simultaneously eliminates complicity.

Purity from complicity is never possible though (Shotwell, 2016). In her celebrated book, *Against Purity: Living Ethically in Compromised Times*, Alexis Shotwell (2016) argues that "it is not possible to avoid complicity, [so] we do better to start from an assumption that everyone is implicated in situations we [...] repudiate. We are compromised and we have made compromises, and this will continue to be the way we craft the worlds to come" (p. 5). Shotwell further suggests that if we want a world with less suffering and more flourishing, it would be useful to perceive complicity as a constitutive part of our lives, rather than as something we should avoid, because it is unavoidable.

There are two important sets of questions that emerge from Shotwell's claims, at least for those of us who do work in democratic education. The first is more philosophical, if you will, and the second is more pedagogical. First, then, if everyone is complicit, are we all complicit in the same manner? Does it make a difference to make this distinction? And if complicity is unavoidable, does it even matter to make an argument that it is still worthwhile to try to cultivate anti-complicity in everyday life, as I have suggested in Chapter 11? If your answer to these questions is that we are not complicit in the same manner (i.e., complicity comes in different degrees and in different kinds) and that it still matters that we cultivate anti-complicity in our everyday lives, then we are together in the efforts to ask pedagogical questions emerging from these assumptions. So, here is my second set of questions: How can we urge ourselves and encourage our students to acknowledge our complicity (e.g., our unearned privilege as members of a group) regardless of our personal circumstances? To what extent is it possible to cultivate anti-complicity in the classroom and beyond through affective pedagogies that nurture democratic education?

What I have emphasized throughout the book as being crucial in these pedagogical efforts is not only to recognize notions such as complicity, populism, and others as embodied and affective practices but also to engage in affirmative critiques that nurture affective solidarity, that is, practical, concrete ways for "standing with" (TallBear, 2014) others to practice democracy and social justice in everyday life. Here is precisely the crucial role of educators around the world: to provide critical resources to younger generations for cultivating an affirmative culture and process of democracy – ones that transcend the negativity of mere critique of either right-wing populists (the likes of Trump) or inadequate forms of democracy in everyday life. Within an affirmative culture and process of democracy, educators and students recognize the weaknesses of democracy, yet they cultivate everyday habits and actions that are committed to enriching and strengthening democracy on its every step – rather than undermining, subverting or mocking democracy's missteps.

The multiple crises that the world currently faces will not be automatically solved by not reelecting populists such as Trump, but that would be a valuable first step. If educators do our job and turn to "our" historical experiences of anti-fascist education in our own countries as well as throughout the world, then another important step will be taken in a long and hard struggle against fascism. As Tooze (2019) writes, paraphrasing T. S. Elliot, "democracy is unlikely to die with a bang. But all the more likely is the possibility that it will expire with a whimper" (n.p.). The "whimper" may suggest that the suffocation of democracy does not happen by a single spectacular event, but as a result of *our* continuing inattention to numerous everyday habits and practices that consistently undermine democracy.

Starting from an understanding of our affective, ethical and political implication in this world, "to recognize the quite vast injustices informing our everyday lives, and from that understanding to act on our wish that it were not so" (Shotwell, 2016, p. 204) is at the heart of (pedagogical) practices "whose point is not only to interpret the world, but to change it" (Shotwell, 2016, p. 204). Solidarity and strategic work in democratic education open spaces for the kind of pedagogical and public interventions that I discussed in several chapters, and call for an explicit conception of what it means to imagine a future that is inclusive for *all*, not only for some. We cannot predict what might emerge, if these interventions actually take place, except holding open some doors through which the world might take a *more* democratic and just path.

References

Adey, P. (2014). Security atmospheres or the crystallization of worlds. *Environment and Planning D: Society and Space, 32*, 834–851.

Adkins, B. (2015). *Deleuze and Guattari's* A Thousand Plateaus: *A critical introduction and guide*. Edinburgh: Edinburgh University Press.

Adler-Nissen, R., Andersen, K. E., & Hansen, L. (2020). Images, emotions, and international politics: The death of Alan Kurdi. *Review of International Studies, 46*, 75–95.

Adorno, T. W., Frenkel-Brunswik, E., Levinson, D. J., & Sanford, R. N. (1950). *The authoritarian personality*. New York: Harper & Brothers.

Afxentiou, A., Dunford, R., & Neu, M. (Eds.). (2017a). *Exploring complicity: Concepts, cases and critique*. London: Rowman & Littlefield.

Afxentiou, A., Dunford, R., & Neu, M. (2017b). Introducing complicity. In A. Afxentiou, R. Dunford & M. Neu (Eds.), *Exploring complicity: Concepts, cases and critique* (pp. 1–15). London: Rowman & Littlefield.

Ahmed, S. (2003). In the name of love. *Borderlands, 2*(3), retrieved from www.borderlands.net.au/vol2no3_2003/ahmed_love.htm

(2004). *The cultural politics of emotion*. Edinburgh: Edinburgh University Press.

(2010). *The promise of happiness*. Durham, NC: Duke University Press.

(2012). *On being included: Racism and diversity in institutional life*. Durham, NC: Duke University Press.

(2013). Critical racism/critical sexism. *feministkilljoys*, retrieved from https://feministkilljoys.com/2013/12/19/critical-racismcritical-sexism/

(2014). Atmospheric walls. *feministkilljoys*, retrieved from https://feministkilljoys.com/2014/09/15/atmospheric-walls/

Alt, S. (2019). Conclusion: Critique and the politics of affirmation in international relations. *Global Society, 33*(1), 137–145.

Amin, A., & Thrift, N. (2013). *Arts of the political: New openings for the left*. Durham, NC: Duke University Press.

Anderson, B. (2009). Affective atmospheres. *Emotion, Space and Society, 2*(2), 77–81.

(2012). Affect and biopower: Towards a politics of life. *Transactions of the Institute of British Geographers, 37*(1), 28–43.

(2014). *Encountering affect: Capacities, apparatuses, conditions*. New York: Routledge.

(2017a). Hope and micropolitics. *Environment and Planning D: Society and Space, 35*(4), 593–595.
(2017b). "We will win again. We will win a lot": The affective styles of Donald Trump. *Society & Space*, retrieved from https://societyandspace.org/2017/02/28/we-will-win-again-we-will-win-a-lot-the-affective-styles-of-donald-trump/
Anderson, B., & Harrison, P. (2010). The promise of non-representational theories. In B. Anderson & P. Harrison (Eds.), *Taking place: Non-representational theories and geography* (pp. 1–34). Farnham: Ashgate.
Andreotti, V. (2014). Conflicting epistemic demands in poststructuralist and postcolonial engagements with questions of complicity in systemic harm. *Educational Studies, 50*(4), 378–397.
Applebaum, B. (2007). White complicity and social justice education: Can one be culpable without being liable? *Educational Theory, 57*(4), 453–467.
(2010). *Being white, being good: White complicity, white moral responsibility and social justice pedagogy*. New York: Lexington Books.
(2012). Reframing responsibility in the social justice classroom. *Race Ethnicity and Education, 15*(5), 615–631.
(2013). Vigilance as a response to white complicity. *Educational Theory, 63*(1), 17–34.
(2017). Comforting discomfort as complicity: White fragility and the pursuit of invulnerability. *Hypatia, 32*(4), 862–875.
Arendt, H. (1958/1998). *The human condition*. Chicago, IL: The University of Chicago Press.
(1959). Reflections on Little Rock. *Dissent, 6*(1), 45–56.
(1963/1977). *Eichmann in Jerusalem: A report on the banality of evil*. London: Penguin.
(1965/2006). *On revolution*. New York: Penguin Books.
(1968). The crisis in education. In H. Arendt (Ed.), *Between past and future: Eight exercises in political thought* (pp. 170–193). New York: Penguin.
(1978). *The life of the mind* (vol. 1). New York: Harcourt Brace Jovanovich.
(1979). *The origins of totalitarianism*. New York: Harcourt, Brace & World.
(1987). Collective responsibility. In J. Bernauer (Ed.), *Amor Mundi: Explorations in the faith and thought of Hannah Arendt* (pp. 43–50). Boston, MA: Martinus Nijhoff Publishers.
(1992). Lectures on Kant's political philosophy. In H. Arendt & R. Beiner (Eds.), *Hannah Arendt: Lectures on Kant's political philosophy* (pp. 7–77). Chicago, IL: The University of Chicago Press.
(1994). Organized guilt and universal responsibility. In J. Kohn (Ed.), *Essays in understanding, 1930–1954* (pp. 121–132). New York: Harcourt, Brace & Company.
(2003). *Responsibility and judgment*. New York: Schocken Books.
(2006). *Between past and present*. New York: Penguin.
Ashenden, S. (2014). The persistence of collective guilt. *Economy and Society, 43*(1), 55–82.

Ashmonti, L. (2013). History, democracy and the European Union. *Global Dialogue, 15*(2), 91–102.
Athanasiou, A., Hantzaroula, P., & Yannakopoulos, K. (2008). Towards a new epistemology: The "affective turn." *Historein, 8*, 5–16.
Attwell, D., Pes, A., & Zinato, S. (2019). Introduction: Shame, literature, and the postcolonial. In D. Attwell, A. Pes & S. Zinato (Eds.), *Poetics and politics of shame in postcolonial literature* (pp. 1–42). New York: Routledge.
Badiou, A. (2013). Affirmative dialectics: From logic to anthropology. *The International Journal of Badiou Studies, 2*(1), 1–13.
Baldacchino, J.-P. (2011). The eidetic of belonging: Towards a phenomenological psychology of affect and ethno-national identity. *Ethnicities, 11*(1), 80–106.
Ball, J. (2017). *Post-truth: How bullshit conquered the world*. London: Biteback.
Ball, S. J. (2013). *Foucault, power, and education*. New York: Routledge.
  (2016). Subjectivity as a site of struggle: Refusing neoliberalism? *British Journal of Sociology of Education, 37*(8), 1129–1146.
  (2017). Education as critique – "Un-thinking" education. In S. J. Ball (Ed.), *Michel Foucault: SpringerBriefs on key thinkers in education* (pp. 35–60). Dordrecht, The Netherlands: Springer.
Barad, K. (2007). *Meeting the universe halfway: Quantum physics and the entanglement of matter and meaning*. Durham, NC: Duke University Press.
Barbalet, J. (1998). *Emotion, social theory and social structure*. Cambridge: Cambridge University Press.
Barnwell, A. (2015). Entanglements of evidence in the turn against critique. *Cultural Studies, 30*(6), 906–925.
Bargués-Pedreny, P. (2019). From critique to affirmation in International Relations. *Global Society, 33*(1), 1–11.
Bar-On, T. (2018). The radical right and nationalism. In J. Rydgren (Ed.), *The Oxford handbook of the radical right* (pp. 17–41). Oxford: Oxford University Press.
Beausoleil, E. (2019). Listening to claims of structural injustice. *Angelaki, 24*(4), 120–135.
Bekerman, Z., & Zembylas, M. (2018). *Psychologized language in education: Denaturalizing a regime of truth*. New York: Palgrave Macmillan-Springer.
Benin, D., & Cartwright, L. (2006). Shame, empathy and looking practices: Lessons from a disability studies classroom. *Journal of Visual Culture, 5*(2), 155–171.
Berezin, M. (1997). *Making the fascist self: The political culture of interwar Italy*. Ithaca, NY: Cornell University Press.
Berlant, L. (2007). Slow death (sovereignty, obesity, lateral agency). *Critical Inquiry, 33*, 754–780.
  (2008). *The female complaint: The unfinished business of sentimentality in American culture*. Durham, NC: Duke University Press.
  (2011). *Cruel optimism*. Durham, NC: Duke University Press.
  (2016). Trump, or political emotions. *The New Inquiry*, August 5, 2016. Retrieved from https://thenewinquiry.com/trump-or-political-emotions/

Bernstein, B. (2001). From pedagogies to knowledges. In A. Morais, I. Neves, B. Davies & H. Daniels (Eds.), *Towards a sociology of pedagogy. The contribution of Basil Bernstein to research* (pp. 363–368). New York: Peter Lang.

Bhanji, N. (2019). Necrointimacies: Affect and the virtual reverberations of violent intimacy. *Capacious, 1*(4), 110–135.

Biesta, G. (2006). *Beyond learning: Democratic education for a human future.* Boulder, CO: Paradigm.

(2010a). *Good education in age of measurement: Ethics, politics, democracy.* Boulder, CO: Paradigm.

(2010b). How to exist politically and learn from it: Hannah Arendt and the problem of democratic education. *Teachers College Record, 112*(2), 558–577.

(2011). The ignorant citizen: Mouffe, Rancière, and the subject of democratic education. *Studies in Philosophy and Education, 30*(2), 141–153.

(2013). *The beautiful risk of education.* Boulder, CO: Paradigm.

(2016). Reconciling ourselves to reality: Arendt, education and the challenge of being at home in the world. *Journal of Educational Administration and History, 48*(2), 183–192.

Bille, M., & Simonsen, K. (2019). Atmospheric practices: On affecting and being affected. *Space and Culture*, DOI: 10.1177/1206331218819711

Bille, M., Bjerregaard, P., & Sørensen, T. (2015). Staging atmospheres: Materiality, culture, and the texture of the in-between. *Emotion, Space and Society, 15*, 31–38.

Bird, G., & Lynch, H. (2019). Introduction to the politics of life: A biopolitical mess. *European Journal of Social Theory, 22*(3), 301–316.

Bissell, D. (2010). Passenger mobilities: Affective atmospheres and the sociality of public transport. *Environment and Planning D: Society and Space, 28*, 270–289.

Bjerg, H., & Staunæs, D. (2011). Self-management through shame – Uniting governmentality studies and the "affective turn." *Ephemera, 11*(2), 138–156.

Blackman, L., & Venn, C. (2010). Affect. *Body & Society, 16*, 7–28.

Blee, K. M. (2002). *Inside organized racism: Women in the hate movement.* Berkeley, CA: University of California Press.

Böhme, G. (1993). Atmosphere as the fundamental concept of a new aesthetics. *Thesis Eleven, 36*, 113–126.

(2017). *The aesthetics of atmospheres.* New York: Routledge.

Boland, T. (2007). Critique as a technique of self: A Butlerian analysis of Judith Butler's Prefaces. *History of the Human Sciences, 20*(3), 105–122.

(2014). Critique is a thing of this world: Towards a genealogy of critique. *History of the Human Sciences, 27*(1), 108–123.

Boler, M., & Davis, E. (2018). The affective politics of the "post-truth" era: Feeling rules and networked subjectivity. *Emotion, Space and Society, 27*, 75–85.

Boltanski, L. (1999). *Distant suffering: Morality, media and politics.* Cambridge: Cambridge University Press.

Bonilla-Silva, E. (2019a). Feeling race: Theorizing the racial economy of emotions. *American Sociological Review*, *84*(1), 1–25.
(2019b). Toward a new political praxis for Trumpamerica: New directions in critical race theory. *American Behavioral Scientist*, *63*(13), 1776–1788.
Bonnell, J., Copestake, P., Kerr, D., Passy, R., Reed. C., Salter, R., Sarwar, S., & Sheikh, S. (2011). *Teaching approaches that help to build resilience to extremism among young people*. London: Department for Education.
Bowell, T. (2017). Response to the editorial "Education in a post-truth world." *Educational Philosophy and Theory*, *49*(6), 582–585.
Bozalek, V., & Zembylas, M. (2017). Towards a "response-able" pedagogy across higher education institutions in post-apartheid South Africa: An ethico-political analysis. *Education as Change*, *21*(2), 62–85.
Braidotti, R. (2013). *The posthuman*. Cambridge: Polity.
Branscombe, N., Slogoski, B., & Kappen, D. (2004). The measurement of collective guilt: What it is and what it is not. In N. R. Branscombe & B. Doosje (Eds.), *Collective guilt: International perspectives* (pp. 16–34). Cambridge: Cambridge University Press.
Brown, S., Kanyeredzi, A., McGrath, L., Reavey, P., & Tucker, I. (2019). Affect theory and the concept of atmosphere. *Distinktion: Journal of Social Theory*, *20*(1), 5–24.
Brown, W. (2015). *Undoing the demos: Neoliberalism's stealth revolution*. Cambridge, MA: MIT Press.
Brøgger, K., & Staunæs, D. (2016). Standards and (self)implosion: How the circulation of affects accelerates the spread of standards and intensifies the embodiment of colliding, temporal ontologies. *Theory & Psychology*, *26*(2), 223–242.
Bruckner, P. (2010). *The tyranny of guilt: An essay on western masochism*. Princeton, NJ: Princeton University Press.
Burdick, J., & Sandlin, J. (2013). Learning, becoming, and the unknowable: Conceptualizations, mechanism, and process in public pedagogy literature. *Curriculum Inquiry*, *43*(1), 142–177.
Buser, M. (2014). Thinking through non-representational and affective atmospheres in planning theory and practice. *Planning Theory*, *13*(3), 227–243.
Butler, J. (2004a). *Precarious life: The powers of mourning and violence*. London: Verso.
(2004b). What is critique? An essay on Foucault's virtue. In S. Salih & J. Butler (Eds.), *The Judith Butler reader* (pp. 301–321). Malden, MA: Blackwell.
(2005). *Giving an account of oneself*. New York: Fordham University Press.
(2009). Critique, dissent, disciplinarity. *Critical Inquiry*, *35*(summer), 773–795.
Butler, J. (2020, March 30). Capitalism has its limits [Blog post]. Retrieved from www.versobooks.com/blogs/4603-capitalism-has-its-limits
Button, M. (2019). Shame, political accountability, and the ethical life of politics: Critical exchange on Jill Locke's *Democracy and the Death of Shame*. *Political Theory*, *47*(3), 391–396.

Carniel, J. (2018). [Insert image here]: A reflection on the ethics of imagery in a critical pedagogy for the humanities. *Pedagogy, Culture & Society, 26*(1), 141–155.

Chouliaraki, L. (2008). Mediation as moral education. *Media, Culture & Society, 30*, 831–847.

——— (2010). Post-humanitarianism: Humanitarian communication beyond a politics of pity. *International Journal of Cultural Studies, 13*(2), 107–126.

——— (2012). *The ironic spectator: Solidarity in the age of post-humanitarianism.* Cambridge: Polity Press.

Chouliaraki, L., & Stolic, T. (2017). Rethinking media responsibility in the refugee "crisis": A visual typology of European news. *Media, Culture & Society, 39*(8), 1162–1177.

Clark, J. N. (2008). Collective guilt, collective responsibility and the Serbs. *East European Politics and Societies, 22*(3), 668–692.

Clarke, M., Schostack, J., & Hammersley-Fletcher, L. (Eds.). (2018). *Paradoxes of democracy, leadership and education: Alternatives to capitalist reproduction.* London: Routledge.

Clarke, S., Hoggett, P., & Thompson, S. (Eds.). (2006). *Emotion, politics and society.* New York: Palgrave Macmillan.

Closs Stephens, A. C. (2016). The affective atmospheres of nationalism. *Cultural Geographies, 23*(2), 181–198.

Closs Stephens, A. C., Hughes, S., Schofield, V., & Sumartojo, S. (2017). Atmospheric memories: Affect, and minor politics at the ten-year anniversary of the London bombings. *Emotion, Space and Society, 23*, 44–51.

Clough, P. (2007). Introduction. In P. Clough, with J. Halley (Eds.), *The affective turn: Theorizing the social* (pp. 1–33). Durham, NC: Duke University Press.

Clough, P. T., & Willse, C. (2011). Introduction. In. T. Clough & C. Willse (Eds.), *Beyond biopolitics: Essays on the governance of life and death* (pp. 1–16). Durham, NC: Duke University Press.

CNN. (2016). Transcript of Republican debate in Miami, full text, *CNN*, March 15, 2016, retrieved from https://edition.cnn.com/2016/03/10/politics/republican-debate-transcript-full-text/index.html

Connolly, W. (2017). *Aspirational fascism: The struggle for multifaceted democracy under Trumpism.* Minneapolis: University of Minnesota Press.

Conovan, M. (1992). *Hannah Arendt: A reinterpretation of her political thought.* New York: Cambridge University Press.

Cossarin, P., & Vallespin, F. (2019). *Populism and passions: Democratic legitimacy after austerity.* Abingdon: Routledge.

Crilley, R. (2018). International relations in the age of "post-truth" politics. *International Affairs, 94*(2), 417–425.

Curtis, B., & Patrick, E. (2014). Implicated: A review paper on guilt. *Economy and Society, 43*(1), 136–152.

Cvetkovich, A. (2003). *An archive of feelings: Trauma, sexuality and lesbian public cultures.* Durham, NC: Duke University Press.

——— (2012). *Depression: A public feeling.* Durham, NC: Duke University Press.

Damluji, H. (2019). *The responsible globalist: What citizens of the world can learn from nationalism*. London: Penguin Books.

Danewid, I. (2017). White innocence in the Black Mediterranean: Hospitality and the erasure of history. *Third World Quarterly, 38*(7), 1674–1689.

Danoff, B. (2012). A school or a stage? Tocqueville and Arendt on politics and education. *Perspectives on Political Science, 41*(3), 117–124.

Davidson, A. (2011). In praise of counter-conduct. *History of the Human Sciences, 24*(4), 25–41.

Davis, E. (2017). *Why we have reached peak bullshit and what we can do about it*. London: Little, Brown.

Davies, L. (2008). *Educating against extremism*. Stoke on Trent: Trentham.

  (2018). *Review of educational initiatives in counter-extremism internationally*. Gothenburg: The Segerstedt Institute.

Davies, W. (2017). A review of Arlie Russell Hochschild's *Strangers in their Own Land: Anger and Mourning on the American Right*. *International Journal of Politics Culture and Society, 30*, 413–420.

  (2020). Anger fast and slow: Mediations of justice and violence in the age of populism. *Global Discourse, 10*(2), 169–185.

d'Ancona, M. (2017). *Post-truth: The new war on truth and how to fight back*. London: Ebury Press.

Degerman, D. (2019a). Brexit anxiety: A case study in the medicalization of dissent. *Critical Review of International Social and Political Philosophy, 22*(7), 823–840.

  (2019b). Within the heart's darkness: The role of emotions in Arendt's political thought. *European Journal of Political Theory, 18*(2), 153–173.

De la Torre, C., & Arnson, C. J. (2013). *Latin American populism in the twenty-first century*. Baltimore, MD: Johns Hopkins University.

Deleuze, G. (1988). *Spinoza: Practical philosophy* (trans. R. Hurley). San Francisco, CA: City Lights Books.

  (1992). Ethology: Spinoza and us. In J. Crary & S. Kwinter (Eds.), *Incorporations* (pp. 625–633). New York: Zone Books.

  (2006). *Two regimes of madness*. New York: Semiotext(e).

Deleuze, G., & Guattari, F. (1983). *Anti-Oedipus: Capitalism and schizophrenia*. Minneapolis: University of Minnesota Press.

  (1987). *A thousand plateaus: Capitalism and schizophrenia*. Minneapolis: University of Minnesota Press.

  (1994). *What is philosophy?* New York: Columbia University Press.

Demertzis, N. (Ed.). (2013). *Emotions in politics: The affect dimension in political tension*. New York: Palgrave Macmillan.

Dewey, J. (1916/1985). Democracy and education. In J. A. Boydston (Ed.), *The middle works, 1899–1924* (vol. 9). Carbondale: Southern Illinois University Press.

DiAngelo, R. (2011). White fragility. *International Journal of Critical Pedagogy, 3*(3), 54–70.

(2015). Why it's so hard to talk to white people about racism. *Huffington Post*, June 30, 2015. Retrieved from www.huffingtonpost.com/good-men-project/why-its-so-hard-to-talk-to-white-people-about-racism_b_7183710.html

Ebner, J. (2017). *The rage: The vicious circle of Islamist and far-right extremism*. London: I. B. Tauris & Co.

Ellis, D., Tucker, I., & Harper, D. (2013). The affective atmospheres of surveillance. *Theory & Psychology, 23*(6), 716–731.

Elshtain, J. B. (1995). Political children. In B. Honig (Ed.), *Feminist interpretations of Hannah Arendt* (pp. 263–284). University Park, PA: Pennsylvania State University Press.

Emcke, C. (2019). *Against hate*. Cambridge: Polity Press.

Englund, T. (2016). On moral education through deliberative communication. *Journal of Curriculum Studies, 48*(1), 58–76.

Erisen, C., Lodge, M., & Taber, C. (2014). Affective contagion in effortful political thinking. *Political Psychology, 35*(2), 187–206.

Evans, B., & Reid, J. (2013). Introduction: Fascism in all its forms. In B. Evans & J. Reid (Eds.), *Deleuze & fascism: Security: War: Aesthetics* (pp. 1–12). New York: Routledge.

Fassin, D. (2017). The endurance of critique. *Anthropological Theory, 17*(1), 4–29.

Feinberg, W. (2012). The idea of a public education. *Review of Research in Education, 36*, 1–22.

Fenwick, T. (2011). Learning "social responsibility" in the workplace: Conjuring, unsettling, and folding boundaries. *Pedagogy, Culture & Society, 19*(1), 41–60.

Ferry, L., & Kingston, R. (Eds.). (2008). *Bringing the passions back in: The emotions in political philosophy*. Vancouver: UBC Press.

Fielding, M., & Moss, P. (2011). *Radical education and the common school: A democratic alternative*. London: Routledge.

Finn, M. (2016). Atmospheres of progress in a data-based school. *Cultural Geographies, 23*(1), 29–49.

Firat, B., de Mul, S., & Van Wichelen, S. (Eds.). (2009). *Commitment and complicity in cultural theory and practice*. London: Palgrave Macmillan.

Fischer, C. (2016). Feminist philosophy, pragmatism, and the "turn to affect": A genealogical critique. *Hypatia, 31*(4), 810–826.

Fitzpatrick, K., & Tinning, R. (2014). Health education's fascist tendencies: A cautionary exposition. *Critical Public Health, 24*(2), 132–142.

Folkers, A. (2016). Daring the truth: Foucault, parrhesia and the genealogy of critique. *Theory, Culture & Society, 33*(1), 3–28.

Ford, D. R. (2019). *Politics and pedagogy in the "post-truth" era: Insurgent philosophy and praxis*. London: Bloomsbury Academic.

Fortier, A.-M. (2010). Proximity by design? Affective citizenship and the management of unease. *Citizenship Studies, 14*(1), 17–30.

(2016). Afterword: Acts of affective citizenship? Possibilities and limitations. *Citizenship Studies, 20*(8), 1038–1044.

Foucault, M. (1980). *The history of sexuality, vol. 1: An introduction*. New York: Vintage.
  (1983). Preface. In G. Deleuze & F. Guattari (Eds.), *Anti-Oedipus: Capitalism & schizophrenia* (pp. xi–xiv). Minneapolis: University of Minnesota Press.
  (1984). What is enlightenment? In P. Rabinow (Ed.), *The Foucault reader* (pp. 32–50). New York: Pantheon.
  (1991). How an "experience-book" is born? In M. Foucault (Ed.), *Remarks on Marx: Conversations with Ducio Trombadori* (pp. 25–42). New York: Semiotext(e).
  (1997a). *Ethics: Subjectivity and truth* (ed. P. Rabinow). New York: The New Press.
  (1997b). What is critique? In S. Lotringer & I. Hochroth (Eds.), *The politics of truth* (pp. 23–82). New York: Semiotext(e).
  (2000). The masked philosopher. In P. Rabinow (Ed.), *Ethics: Essential works of Foucault 1954–1984* (pp. 321–328). London: Penguin Books.
  (2001). *Fearless speech* (ed. J. Pearson). Los Angeles: Semiotext(e).
  (2003). *Society must by defended: Lectures at the College de France 1975–1976*. London: Penguin.
  (2008). *The birth of biopolitics: Lectures at the Collège de France, 1978–1979*. New York: Picador.
  (2009). *Security, territory, population: Lectures at the Collége de France 1977–1978* (vol. 4). New York: Macmillan.
  (2010). *The government of self and others. Lectures at the College de France*. New York: Palgrave Macmillan.
  (2014). *Wrong-doing, truth-telling: The function of avowal in justice*. Chicago, IL: The Chicago University Press.
Fox, N. J., & Alldred, P. (2017). *Sociology and the new materialism*. London: Sage.
Freeden, M. (2017). After the Brexit referendum: Revisiting populism as an ideology. *Journal of Political Ideologies*, 22(1), 1–11.
Freire, P. (1970/2003). *Pedagogy of the oppressed*. New York: Continuum.
  (1994). *Pedagogy of hope: Reliving pedagogy of the oppressed*. New York: Continuum.
Fregonese, S. (2017). Affective atmospheres, urban geopolitics and conflict (de)escalation in Beirut. *Political Geography*, 61, 1–10.
Galston, W. (2018). *Anti-pluralism: The populist threat to liberal democracy*. New Haven, CT: Yale University Press.
Gandy, M. (2017). Urban atmospheres. *Cultural Geographies*, 24(3), 353–374.
Gebhardt, M. (2019). The populist moment: Affective orders, protest, and politics of belonging. *Distinktion: Journal of Social Theory*, DOI: 10.1080/1600910X.2019.1653346
Genosko, G. (2017). Black holes of politics: Resonances of microfascism. *La Deleuziana*, 5, 59–67.
Gilbert, C. (2016). #NotIntendedToBeAFactualStatement: On truth and lies in an affective sense. In J. Hannan (Ed.), *Truth in the public sphere* (pp. 93–114). Lanham, MD: Lexington Books.

Gillies, D. (2016). Visiting good company: Arendt and the development of reflective practitioner. *Journal of Educational Administration and History, 48*(2), 148–159.

Giroux, H. (2019). Authoritarianism and the challenge of higher education in the age of Trump. *Action, Criticism, and Theory for Music Education, 18*(1), 6–25.

Glynos, J. (2001). The grip of ideology: A Lacanian approach to the theory of ideology. *Journal of Political Ideologies, 6*(2), 191–214.

Godfrey, P. (2004). "Sweet little (white) girls"? Sex and fantasy across the color line and the contestation of patriarchal white supremacy. *Equity & Excellence in Education, 37*, 204–218.

Goldstein, L. S. (2009). *Teaching with love: A feminist approach to early childhood education.* New York: Peter Lang.

Goodwin, J., Jasper, J., & Polletta, F. (Eds.). (2001). *Passionate politics: Emotions and social movements.* Chicago, IL: The University of Chicago Press.

Gordy, E. (2003). Accounting for a violent past by other than legal means. *Southeast European and Black Sea Studies, 3*(1), 1–24.

Gould, D. (2012). Political despair. In P. Hoggett & S. Thompson (Eds.), *Politics and the emotions: The affective turn in contemporary political studies* (pp. 95–111). London: Bloomsbury.

Gutmann, A. (1996). *Democratic education.* Princeton, NJ: Princeton University Press.

Gray, B. J. (2018). The politics of shame. *Current Affairs*, March 11, 2018. Retrieved from www.currentaffairs.org/2018/03/the-politics-of-shame

Gregg, M., & Seigworth, G. (Eds.). (2010). *The affect theory reader.* Durham, NC: Duke University Press.

Griffin, R. (1991). *The nature of fascism.* New York: St. Martin's Press.

Guattari, F. (1984). *Molecular revolution: Psychiatry and politics* (trans. R. Sheed). Harmondsworth: Penguin Books.

(2009). Everybody wants to be a fascist. In S. Lotringer (Ed.), *Chaosophy* (pp. 154–175). New York: Semiotext(e).

(2016). *Lines of flight: For another world of possibilities* (trans. A. Goffey). London: Bloomsbury Academic.

Guenther, L. (2011). Shame and the temporality of social life. *Continental Philosophy Review, 44*(1), 23–39.

Gunnarsson, K., & Hohti, R. (2018). Editorial: Why affirmative critique? *Reconceptualizing Educational Research Methodology, 9*(1), 1–5.

Hage, G. (2000). *White nation: Fantasies of white supremacy in a multicultural society.* New York: Routlege.

Håkansson, M., & Östman, L. (2019). The political dimension in ESE: The construction of a political moment model for analyzing bodily anchored political emotions in teaching and learning of the political dimension. *Environmental Educational Research, 25*(4), 585–600.

Hållander, M. (2019). On the verge of tears: The ambivalent spaces of emotions and testimonies. *Studies in Philosophy and Education, 38*, 467–480.

References

Haney-López, I. (2013). *Dog whistle politics: How coded racial appeals have reinvented racism and wrecked the middle class*. Oxford: Oxford University Press.

Haraway, D. (2016). *Staying with the trouble: Making kin in the chthulucene*. Durham, NC: Duke University Press.

Haritaworn, J., Kuntsman, A., & Posocco, S. (2014). Introduction. In J. Haritaworn, A. Kuntsman & S. Posocco (Eds.), *Queer necropolitics* (pp. 1–27). New York: Routledge.

Hartman, S. V. (1997). *Scenes of subjection: Terror, slavery, and self-making in nineteenth-century America*. New York, Oxford: Oxford University Press.

Harwood, V., & Rasmussen, M. L. (2013). Practicing critique, attending to truth: The pedagogy of discriminatory speech. *Educational Philosophy and Theory*, *45*(8), 874–884.

Haslett, A. (2016). Donald Trump, shamer in chief. *The Nation*, October 14, 2016. Retrieved from www.thenation.com/article/donald-trump-shamer-in-chief/

Heaney, J. (2011). Emotions and power: Reconciling conceptual twins. *Journal of Political Power*, *4*(2), 259–277.

(2013). Emotions and power: A bifocal prescription to cure theoretical myopia. *Journal of Political Power*, *6*(3), 355–362.

Heins, V. (2007). Reasons of the heart: Weber and Arendt on emotion in politics. *The European Legacy*, *12*(6), 715–728.

Hemmings, C. (2005). Invoking affect: Cultural theory and the ontological turn. *Cultural Studies*, *19*(5), 548–567.

(2012). Affective solidarity: Feminist reflexivity and political transformation. *Feminist Theory*, *13*(2), 147–161.

Hochschild, A. (2016). *Strangers in their own land: Anger and mourning on the American right*. New York: New Press.

Hodgson, N., Vlieghe, J., & Zamojski, P. (2017). Manifesto for a post-critical pedagogy. In N. Hodgson, J. Vlieghe & P. Zamojski (Eds.), *Manifesto for a post-critical pedagogy* (pp. 15–19). Brooklyn, NY: Punctum Books.

(2018). Education and the love of the world: Articulating a post-critical educational philosophy. *Foro de Educación*, *16*(24), 7–20.

Hoggett, P., & Thompson, S. (Eds.). (2012). *Politics and the emotions: The affective turn in contemporary political studies*. London: Continuum.

Holland, E. (2008). Schizoanalysis, nomadology, fascism. In I. Buchanan & N. Thoburn (Eds.), *Deleuze and politics* (pp. 74–98). Edinburgh: Edinburgh University Press.

Holmes, M. (2010). The emotionalization of reflexivity. *Sociology*, *44*(1), 139–154.

Horsthemke, K. (2017). "#FactsMustFall"?-Education in a post-truth, post-truthful world. *Ethics and Education*, *12*(3), 273–288.

Howard, J. (1999). What is sentimentality? *American Literary History*, *11*(1), 63–81.

Hutchison, E. (2016). *Affective communities in world politics*. Cambridge: Cambridge University Press.

Hynes, M. (2013). Reconceptualizing resistance: Sociology and the affective dimension of resistance. *The British Journal of Sociology*, 64(4), 559–577.

Ioanide, P. (2015). *The emotional politics of racism: How feelings trump facts in an era of colorblindness*. Stanford, CA: Stanford University Press.

IOM (International Office of Migration). (2019 November). Press release: Mediterranean migrant arrivals reach 76,558 in 2019; deaths reach 1,071. Retrieved from www.iom.int/news/mediterranean-migrant-arrivals-reach-76558-2019-deaths-reach-1071

jagodzinski, J. (2019). *Schizoanalytic ventures at the end of the world: Film, video, art, and pedagogical challenges*. Cham, Switzerland: Springer Nature.

Jaspers, K. (1947/2000). *The question of German guilt*. New York: Fordham University Press.

(1961). *The atom bomb and the future of man*. Chicago, IL: The University of Chicago Press.

Johnson, C. (2010). The politics of affective citizenship: From Blair to Obama. *Citizenship Studies*, 14(5), 495–509.

Juelskjær, M., & Staunæs, D. (2016a). Orchestrating intensities and rhythms: How post-psychologies are assisting new educational standards and reforming subjectivities. *Theory & Psychology*, 26(2), 182–201.

(2016b). Designing leadership chairs: Experiments with affirmative critique of leadership and environmentality. *Reconceptualizing Educational Research Methodology*, 7(2), 35–51.

Juelskjær, M., Staunæs, D., & Ratner, H. (2013). The return of the Freudian couch: Managing affectivity through technologies of comfort. *International Journal of Qualitative Studies in Education*, 26(9), 1132–1152.

Karhu, S. (2017). *From violence to resistance: Judith Butler's critique of norms*. Unpublished doctoral dissertation, University of Helsinki.

Kerr, D. (2005). Citizenship education in England – Listening to young people: New insights from the citizenship education longitudinal study. *International Journal of Citizenship and Teacher Education*, 1(1), 74–96.

Kemmer, L., Peters, C. H., Weber, V., Anderson, B., & Mühlhoff, R. (2019). On right-wing movements, spheres, and resonances: An interview with Ben Anderson and Rainer Mühlhoff. *Distinktion: Journal of Social Theory*, 20(1), 25–41.

Keyes, R. (2004). *The post-truth era: Dishonesty and deception in contemporary life*. New York: St. Martin's Press.

Kinnvall, C. (2018). Ontological insecurities and postcolonial imaginaries: The emotional appeal of populism. *Humanity & Society*, 42(4), 523–543.

Kølvraa, C. (2015). Affect, provocation, and far right rhetoric. In B. T. Knudsen & C. Stage (Eds.), *Affective methodologies: Developing cultural research strategies for the study of affect* (pp. 183–200). New York: Palgrave Macmillan.

Kølvraa, C., & Ifversen, J. (2017). The attraction of ideology: Discourse, desire and the body. *Journal of Political Ideologies*, 22(2), 182–196.

Korsgaard, M. T. (2016). An Arendtian perspective on inclusive education: Towards a reimagined vocabulary. *International Journal of Inclusive Education*, *20*(9), 934–945.
Krasmann, S. (2019). Secrecy and the force of truth: countering post-truth regimes. *Cultural Studies*, *33*(4), 690–710.
Krauel, J. (2014). Emotions and nationalism: The case of Joan Maragall's compassionate love of country. *Hispanic Research Journal*, *15*(3), 191–208.
Kreiss, D., Barker, J., & Zenner, S. (2017). Trump gave them hope: Studying the strangers in their own land. *Political Communication*, *34*, 470–478.
Kurunczi, A., Martinkowski, A., Rösen, K., Sper, V., & Wächter, C. (2018). Social representations: Between complicity and resistance. *Kultur & Geschlecht*, *20*, 1–3.
Kutz, C. (2000). *Complicity: Ethics and law for a collective age*. Cambridge: Cambridge University Press.
 (2007). Causeless complicity. *Criminal Law and Philosophy*, *1*(3), 289–305.
Kymlicka, W., & Norman, W. (1994). Return of the citizen: A survey of recent work on citizenship theory. *Ethics*, *104*(2), 352–381.
Laclau, E. (2005a). *On populist reason*. London: Verso.
 (2005b). Populism: What's in a name? In F. Panizza (Ed.) Populism and the mirror of democracy (pp. 32–49). London: Verso.
Larsen, L. T. (2011). Turning critique inside out: Foucault, Boltanski and Chiapello on the tactical displacement of critique and power. *Distinktion: Scandinavian Journal of Social Theory*, *12*(1), 37–55.
Latour, B. (2004). Why has critique run out of steam?: From matters of fact to matters of concern. *Critical Inquiry*, *30*(Winter), 225–248.
Lebron, C. J. (2013). *The color of our shame: Race and justice in our time*. Oxford: Oxford University Press.
Lemke, T. (2011). Critique and experience in Foucault. *Theory, Culture & Society*, *28*(4), 26–48.
Lenette, C., & Miskovic, N. (2016). Some viewers may find the following images disturbing: Visual representations of refugee deaths at border crossings. *Crime, Media, Culture*, *14*(1), 111–120.
Leonardo, Z. (2011). After the glow: Race ambivalence and other educational prognoses. *Educational Philosophy and Theory*, *43*, 675–698.
Leonardo, Z., & Zembylas, M. (2013). Whiteness as technology of affect: Implications for educational theory and praxis. *Equity & Excellence in Education*, *46*(1), 150–165.
Lepora, C., & Goodin, R. (2013). *On complicity and compromise*. Oxford: Oxford University Press.
Leys, R. (2011). The turn to affect: A critique. *Critical Inquiry*, *37*(3), 434–472.
Lindquist, J. (2004). Class affects, classroom affectations: Working through the paradoxes of strategic empathy. *College English*, *67*(2), 187–209.
Locke, J. (2007). Shame and the future of feminism. *Hypatia*, *22*(4), 146–162.
 (2016). *Democracy and the death of shame: Political equality and social disturbance*. New York: Cambridge University Press.
Loreman, T. (2011). *Love as pedagogy*. Rotterdam, The Netherlands: Sense Publishers.

Lorimer, H. (2005). Cultural geography: The busyness of being "more-than-representational". *Progress in Human Geography*, *29*(1), 83–94.
Lowe, L. (2015). *The intimacies of four continents*. Durham, NC: Duke University Press.
Lu, C. (2008). Shame, guilt and reconciliation after war. *European Journal of Social Theory*, *11*(3), 367–383.
Lupton, D. (1995). *The imperative of health: Public health and the regulated body*. London: Sage.
(1998). *The emotional self: A sociocultural exploration*. London: Sage.
Lyman, P. (2004). The domestication of anger: The use and abuse of anger in politics. *European Journal of Social Theory*, *7*(2), 133–147.
MacLean, N. (2017). *Democracy in chains: The deep history of the radical right's stealth plan for America*. New York: Penguin Random House.
Macoun, A. (2016). Colonizing white innocence: Complicity and critical encounters. In S. Maddison, T. Clark & R. de Costa (Eds.), *The limits of settler colonial reconciliation: Non-Indigenous people and the responsibility to engage* (pp. 85–102). Singapore: Springer Nature.
Maddison, S. (2012). Postcolonial guilt and national identity: Historical injustice and the Australian settler state. *Social Identities*, *18*(6), 695–709.
Manning, N., & Holmes, M. (2014). Political emotions: A role for feelings of affinity in citizens' (dis)engagements with electoral politics? *Sociology*, *48*(4), 698–714.
Mårdh, A., & Tryggvason, A. (2017). Democratic education in the mode of populism. *Studies in Philosophy and Education*, *36*, 601–613.
Marotta, S., & Cummings, A. (2019). Planning affectively: Power, affect, and images of the future. *Planning Theory*, *18*(2), 191–213.
Martin, J. (2013). A feeling for democracy? Rhetoric, power and the emotions. *Journal of Political Power*, *6*(3), 461–476.
Martin, J. L., Nickels, A. E., & Sharp-Grier, M. (2017). Editors' introduction. In J. L. Martin, A. E. Nickels & M. Sharp-Grier (Eds.), *Feminist pedagogy, practice, and activism: Improving lives for girls and women* (pp. xxi–xxiv). New York: Routledge.
Massumi, B. (1987). Notes on the translation and acknowledgments. In G. Deleuze & F. Guattari (Eds.), *A thousand plateaus: Capitalism & schizophrenia* (pp. xvi–xix). Minneapolis, MN: University of Minnesota Press.
(2002a). Navigating movements. In M. Zournazi (Ed.), *Hope: New philosophies for change* (pp. 210–242). Annandale: Pluto Press.
(2002b). *Parables for the virtual: Movement, affect, sensation*. Durham, NC: Duke University Press.
(2010). The future birth of the affective fact: The political ontology of threat. In M. Gregg & G. J. Seigworth (Eds.), *The affect theory reader* (pp. 52–70). Durham, NC: Duke University Press.
(2015a). *Politics of affect*. London: Polity.
(2015b). Q & A with Brian Massumi, by Laura Sell. Duke University Press blog. https://dukeupress.wordpress.com/2015/08/19/qa-with-brian-massumi/

Matias, C. (2016a). *Feeling white: Whiteness, emotionality, and education*. Rotterdam, The Netherlands: Sense Publishers.
  (2016b). White skin, Black friend. A Fanonian application to theorize racial fetish in teacher education. *Educational Philosophy and Theory*, *48*(3), 221–236.
Maudlin, J. G. (2014). The abandonment of hope: Curriculum theory and white moral responsibility. *Journal of Curriculum and Pedagogy*, *11*(2), 136–153.
May, T. (2013). Desire and ideology in fascism. In B. Evans & J. Reid (Eds.), *Deleuze & fascism: Security: War: Aesthetics* (pp. 13–26). New York: Routledge.
Mayer, J. (2016). *Dark money: The hidden history of the billionaires behind the rise of the radical right*. New York: Penguin Random House.
Mbembe, A. (2003). Necropolitics. *Public Culture*, *15*(1), 11–40.
  (2019). *Necropolitics*. Durham, NC: Duke University Press.
McCarty, T. W. (2018). Insisting on complicity. *Contemporary Political Theory*, *18*(1), 1–21.
McCormack, D. (2003). An event of geographical ethics in spaces of affect. *Transactions of the Institute of British Geographers*, *28*(4), 488–507.
  (2008). Engineering affective atmospheres on the moving geographies of the 1897 Andrée expedition. *Cultural Geographies*, *15*, 413–430.
  (2018). *Atmospheric things: On the allure of environmental envelopment*. Durham, NC: Duke University Press.
McDonnell, J. (2014). Reimagining the role of art in the relationship between democracy and education. *Educational Philosophy and Theory*, *46*(1), 46–58.
McLeod, J. (2017). Reframing responsibility in an era of responsibilization: Education, feminist ethics. *Discourse: Studies in the Cultural Politics of Education*, *38*(1), 43–56.
Mejia, R., Beckermann, K., & Sullivan, C. (2018). White lies: A racial history of the (post)truth. *Communication and Critical/Cultural Studies*, *15*(2), 109–126.
Michels, C., & Steyaert, C. (2017). By accident and by design: Composing affective atmospheres in an urban art intervention. *Organization*, *24*(1), 79–104.
Mihai, M. (2019). Understanding complicity: Memory, hope and the imagination. *Critical Review of International Social and Political Philosophy*, *22*(5), 504–522.
Milazzo, M. (2017). On white ignorance, white shame, and other pitfalls in critical philosophy of race. *Journal of Applied Philosophy*, *34*(4), 557–572.
Miller, A. (1983). *For your own good: Hidden cruelty in child-rearing and the roots of violence*. New York: Farrar, Straus, Giroux.
Miller-Idriss, C. (2017). Soldier, sailor, rebel, rule-breaker: Masculinity and the body in the German far right. *Gender and Education*, *29*(2), 199–215.
Miller-Idriss, C. (2018). Youth and the radical right. In J. Rydgren (Ed.), *The Oxford handbook of the radical right* (pp. 348–365). Oxford: Oxford University Press.

Miller-Idriss, C., & Pilkington, H. (2017). In search of the missing link: Gender, education and the radical right. *Gender and Education, 29*(2), 133–146.

(2014). Theorizing agonistic emotions. *Parallax, 20*(2), 31–48.

Mishra, P. (2017). *Age of anger: A history of the present.* London: Macmillan.

Mohammed, S. (2020). Understanding microfascism: Reading Deleuze and Guattari alongside management guru texts. *Culture and Organization, 26*(3), 196–210.

Mönig, J. M. (2012). Possibly preventing catastrophes: Hannah Arendt on democracy, education and judging. *Ethics and Education, 7*(3), 237–249.

Morrow, A. (2019). Layers of affect: The liminal sites of method. *Critical Studies on Security, 7*(1), 18–33.

Mosse, G. L. (1996). Fascist aesthetics and society: Some considerations. *Journal of Contemporary History, 31*(2), 245–252.

Mouffe, C. (2000). *The democratic paradox.* London: Verso.

(2005). *On the political.* New York: Routledge.

(2013). *Agonistics.* London: Verso.

(2014). By way of postscript. *Parallax, 20*(2), 149–157.

Mudde, C. (2000). *The ideology of extreme right.* Manchester: Manchester University Press.

(2007). *Populist radical right parties in Europe.* Cambridge: Cambridge University Press.

Mudde, C., & Kaltwasser, C. R. (Eds.). (2012). *Populism in Europe and the Americas: Threat or corrective for democracy?* Cambridge: Cambridge University Press.

Mudde, C., & Kaltwasser, C. R. (2017). *Populism: A very short introduction.* Oxford: Oxford University Press.

Mühlhoff, R. (2019). Affective dispositions. In J. Slaby & C. von Scheve (Eds.), *Affective societies-key concepts.* New York: Routledge.

Müller, J.-W. (2016). *What is populism?* Philadelphia, PA: University of Pennsylvania Press.

Mulcahy, D. (2019). Pedagogic affect and its politics: Learning to affect and be affected in education. *Discourse: Studies in the Cultural Politics of Education, 40*(1), 93–108.

Nathanson, D. (2008). Prologue: Affect imagery consciousness. In B. P. Karon (Ed.), *S. S. Tomkins Affect imagery consciousness: The complete edition* (pp. xi–xxvi). New York: Springer.

Nelson, D. (2004). Suffering and thinking: The scandal of tone in Jerusalem. In L. Berlant (Ed.), *Compassion: The culture and politics of an emotion* (pp. 219–244). New York: Routledge.

(2006). The virtues of heartlessness: Mary McCarthy, Hannah Arendt, and anesthetics of empathy. *American Literary History, 18*(1), 86–101.

(2017). *Tough Enough: Arbus, Arendt, Didion, McCarthy, Sontag, Weil.* Chicago, IL: The University of Chicago Press.

Nixon, R. (2011). *Slow violence and the environmentalism of the poor.* Cambridge, MA: Harvard University Press.

Nussbaum, M. (2013). *Political emotions: Why love matters for justice*. Cambridge, MA: Belknap Press of Harvard University.

Odysseos, L. (2016). Human rights, self-formation and resistance against disposability: Grounding Foucault's "theorizing practice" of counter-conduct in Bhopal. *Global Society, 30*(2), 179–200.

Odysseos, L., Death, C., & Malmvig, H. (2016). Interrogating Michel Foucault's counter-conduct: Theorizing the subjects and practices of resistance in global politics. *Global Society, 30*(2), 151–156.

Okoth, G. O., & Anyango, C. (2014). The crisis of democratic education: Building on African Indigenous principles and social science studies in developing sustainable democratic education in Kenya. *International Journal of Education and Research, 2*(3), 1–10.

Olesen, T. (2018). Memetic protest and the dramatic diffusion of Alan Kurdi. *Media, Culture & Society, 40*(5), 656–672.

Olssen, M. (2003). Foucault's conception of critique: Kant, humanism and the human sciences. In M. Peters, M. Olssen & C. Lankshear (Eds.), *Futures of critical theory: Dreams of difference* (pp. 73–102). New York: Rowman & Littlefield.

Osborne, T. (2009). Foucault as educator. In M. A. Peters, A. C. Besley, M. Olssen, S. Maurer & S. Weber (Eds.), *Governmentality studies in education* (pp. 125–136). Rotterdam, The Netherlands: Sense Publishers.

Osuri, G. (2009). Necropolitical complicities: (Re)constructing a normative somatechnics of Iraq. *Social Semiotics, 19*(1), 31–45.

Ott, B., & Dickinson, G. (2019). *The twitter presidency: Donald J. Trump and the politics of white rage*. New York: Routledge.

Oxford Dictionaries. (n.d.a). Oxford Dictionaries Word of the Year 2016. Retrieved from https://en.oxforddictionaries.com/word-of-the-year/word-of-the-year-2016

Panizza, F. (Ed.). (2005). *Populism and the mirror of democracy*. London: Verso.

Papacharissi, Z. (2015). *Affective publics: Sentiment, technology, and politics*. Oxford: Oxford University Press.

Papailias, P. (2019). (Un)seeing dead refugee bodies: Mourning memes, spectropolitics, and the haunting of Europe. *Media, Culture & Society, 41*(8), 1048–1068.

Paxton, R. (2004). *The anatomy of fascism*. New York: Alfred A. Knopf.

Paz, A. (2020). In the shadow of dark times: Hannah Arendt's *Eichmann in Jerusalem* and the problem of thinking in modern era. *Holocaust Studies, 26*(3), 354–380.

Peck, C., & Epstein, T. (Eds.). (2017). *Teaching and learning difficult histories in international contexts: A critical sociocultural approach*. New York: Routledge.

Pedwell, C. (2012). Affective (self-) transformation: Empathy, neoliberalism and international development. *Feminist Theory, 13*(2), 163–179.

(2014). Cultural theory as mood work. *New Formations, 82*(1), 47–63.

Pedwell, C., & Whitehead, A. (2012). Affecting feminism: Questions of feeling in feminist theory. *Feminist Theory, 13*(2), 115–129.

Pelinka, A. (2013). Right-wing populism: Concept and typology. In R. Wodak, M. Khosravnik & B. Mral (Eds.), *Right-wing populism in Europe politics and discourse* (pp. 3–22). New York: Bloomsbury Academic.
Pennington, M. (2014). Against democratic education. *Social Philosophy & Policy*, *31*(1), 1–35.
Peters, C. H., & Protevi, J. (2017). *Affective ideology and Trump's popularity*. Unpublished paper. Retrieved from www.protevi.com/john/TrumpAffect.pdf
Peters, M. (2017). Education in a post-truth world. *Educational Philosophy and Theory*, *49*(6), 563–566.
Petrie, M., McGregor, C., & Crowther, J. (2019). Populism, democracy and a pedagogy of renewal. *International Journal of Lifelong Learning*, *38*(5), 488–502.
Pfister, J. (2006). *Critique for what? Cultural studies, American studies, left studies*. New York: Routledge.
Philippopoulos-Mihalopoulos, A. (2016). Withdrawing from atmosphere: An ontology of air partitioning and affective engineering. *Environment and Planning D: Society and Space*, *34*(1), 150–167.
Pile, S. (2010). Emotions and affect in recent human geography. *Transactions of the Institute of British Geographers*, *35*, 5–20.
Piliero, E. (2017). Debating collective responsibility: Arendt and Young. *Social Philosophy Today*, *33*, 175–186.
Pinar, W. (2006). *The synoptic text today and other essays: Curriculum development after the reconceptualization*. New York: Peter Lang.
Pomante, L. (2017). "Italy, the land of beauty and art." The Italian landscape and cultural heritage in the books and the primary school textbooks from the Fascist period to the II postwar period: Between national identity and sense of citizenship. *History of Education & Children's Literature*, *12*(1), 157–211.
Povinelli, E. (2005). What's love got to do with it? The race of freedom and the drag of descent. *Social Analysis*, *49*(2), 173–181.
  (2011). *Economies of abandonment: Social belonging and endurance in late liberalism*. Durham, NC: Duke University Press.
Probyn, E. (2005). *Blush: Faces of shame*. Minneapolis and London: University of Minnesota Press.
Puar, J. (2007). *Terrorist assemblages: Homonationalism in queer times*. Durham, NC: Duke University Press.
  (2017). *The right to maim: Debility, capacity, disability*. Durham, NC: Duke University Press.
Quinan, C., & Thiele, K. (2020). Biopolitics, necropolitics, cosmopolitics – Feminist and queer interventions: An introduction. *Journal of Gender Studies*, *29*(1), 1–8.
Ranciére, J. (1991). *The ignorant schoomaster: Five lessons in intellectual emancipation*. Stanford, CA: Stanford University Press.
Rebughini, P. (2018). Critical agency and the future of critique. *Current Sociology*, *66*(1), 3–19.

Reckwitz, A. (2012). Affective spaces: A praxeological outlook. *Rethinking History*, *16*(2), 241–258.
Reynolds, P. (2017). Complicity as political rhetoric: Some ethical and political reflections. In A. Afxentiou, R. Dunford & M. Neu (Eds.), *Exploring complicity: Concepts, cases and critique* (pp. 35–52). London: Rowman & Littlefield.
Rice, J. (2008). The new "new": Making a case for critical affect studies. *Quarterly Journal of Speech*, *94*(2), 200–212.
Riedel, F. (2019). Atmosphere. In J. Slaby & C. von Scheve (Eds.), *Affective societies: Key concepts* (pp. 85–95). London: Routledge.
Ringrose, J. (2018). Digital feminist pedagogy and post-truth misogyny. *Teaching in Higher Education*, *23*(5), 647–656.
Robinson, J. (2012). Sentimentality in life and literature. In K. M. Higgins & D. Sherman (Eds.), *Passion, death, and spirituality: The philosophy of Robert C. Solomon* (pp. 67–92). London: Springer.
Rose, N. (2007). *The politics of life itself: Biomedicine, power, and subjectivity in the twenty-first century*. Princeton, NJ: Princeton University Press.
Rossdale, C., & Stierl, M. (2016). Everything is dangerous: Conduct and counter-conduct in the Occupy Movement. *Global Society*, *30*(2), 157–178.
Roudinesco, E. (2008). *Philosophy in turbulent times: Canguilhem, Sartre, Foucault, Althusser, Deleuze, Derrida* (trans. W. McCuaig). New York: Columbia University Press.
Ruitenberg, C. W. (2009). Educating political adversaries: Chantal Mouffe and radical democratic citizenship education. *Studies in Philosophy and Education*, *28*(3), 269–281.
Runciman, D. (2018). *How democracy ends*. London: Profile Books.
  (2010). Conflict, affect and the political: On disagreement as democratic capacity. *In Factis Pax*, *4*(1), 40–55.
Rydgren, J. (2007). The sociology of the radical right. *Annual Review of Sociology*, *33*, 241–262.
  (2018). The radical right: An introduction. In J. Rydgren (Ed.), *The Oxford handbook of the radical right* (pp. 1–16). Oxford: Oxford University Press.
Saar, M. (2002). Genealogy and subjectivity. *European Journal of Philosophy*, *10*(2), 231–245.
  (2008). Understanding genealogy: History, power, and the self. *Journal of Philosophy of History*, *2*(3), 295–314.
Salazar, M. (2013). A humanizing pedagogy: Reinventing the principles and practice of education as a journey toward liberation. *Review of Research in Education*, *37*, 121–148.
Salmela, M., & von Scheve, C. (2017). Emotional roots of right-wing political populism. *Social Science Information*, *56*(4), 567–595.
  (2018). Emotional dynamics of right- and left-wing political populism. *Humanity & Society*, *42*(4), 434–454.
Samoya, A. C., & Nicolazzo, Z. (2017). Affect and/as collective resistance in a post-truth moment. *International Journal of Qualitative Studies in Education*, *30*(1), 988–993.

Sanders, M. (2002). *Complicities*. Durham, NC: Duke University Press.
Sandlin, J. A., O'Malley, M. P., & Burdick, J. (2011). Mapping the complexity of public pedagogy scholarship: 1894–2010. *Review of Educational Research, 81* (3), 338–375.
Sant, E. (2019). Democratic education: A theoretical review (2006–2017). *Review of Educational Research, 89*(5), 655–696.
Sanyal, D. (2015). *Memory and complicity: Migrations of Holocaust remembrance*. New York: Fordham University Press.
Sauer, B. (2013). Bringing emotions back in. Gefühle als Regierungstechnik: Geschlechter- und demokratietheoretische Überlegungen. In C. Jarzebowski & A. Kwaschik (Eds.), *Performing emotions. Interdisziplinäre Perspektiven auf das Verhältnis von Politik und Emotionen in der Frühen Neuzeit und in der Moderne* (pp. 241–258). Göttingen: V&R unipress.
Schaap, A. (2001). Guilty subjects and political responsibility: Arendt, Jaspers and the resonance of the "German question" in politics of reconciliation. *Political Studies, 49*(4), 749–766.
Schaefer, D. (2019). *The evolution of affect theory: The humanities, the sciences, and the study of power*. Cambridge: Cambridge University Press.
(2020). Whiteness and civilization: Shame, race, and the rhetoric of Donald Trump. *Communication and Critical/Cultural Studies, 17*(1), 1–18.
Scheff, T. J., & Retzinger, S. M. (1991). *Emotions and violence: Shame and rage in destructive conflicts*. Lexington, MA: D. C. Heath.
Scheper-Hughes, N. (2014). The militarization and madness of everyday life. *South Atlantic Quarterly, 113*(3), 640–655.
Schlink, B. (2010). *Guilt about the past*. London: Beautiful Books.
Schrock, D., Dowd-Arrow, B., Erichsen, K., Gentile, H., & Dignam, P. (2017). The emotional politics of making America Great Again: Trump's working class appeals. *Journal of Working-Class Studies, 2*(1), 5–22.
Schuller, K. (2018). *The biopolitics of feeling: Race, sex, and science in the nineteenth century*. Durham, NC: Duke University Press.
Schutz, A. (2002). Is political education an oxymoron? Hannah Arendt's resistance to public spaces in schools. In S. Rice (Ed.), *Philosophy of Education 2001* (pp. 324–332). Urbana, IL: Philosophy of Education Society.
Schutz, A., & Sandy, N. G. (2015). Friendship and the public stage: Revisiting Hannah Arendt's Resistance to "political education." *Educational Theory, 65* (1), 21–38.
Scott, D. (1999). *Refashioning futures: Criticism after postcoloniality*. Princeton, NJ: Princeton University Press.
(2004). *Conscripts of modernity: The tragedy of colonial Enlightenment*. Durham, NC: Duke University Press.
Sedgwick-Kosofsky, E. (2003). *Touching feeling: Affect, pedagogy, performativity*. Durham, NC: Duke University Press.
Seigworth, G., & Gregg, M. (2010). An inventory of shimmers. In M. Gregg & G. Seigworth (Eds.), *The affect theory reader* (pp. 1–28). Durham, NC: Duke University Press.

Serpell, N. (2019, March). The banality of empathy. *NYR Daily*, March 2, 2019.
Shelby, T. (2003). Ideology, racism, and critical social theory. *Philosophical Forum*, 34(2), 153–188.
Shore, C., & Wright, S. (2015). Governing by numbers: Audit culture, rankings and the new world order. *Social Anthropology*, 23, 22–28.
Shotwell, A. (2016). *Against purity: Living ethically in compromised times*. Minneapolis: University of Minnesota Press.
Smith, W. D. (2012). The place of ethics in Deleuze's philosophy: Three questions of immanence. In D. W. Smith (Ed.), *Essays on Deleuze* (pp. 146–159). Edinburgh: Edinburgh University Press.
Snir, I. (2017). Education and articulation: Laclau and Mouffe's radical democracy in school. *Ethics and Education*, 12, 351–363.
Spinks, L. (2001). Thinking the post-human: Literature, affect, and the politics of style. *Textual Practice*, 15(1), 23–46.
Stanley, J. (2018). *How fascism works: The politics of us and them*. New York: Random House.
Stavrakakis, Y. (1999). *Lacan and the political*. London: Routledge.
Staunæs, D. (2011). Governing the potentials of life Itself? Interrogating the promises in affective educational leadership. *Journal of Educational Administration and History*, 43(3), 227–247.
   (2016). Notes on inventive methodologies and affirmative critiques of an affective edu-future. *Research in Education*, 96(1), 62–70.
   (2018). Green with envy: Affects and gut feelings as an affirmative, immanent, and trans-corporeal critique of new motivational data visualizations. *International Journal of Qualitative Studies in Education*, 31(5), 409–421.
Staunæs, D., & Conrad, J. S. B. (2020). The will not to know: Data leadership, necropolitics and ethnic-racialized student subjectivities. In R. Niesche & A. Heffernan (Eds.), *Theorizing identity and subjectivity in educational leadership research* (pp. 126–140). New York: Routledge.
Steyn, M. (2012). The ignorance contract: Recollections of apartheid childhoods and the construction of epistemologies of ignorance. *Identities: Global Studies in Culture and Power*, 19(1), 8–25.
Stoler, A. (2002). *Carnal knowledge and imperial power: Race and the intimate in colonial rule*. Berkeley, CA: University of California Press.
Straker, G. (2011). Unsettling whiteness. *Psychoanalysis, Culture & Society*, 16(1), 11–26.
Striblen, C. (2007). Guilt, shame, and shared responsibility. *Journal of Social Philosophy*, 38(3), 469–485.
Strick, S. (2014). *American dolorologies: Pain, sentimentalism, biopolitics*. Albany, NY: State University of New York Press.
Sullivan, S. (2014). *Good white people: The problem with middle-class white anti-racism*. Albany, NY: SUNY Press.
Sumartojo, S. (2016). Commemorative atmospheres: Memorial sites, collective events and the experience of national identity. *Transactions of the Institute of British Geographers*, 41(4), 541–553.

Swift, S. (2011). Hannah Arendt's tactlessness: Reading Eichmann in Jerusalem. *New Formations, 71,* 79–94.
TallBear, K. (2014). Standing with and speaking as faith: A feminist-Indigenous approach to inquiry. *Journal of Research Practice, 10*(2), Article N17. Retrieved from http://jrp.icaap.org/index.php/jrp/article/view/405/371
Tarc, A. M. (2011). Reparative curriculum. *Curriculum Inquiry, 41*(3), 350–372.
Tarnopolsky, C. (2010). *Prudes, perverts and tyrants: Plato's Gorgias and the politics of shame.* Princeton, NJ: Princeton University Press.
Tate, S. A. (2014). Racial affective economies, disalienation and "race made ordinary." *Ethnic and Racial Studies, 37*(13), 2475–2490.
Taubman, P. (2009). *Teaching by numbers: Deconstructing the discourse of standards and accountability in education.* New York: Routledge.
Taylor, G. (1985). *Pride, shame, and guilt: Emotions of self-assessment.* Oxford: Clarendon Press.
Taylor, L. (2011). Feeling in crisis: Vicissitudes of response in experiments with global justice education. *Journal of the Canadian Association for Curriculum Studies, 9*(1), 6–65.
Tesich, S. (1992, January). A government of lies. *The Nation.* Retrieved from https://drive.google.com/file/d/0BynDrdYrCLNtdmtoSFZFeGMtZUFsT1NmTGVTQmc1dEpmUC1z/view
Thiele, K. (2017). Affirmation. In M. Bunz, B. M. Kaiser & K. Thiele (Eds.), *Symptoms of the planetary condition: A critical vocabulary* (pp. 25–29). Meson Press: Lüneburg.
Thrift, N. (1996). *Spatial formations.* London: Sage.
  (2004). Intensities of feeling: Toward a spatial politics of affect. *Geografiske Annaler, 86B,* 57–78.
  (2008). *Non-representational theory: Space, politics, affect.* London: Routledge.
Todd, S. (2003). *Learning from the Other: Levinas, psychoanalysis, and ethical possibilities in education.* Albany, NY: State University of New York Press.
Tomkins, S. (1963). *Affect-imagery-consciousness* (vol. 2). New York: Springer.
  (1995). Shame-humiliation and contempt-disgust. In E. Sedgwick & A. Frank (Eds.), *Shame and its sisters: A Silvan Tomkins reader* (pp. 133–179). Durham, NC: Duke University Press.
Tooze, A. (2019). Democracy and its discontents. *The New York Review of Books,* June 6, 2019, Retrieved from www.nybooks.com/articles/2019/06/06/democracy-and-its-discontents/
Topolski, A. (2008). Creating citizens in the classroom: Hannarh Arendt's political critique of education. *Ethical Perspectives: Journal of the European Ethics Network, 15*(2), 259–282.
  (2015). *Arendt, Levinas and a politics of relationality.* London: Rowman & Littlefield.
Trump, D. (1987). *Trump: The art of the deal.* New York: Random House.
  (2015). *Crippled America: How to make America great again.* New York: Threshold Editions.

Tryggvason, A. (2017). The political as presence: On agonism in citizenship education. *Philosophical Inquiry in Education*, 24(3), 252–265.
   (2018). Democratic education and agonism. *Democracy & Education*, 26(1), 1–9.
Vlieghe, J. (2014). Foucault, Butler and corporeal experience: Taking social critique beyond phenomenology and judgment. *Philosophy and Social Criticism*, 40(1), 1019–1035.
Vogelmann, F. (2017). Critique as a practice of prefigurative emancipation, *Distinktion: Journal of Social Theory*, 18(2), 196–214.
Vrasti, W., & Dayal, S. (2016). Cityzenship: Rightful presence and the urban commons. *Citizenship Studies*, 20(8), 994–1011.
Wächter, C. (2019). Introduction: Complicity and the politics of representation. In C. Wächter & R. Wirth (Eds.), *Complicity and the politics of representation* (pp. 1–8). London: Rowman & Littlefield.
Wächter, C., & Wirth, R. (Eds.). (2019). *Complicity and the politics of representation*. London: Rowman & Littlefield.
Wahl-Jorgensen, K. (2018). Media coverage of shifting emotional regimes: Donald Trump's angry populism. *Media, Culture & Society*, 40(5), 766–778.
Wallace, R. J. (1994). *Responsibility and the moral sentiments*. Cambridge, MA: Harvard University Press.
Watkins, Megan. (2006). Pedagogic affect/effect: Embodying a desire to learn. *Pedagogies: An International Journal*, 1(4), 269–282.
   (2016). Gauging the affective: Becoming attuned to its impact in education. In M. Zembylas & P. A. Schutz (Eds.), *Methodological Advances in Research on Emotion and Education* (pp. 71–81). Dordrecht, The Netherlands: Springer.
Watkins, Mary. (2018). The social and political life of shame: The U.S. 2016 presidential election. *Psychoanalytic Perspectives*, 15(1), 25–37.
Webb, P. T. (2015). Fucking teachers. *Deleuze Studies*, 9(3), 437–451.
Weheliye, A. (2014). *Habeas viscus: Racializing assemblages, biopolitics, and Black feminist theories of the human*. Durham, NC: Duke University Press.
Westheimer, J. (2008). What kind of citizen? Democratic dialogues in education. *Education Canada*, 48(3), 6–10.
Wetherell, M. (2012). *Affect and emotion: A new social science understanding*. London: Sage.
   (2013). Affect and discourse – What's the problem? From affect as excess to affective/discursive practice. *Subjectivity*, 6(4), 349–368.
   (2015). Trends in the turn to affect: A social psychological critique. *Body & Society*, 21(2), 139–166.
Wetherell, M., McCreanor, T., McConville, A., & Moewaka Barnes, H. (2015). Settling space and covering the nation: Some conceptual considerations in analyzing affect and discourse. *Emotion, Space and Society*, 16, 58–64.
Whitt, M. (2016). Other people's problems: Student distancing, epistemic responsibility, and injustice. *Studies in Philosophy and Education*, 35, 427–444.
Williams, R. (1961). *The long revolution*. London: Chatto and Windus.

Williamson, J. A., Larson, J., & Reed, A. (Eds.). (2014). *The sentimental mode: Essays in literature, film and television*. Jefferson, NC: McFarland.

Wodak, R. (2015). *The politics of fear: What right-wing populist discourses mean*. London: Sage.

Woodley, D. (2010). *Fascism and political theory: Critical perspectives on fascist ideology*. New York: Routledge.

Woodward, K. (2009). *Statistical panic: Cultural politics and poetics of emotion*. Durham, NC: Duke University Press.

Yancy, G. (2015). Introduction-un-sutured. In G. Yancy (Ed.), *White self-criticality beyond anti-racism: How does it feel to be a white problem?* (pp. xi–xxvii). London: Lexington Books.

Youdell, D. (2006). Subjectivation and performative politics – Butler thinking Althusser and Foucault: Intelligibility, agency and the raced–nationed–religioned subjects of Education. *British Journal of Sociology of Education, 27*(4), 511–528.

Young, I. M. (2004). Responsibility and global labor justice. *The Journal of Political Philosophy, 12*, 365–388.

(2011). *Responsibility for justice*. Oxford: Oxford University Press.

Zembylas, M. (2008). Trauma, justice and the politics of emotion: The violence of sentimentality in education. *Discourse: Studies in the Cultural Politics of Education, 29*(1), 1–17.

(2009). Affect, citizenship, politics: Implications for education. *Pedagogy, Culture & Society, 17*(3), 369–384.

(2011a). Ethnic division in Cyprus and a policy initiative on promoting peaceful coexistence: Toward an agonistic democracy for citizenship education. *Education, Citizenship and Social Justice, 6*(1), 53–67.

(2011b). Investigating the emotional geographies of exclusion in a multicultural school. *Emotion, Space and Society, 4*, 151–159.

(2012). Pedagogies of strategic empathy: Navigating through the emotional complexities of antiracism in higher education. *Teaching in Higher Education, 17*(2), 113–125.

(2013a). The "crisis of pity" and the radicalization of solidarity: Towards critical pedagogies of compassion. *Educational Studies: A Journal of the American Educational Studies Association, 49*, 504–521.

(2013b). Memorial ceremonies in schools: Analyzing the entanglement of emotions and power. *Journal of Political Power, 6*(3), 477–493.

(2014). Affective citizenship in multicultural societies: Implications for critical citizenship education. *Citizenship Teaching & Learning, 9*(1), 5–18.

(2015a). *Emotion and traumatic conflict: Re-claiming healing in education*. Oxford: Oxford University Press.

(2015b). Exploring the implications of citizenship-as-equality in critical citizenship education. *Democracy & Education, 23*(1), 1–6.

(2016). Toward a critical-sentimental orientation in human rights education. *Educational Philosophy and Theory, 48*(11), 1151–1167.

(2017a). Love as ethico-political practice: Inventing reparative pedagogies of aimance in "disjointed" times. *Journal of Curriculum and Pedagogy*, *14*(1), 23–38.

(2017b). Re-envisioning human rights in the light of Arendt and Rancière: Towards an agonistic account of human rights education. *Journal of Philosophy of Education*, *51*(4), 709–724.

(2017c). Wilful ignorance and the emotional regime of schools. *British Journal of Educational Studies*, *65*(4), 499–515.

(2018a). Political depression, cruel optimism and pedagogies of reparation: Questions of criticality and affect in human rights education. *Critical Studies in Education*, *59*(1), 1–17.

(2018b). Reinventing critical pedagogy *as* decolonizing pedagogy: The education of empathy. *Review of Education, Pedagogy, and Cultural Studies*, *40*(5), 404–421.

(2018c). Political emotions in the classroom: How affective citizenship education illuminates the debate between agonists and deliberators. *Democracy & Education*, *26*(1), 1–5. Retrieved from https://democracyeducationjournal.org/home/vol26/iss1/6/.

(2018d). Affect, race, and white discomfort in schooling: Decolonial strategies for "pedagogies of discomfort." *Ethics and Education*, *13*(1), 86–104.

(2018e). Professional standards for teachers and school leaders: Interrogating the entanglement of affect and biopower in standardizing processes. *Journal of Professional Capital and Community*, *3*(3), 142–156.

(2018f). Affective citizenship and education in multicultural societies: Tensions, ambivalences and possibilities. In A. Peterson, G. Stahl & H. Soong (Eds.), *The Palgrave handbook of citizenship and education*. Cham, Switzerland: Palgrave Macmillan.

(2019). "Shame at being human" as a transformative political concept and praxis: Pedagogical possibilities. *Feminism & Psychology*, *29*(2), 303–321.

(2020a). Affect/emotion and securitising education: Re-orienting the methodological and theoretical framework for the study of securitisation in education. *British Journal of Educational Studies*, *68*(4) 487–506.

(2020b). Emotions, affects and trauma in classrooms: Moving beyond the representational genre. *Research in Education*, *106*(1), 59–76.

(2020c). The ethics and politics of traumatic shame: Pedagogical insights. In B. Dernikos, N. Lesko, S. D. McCall & A. Niccolini (Eds.), *Mapping the affective turn in education: Theory, research, pedagogy* (pp. 54–68). New York: Routledge.

Zembylas, M., & Keet, A. (2019). *Critical human rights education: Advancing social-justice-oriented educational praxes*. Dordrecht, The Netherlands: Springer.

Index

accountability, culture of, democratic education and, 6
Adorno, Theodor, 114
affective atmospheres
   challenging right-wing populism and, 135–138
   defined, 124–125
   in democratic education, 13, 129–135
   relevance of, 124–129
   staging of, in democratic education, 132–135
affective contagion, far-right rhetoric and, 113
affective counterpolitics
   in democratic education, 49–53
   pedagogical space for, 4–5
   risks of, 52–53
affective economies, 23
affective ideology
   far-right rhetoric and, 110–114
   political appeal and, 26–27
   of Trump pedagogy, 45–48
   Trump pedagogy and, 46–48
   Trump's politics of shame and, 24–28
affective-political contingency, anti-complicity pedagogy and, 205–206
affective style, Trump's establishment of, 42–43
affect theory
   agonistic pluralism and, 13
   citizenship and, 82–83
   complicity and, 192–194, 200–203
   dead bodies of children and, 186
   defined, 22
   evolution of, 124–129
   far-right rhetoric and, 109–110, 112–114
   fascism and, 71–73
   governmentality and, 61–63
   Laclau's discussion of populism and, 41
   microfascism and, 74–80
   as political and pedagogic practice, 22–24
   post-truth and, 54–61
   right-wing populism linked to, 2–7, 41–45
   sentimentality and, 182
   shame and, 10–11
   social, political and embodied aspects of, 7–10
   truthiness and, 56–61
   truth regimes and, 66
   white shame and, 19–22
affirmative critique
   critical theory's focus on, 95–97
   defined, 91–94
   development of, 11
   discourse on, 94–97
   pedagogical formulation of, 93–94, 103–107
   pedagogues for, 12–13
   philosophical discourse on, 92–93
   response-able pedagogy and, 103–105
   of right-wing populism, 51–52
   unmaking microfascist subjectivity with, 84–88
Afxentiou, A., 197–200
Against Purity: Living Ethically in Compromised Times (Shotwell), 212–213
agency, microfascism and, 80
agonism, far-right rhetoric and, 113–114
agonistic democratic education, 5–6
agonistic emotion, 13
   affects in pedagogy and, 118–122
   far-right rhetoric and, 109–110
agonistic pluralism
   collective identification and, 114–118
   democracy and, 116–117
Ahmed, S.
   affect theory and, 7–10, 23
   on angry populism, 42–43
   on atmospheres, 128, 130–132
   economies of shame and, 25–26
alternative belongings
   affective counterpolitics and, 52–53
   atmospheres and, 137–138
ambivalence of shame, 31–35
Amin, A., 137
Anderson, B.
   affective counterpolitics and, 49–53

Index

on angry populism, 42–43
on atmospheric walls, 124–129
complicity and, 200–203
Andreotti, V., 196
anger, right-wing populism and, 1–2
angry populism, mechanisms of, 42–43
anti-complicity pedagogy
   democratic education and, 15
   development of, 203–207
   emergence of, 192–194
anti-immigrant ideology
   dead bodies of migrants and, 184–187
   far-right rhetoric and, 110–114
anti-racism
   politics of shame and, 19–22
   redemption and, 28
   reparative pedagogy and, 32–33
   shame and, 30–31
   white guilt and, 162
apartheid
   complicity and, 192
   necropower and, 179–180
Appelbaum, B., 171–172, 192, 194–197, 206
Arendt, Hannah
   on collective guilt, 163–164
   on collective responsibility, 166–169
   critique of emotion by, 143–147
   on education, 14, 150–153
   pedagogy and influence of, 153–156
   on political consequences of compassion and pity, 147–150
   political philosophy of, 142–143
   on shared responsibility, 14–15, 169–170
Ashenden, S., 163, 165–166
atmospheres, philosophical concept of, 124–129
   staging in democratic education of, 132–135
atmospheric intervention, challenging right-wing populism and, 135–138
attunement, affective ideology and, 46–48
The Authoritarian Personality (Adorno), 114
authority, Arendt on role of, 151–152

backfire effect, post-truth pedagogy and, 67–69
Badiou, A., 92–93
Barad, K., 103–105
Barnwell, A., 95–97
Bar-On, T., 111
Beausoleil, E., 210–211
Beckermann, K., 92–93
belonging
   alternative belongings, 52–53
   citizenship education and, 82–83
   collective guilt and responsibility and, 168–169
Benin, D., 24–28

Berlant, L., 22–23, 50, 182–184, 189–190
Bernstein, B., 46
Bhanji, N., 180
Biesta, G., 174
Bille, M., 124–133, 138
biopolitics
   microfascism and, 79
   necropolitics and, 177
   sentimentality and, 182–184
biopower
   in educational institutions, 86–87
   microfascism and, 77–80
   necropolitics and, 178–181
   sentimentality and, 181–184
Bjerg, H., 62
Black Lives Matter, 15
blame, complicity and, 198–199
bodies
   affect-affected duality in, 78
   affect and role of, 8–10
   atmospheres and, 129–130
   complicity and, 200–203
   dead bodies in classrooms, ethical, political and pedagogical dilemmas and, 184–187
   health education and cult of, 80–82
   in necropolitics, 179–180
   sentimentality and, 182
Böhme, Gernot, 127
Boland, G., 101
Boler, M., 55
Bowell, T., 64
Braidotti, Rosi, 92–93
Brexit discourse, far-rhetoric concerning, 111n.8
British First movement, 111n.9
Brown, W., 129–130
Buser, M., 132–135
Butler, Judith
   analysis of critique by, 12–13, 92–94
   on Covid-19, 209–214
   on Foucault's critique theory, 100–103
Button, M., 29

Carniel, J., 186
Cartwright, L., 24–28
character education, risks of, 170–172
children
   Arendt education for, 14, 150–153
   dead bodies of, 184–187
   necropolitics and, 184
Christian theology, guilt in, 163–166
citizenship
   microfascism in education about, 82–83
   political emotion and education in, 156
Clark, J. N., 164–165
Clarke, M., 141

class politics
  atmospheres and, 131–132
  politics of shame and, 19–22
classroom atmosphere, democratic education and, 130–132
Clough, P., 7–10
Colbert, Stephen, 54–56
collective affect
  agonistic pluralism and, 114–118
  creation of, 64–65
collective guilt
  democratic education and, 14–15, 158–159
  shared responsibility and, 170–172
  understanding of, 163–166
collective identification
  Mouffe on passion and, 115–116
  promotion of, 117–118
collective responsibility, Arendt & Young on, 166–169
colonialism. *See* settler colonialism
common space, political emotion and, 155–156
community of responsibility, collective guilt and, 164–165
compassion, political consequences of, 147–150
complicity
  affect theory and, 192–194
  as embodied and affective practice, 200–203
  necropolitics and, 188
  non-representational theory and, 200–203
  as political concept and act, 197–200
  scholarship on, 192
Conovan, M., 151–152
context
  political emotion and, 154–155
  shared responsibility and, 172
countering violent extremism (CVE) pedagogy, 111–112
counterpolitical response and resource, Trump politics and, 49–50
Covid-19 pandemic, democratic education and impact of, 209–214
The Crisis in Education (Arendt), 150–153
critical theory
  affect and, 7–10
  anti-complicity pedagogy and, 203–207
  counterpolitical response and resource and, 49–50
  critique and, 99–100
  dead bodies of children and, 186
  Latour's discussion of, 94–97
  pedagogies of shame and, 33–34
  post-critical pedagogy and, 103–105
  post-truth and, 55
  shared responsibility and, 173

critical thinking pedagogy, post-truth politics and, 64
"Critique, Dissent, Disciplinary" (Butler), 92–93, 101
critique theory
  Butler's analysis of Foucault's work on, 100–103
  Foucault on, 12–13, 92–94, 97–100
  Latour's discussion of, 91–92
  negative and affirmative critique, 94–97
  philosophical discourse on, 92–93
  virtue and, 100–103
cruel optimism, right-wing populism and, 50
culpability, degrees of
  anti-complicity pedagogy and, 192–194
  complicity and, 198–199
  guilt pedagogy and, 170–172
Cummings, A., 133
current affirmative turn, 95–97
Cvetkovich, A., 7–10, 23–24

Davies, L., 111–112, 120–121
Davis, E., 55
death
  dead bodies in classrooms, dilemma of, 184–187
  democratic education and, 15
  necropower and, 179–180
  pedagogic practice and visibility of, 187–191
decolonial pedagogy, shared responsibility and, 173
defensive response, to guilt, 160–163
Degerman, D., 142–147, 149
Deleuze, Gilles
  on affect and biopower, 77–80
  on body and affect, 201
  on desire and fascism, 74–76, 80–82
  on limits of moral terminology, 116–117
  on microfascism, 12, 71–77
  on micropolitics, 49
  on resistance to microfascism, 86
democracy
  agonistic pluralism and, 116–117
  Arendt on emotions and, 148–149
  atmospheres and values of, 130–132
  Mouffe's theory on, 114–115
  populism and future of, 1–7
  reparative pedagogy and, 32–33
democratic education
  affective atmospheres and, 13, 129–132
  affective counterpolitics pedagogy in, 49–53
  agonistic emotion and, 120–121
  anti-complicity pedagogy and, 15
  Arendt on, 150–156
  biopower and affect in, 80

collective guilt and, 14–15
complicity pedagogy and, 196–197
death and, 15
guilt in, 158–160
microfascism and, 73
political emotions and, 14
politicization of, 52–53
as response to Trump pedagogy, 48
rise of right-wing populism and, 2–7, 11, 124–126
risks of, 52–53
spatialities of, 125
staging of atmospheres in, 132–135
Trump Pedagogy and, 37–38
denial
complicity pedagogy and, 194–197
as response to guilt, 160–163
desire
educators' microfascism and, 85–86
microfascism and, 74–76
desubjectivation, response-able pedagogy and, 106–107
Dewey, John, 210–211
DiAngelo, R., 24
Dickinson, G., 24
disenfranchisement, shame and, 30
disobedience, critique as, 102
distancing strategies, complicity pedagogy and, 196–197

economies of shame, 25–26
educational interventions, in far-right rhetoric, 112–114
educational theory, agonistic pluralism and, 114–115
education and educational institutions
Arendt on, 142–143, 150–153
atmospheres in, 130
far-right rhetoric and, 110–114
microfascism in, 76–77, 80–84
post-truth and, 11–12
post-truth politics in, 63–66
rise of populism and, 2–7
unmaking of microfascist subjectivities in, 84–88
Eichmann, trial of, Arendt on, 142–143
Eichmann in Jerusalem (Arendt), 145–147, 168–169
elites
populist classification of, 39
resentment of, 42–43
Elliot, T. S., 213–214
emotion. *See also* political emotions
affective atmospheres and, 125
affect theory and, 124–129

agonistic emotion, 13, 118–122
Arendt's critique of, 143–147
citizenship education and, 82–83
politics and, 58–59
post-truth and, 54–58
right-wing populism and, 1–2
sentimentality and, 182–184
social, political, and embodied aspects of, 7–10
empathy
banality of, 184–185
pedagogies of shame and, 33–34
promotion of, 65–66
reciprocities in, 34
empathy wall, Hochschild's concept of, 59–61
engineered atmospheres, in democratic education, 132–135
enlarged thought, Arendt's concept of, 153–156
ethical practice
complicity denial and, 196
critique as, 100–103
dead bodies in classrooms, dilemma of, 184–187
ethical responsibility, 159
ethno-nationalism, far-right rhetoric and, 110–114
European populism, attributes of, 39–40
Evans, B., 73–77, 83–85
everyday life, microfascism in, 76–77
existence, aesthetics of, 100–103
Exploring Complicity: Concept, Case, and Critique (Afxentiou), 197–200
extremism
CVE and PVE pedagogy, 111–112
moralization about, 116–117, 120–121
pedagogical and political intervention in, 13, 109–110
youth identification with, 115–116

far right movements, global emergence of, 109–110
far right rhetoric
affective dimension of, 110–114
ideologies of, 109–110
fascism
Adorno on acceptability of, 114
citizenship fascism, 82–83
current rise of, 1
definition and analysis of, 71–73
Deleuze & Guattari on, 71–73
micropolitics of, 73–77
fear, right-wing populism and, 1–2
feminist theory, post-truth and, 55
fetishistic commodities, bodies as, necropolitics and, 180
Finn, M., 131

Fitzpatrick, K., 80–82
Fortier, A.-M., 82–83
forward-looking model, collective responsibility, 166–169
Foucault, Michel
  on biopolitics, 79
  on biopower, 78–79, 178–181
  Butler's analysis of, 100–103
  on critique, 12–13, 92–94, 97–100
  on emotion, 57–58
  on fascism, 71–73
  on truth, 66
Frankfurt School, 99–100
  critical theory and, 95
Freeden, M., 38–41
freedom, critique and, 98
Freire, Paolo, 211–212
French Revolution, Arendt on, 147–150
functionality, affective ideology and, 46–48

Gebhardt, M., 22–23
gender
  atmospheres and, 131–132
  sentimentality and, 183–184
*Giddens, 116
Gilbert, C., 56
"Giving and Account of Oneself" (Butler), 101–102
globalization, rise of populism and, 1–2
Goodin, R., 192, 212
good in the present, response-able pedagogy and, 105–106
governing-through-affect, citizenship education and, 82–83
governmentality
  critique and, 99
  post-truth politics and, 61–63
Gray, B. J., 28–32
Gregg, M., 136
Guattari, Felix, 12
  on affect and biopower, 77–80
  on desire and fascism, 74–76, 80–82
  on microfascism, 73–77
  on micropolitics, 49
  on resistance to microfascism, 86
Guenther, L., 24–28, 31–32
guilt
  collective responsibility and, 166–169
  in democratic education, 158–160
  pedagogical tensions and risk in education about, 160–163
  shared responsibility and, 169–173
  student responses to, 160–163

Hage, G., 31–32
Hållander, 186
Hartman, S. V., 182–184
Harwood, V., 106–107
health education, microfascism and, 80–82
Hegelian thought, critique theory and, 95
Heins, V., 147–148
Hitler Youth, indoctrination and, 150–153
Hochschild, empathy wall concept of, 59–61
Hochschild, A.
  economies of shame and, 25–26
  response-able pedagogy and work of, 105–106
Hodgson, N., 94, 103–104, 106
Holland, E., 74–76
homophobia, populism and, 39–40
hope
  complicity pedagogy and, 195–196
  in democratic education, 52–53
  Trump pedagogy and, 45–48
hopeful criticism, affective counterpolitics pedagogy, 49–53
humanities, affirmative critique in, 95–97

identity
  affect and, 62–63
  collective identification and, 115–116
  shame and, 25
  shared responsibility and, 170
ignorance explanation, post-truth pedagogy and, 67–69
immigration
  dead bodies of migrants, ethical-political dilemma of, 184–187
  sentimentality in pedagogy about, 176–187
individual shame, limits of, 29
indoctrination
  Arendt on education as, 152–153
  Arendt on emotions and, 144–145
  democratic education and risk of, 142
intensity of affectivity, self-management and, 62–63
interculturalism
  rise of populism and, 2–7
  rise of right-wing populism and, 124–126
interest, shame and, 19–22, 25
intimacy
  necrointimacies and, 180
  sentimentality and racialization of, 182–184

Jaspers, Karl, 163–164
judgment
  critique and, 101
  political emotion and, 154
juridico-discursive thought, critique and, 97–100
justice, complicity with injustice and, 198–199

Kant, Immanuel, 154
Kinnval, C., 44
Klein, Melanie, 158, 161–162
Kølvraa, C., 109–110, 112–114
Krasmann, S., 66
Kurdi, Alan, 184–187

Lacan, Jacques, 115–116
Laclau, E., 40–41
Latour, Bruno, 91–97
Lebron, C. J., 210–211
Lemke, T., 97–100
Lepora, C., 192, 212
Levinas, Emmanuel, 158–159, 161–162
liberal democracy
  post-truth and, 59–61
  rise of populism as threat to, 2–7, 124–126
liberal guilt, risks of, 161
Locke, J., 24–29
logic of difference, populism and, 40–41
logic of equivalence, populism and, 40–41
Lorimer, H., 200–203
Lowe, L., 180
Lupton, D., 80–82
lynchings, necropolitics of, 180

Maddison, S., 163–166
Mårdh, A., 41, 48, 138
Marotta, S., 133
Martin, J. L., 125
Massumi, B., 44–45, 49, 77–80
*Maudlin, 195–196
Mbembe, Achille, 177–181
McCarty, T. W., 198–199, 203–207
media literacy, post-truth politics and, 63–64
Mejia, R., 92–93
Michels, C., 137
microfascism
  affect and, 12
  biopower and affect in, 77–80
  citizenship education and, 82–83
  definition of, 71–73
  health education practices and, 80–82
  reparative pedagogy and, 87–88
  unmaking subjectivities in, educational pedagogy for, 84–88
micropolitics
  affective counterpolitics pedagogy and, 49–53
  citizenship education and, 82–83
  far-right rhetoric and, 113–114
  of fascism, 73–77
Mihai, M., 118, 121–122, 197–198
Milazzo, M., 28
Miller-Idriss, C., 111–112
modernity, biopolitics and, 182–184

Mohammed, S., 86
monopolistic representation of people, populist claim to ownership of, 39
morality
  death images and, 189
  far right ideologies in frame of, 121–122
  guilt and, 161–162
  limits of, 116–117
  pedagogic practice and, 212
  populists' claim to ownership of, 39
  shared responsibility and, 169–173
  suffering and compassion and, 149–150
moral responsibility, complicity and, 194–197
moral spectatorship, death images and, 189
Morrow, A., 8–10
Mouffe, Chantal, 5–6, 114–118
  on agonistic pluralism, 13
Mühlhoff, R., 41–42
Mulcahy, D., 24
multiculturalism
  far-right rhetoric as response to, 111
  rise of populism and, 2–7, 124–126

narcissism, shame and, 30
Nathanson, D., 25
national identification, collective guilt and, 164–165
nationalist politics
  far-right rhetoric and, 110–114
  fascism and, 71–73
National Socialism (Nazism)
  Arendt on, 142–143
  citizenship education under, 82–83
  collective guilt and, 163–168
  'ideal' body stereotypes of, 81–82
nativism
  origins of danger and, 44–45
  populism and, 39–40
necrointimacies, Mbembe's concept of, 180
necropolitics
  biopower and, 178–181
  bodies in, 179–180
  complicity in, 188
  defined, 176
  populism and, 15
  queer theory and, 180–181
"Necropolitics" (Mbembe), 178–181
necropower
  Mbembe's discussion of, 179–180
  visibility of, 187–191
negative critique
  discourse on, 94–97
  philosophical discourse on, 92–93
  of right-wing populism, limits of, 51–52

negative emotions, right-wing populism and, 44–45
Nelson, D., 145
neoliberalism
  health education and, 80–82
  rise of populism and, 1–2
new prudentialism, health education and, 80–82
Nicolazzo, Z., 64–65
non-representational theory (NRT), complicity and, 200–203
nostalgia, Trump pedagogy and, 45–48
Nussbaum, Martha, 120, 149

oppression
  historicization of, 32–33
  legitimization of, 45–48
origins of danger, nativist ideology and, 44–45
Osuri, G., 188
Ott, B., 24

Palestinian occupation, necropower and, 179–180
Papailias, P., 188, 190–191
parrhesia, Foucault's concept of, 100n.5
passions
  Mouffe's critique of rationalist politics and, 115–116
  taming of, 117–118
pedagogic practice
  affective counterpolitics pedagogy, 49–53
  affect theory and, 22–24
  affirmative critique and, 103–107
  agonistic emotion and, 118–122
  anti-complicity pedagogy, 192–194, 203–207
  complicity issues and, 194–197
  counter-extremist pedagogy, 111–112
  dead bodies in classrooms, dilemma of, 184–187
  empathy and solidarity development and, 65–66
  Freire's discussion of, 211–212
  guilt phenomenon as risk in, 160–163
  limits of shame and shaming in, 28–31
  necropower visibility and, 187–191
  political emotion and, 153–156
  post-truth and, 55–56
  sentimentality in, 176–187
  shared responsibility, 169–173
  staging of atmosphere and, 132–135
  strategic restructuring of, 31–35
  unmaking microfascist subjectivity with, 84–88
pedagogies of shame, invocation of, 33–34
Pelinka, A., 42–43

people, populists as exclusive representatives of, 39
performativity of affect, 61–63
  critique and, 101
Peters, C. H., 44, 46–48
Peters, M., 103–104
Petrie, M., 4, 48
Philippopoulos-Mihalopoulos, A., 132–135
Pilkington, H., 111–112
pity
  political consequences of, 147–150
  visibility of necropower and, 187–191
police violence, democratic education and impact of, 209–214
political emotions. *See also* emotion
  agonistic pluralism and, 118–122
  classroom nurturing of, 141–143
  cognitivist framework for, 120
  consequences of compassion and pity and, 147–150
  dead bodies in classrooms, dilemma of, 184–187
  definition of, 141–142
  pedagogy and, 153–156
Political Emotions (Nussbaum), 120
politics
  affective atmospheres and, 136
  affect theory and, 8–10, 22–24, 113
  Arendt on emotion and, 143–147
  complicity as act and concept of, 197–200
  democratic education and, 14
  limits of shame and shaming in, 28–31
  post-truth and, 58–59
  sentimental structures of, 182
  shame as, 25–26
  shared responsibility and, 169–173
politics of shame
  Trump's affective rhetoric and, 24–28
  Trump's impact on, 19–22
populism
  core attributes of, 38–41
  current scholarship on rise of, 1–7
  in democratic education, 48
  Laclau's theory of, 40–41
post-critical philosophy, 94
  pedagogy and, 103–105
post-truth politics
  affective grounding of, 56–61
  affirmative critique of, 93–94, 103–107
  context for, 69
  critique theory and, 102–103
  definitions of, 54–56
  in educational settings, 63–66
  Foucault on critique and, 100
  governmentality and affect in, 61–63

Index

material-affective infrastructure of, 61–63
populism and, 11–12
risks in pedagogy for, 67–69
Trump's claims as, 57
power
affectiveness of, 44–45
complicity invisibility and, 199–200
far-right rhetoric and, 113
microfascism, affect and biopower and, 77–80
right-wing populism and resonance of, 44
power-affect, defined, 8–10
prescriptive aspects of shame, 28
preventing violent extremism (PVE) pedagogy, 111–112
Prevent strategy (UK), 112n.10
Probyn, E., 25–26, 28
progressive politics, shame in, 26–27
propaganda, affective atmosphere and risk of, 134–135
Protevi, J., 44, 46–48
provocative politics, far-right rhetoric and, 111
psychology, affective ideology and, 46–48
Puar, J., 180–181
public feelings, affect theory and, 23–24
public intimacy, death images and, 189–190
public performances, Trump's mobilization of support through, 42–43

queer necropolitics, 180–181
The Question of the German Quilt (Jaspers), 163–164

racial capitalism
necropolitics and, 180
Trump's politics and, 29
white shame and, 21
racialized assemblages theory, 180–181
racism
affect theory and, 23–24
Arendt on segregation and, 150–153
atmospheres and, 131–132
complicity and, 192
degrees culpability and, 171–172
historicization of, 32–33
intimacy and, 182–184
necropolitics and, 180
populism and, 39–40
post-truth as symptom of, 63–64
sentimentality and, 182–184
Trump pedagogy and, 45–48
white shame and, 19–22
rage, shame and, 26–27
Rassmussen, M. L., 106–107
rationalist politics, Mouffe on passions and, 115–116

reason, Arendt on emotion and, 145–147
Rebughini, P., 51–52, 95–97
redemption
in anti-racist theory, 28
Trump pedagogy and, 45–48
Reflections on Little Rock (Arendt), 150–153
Reich, Wilhelm, 74–76
Reid, J., 73–77, 83–85
relational aspects of affect, 61–63
relief and redemption, right-wing populism as relief from, 44
reparative pedagogy
microfascism and, 87–88
white shame and, 32–33
resentment *(ressentiment)*, right wing populism and, 41–45
residual tendency, Trump pedagogy and, 45–48
resistance, to complicity, 200
response-able pedagogy, 103–105
responsibility
Arendt on role of, 151–152
collective guilt and, 165–166
Retzinger, S. M., 26–27
Reynolds, P., 198–199
right-wing populism
affective atmospheres as challenge to, 135–138
affect theory and, 1–7, 41–45
affirmative critique of, 51–52
alternative belongings as counterpolitics to, 52–53
cruel optimism and, 50
current rise of, 1
global emergence of, 109–110
post-truth as catalyst for, 54–56
Roman law, guilt in, 163–166
Ruitenberg, C. W., 118–122, 141–142
Runciman, David, 1
Rydgren, J., 110–114

Salmela, M., 1–2, 41–42
Samayoa, A. C., 64–65
Sanders, M., 198–199
Sandy, N. G., 150–153
Schaap, A., 163–164
Schaefer, D., 26–28
Scheff, T. J., 26–27
Schlink, B., 164–165
Schuller, K., 181–184
Schutz, A., 150–153
Scott, D., 205
Sedgwick-Kosofsky, E., 24–28, 32–33
Seigworth, G., 136
self-management, affect and, 62–63
self-transformation, critique as, 102
sensationalism, pedagogy of, 45–48

sentimentality
  Arendt on dangers of, 155
  biopower and, 181–184
  cultural practices of, 182
  defined, 177
  pedagogical practice and, 176–187
  populism and, 15
  reclamation of, 187–191
settler colonialism
  complicity and, 192
  historicization of, 32–33
  land dispossession and, 21
  necropower and, 179–180
  shared responsibility pedagogy and, 173
sexism
  atmospheres and, 131–132
  post-truth as symptom of, 63–64
  Trump pedagogy and, 45–48
shame and shaming
  affect and, 10–11
  ambivalence of, 31–35
  defined, 24–28
  pedagogies of shame, 33–34
  political and pedagogical limits of, 28–31
  political aspects of, 25–26
  resentment *(ressentiment)* and, 41–42
  Trump's weaponization of, 19–22
  unlearning affects of, 34–35
shame-anger loops, as political strategy, 26–27
shamelessness, Trump's use of, 19–22
shared responsibility
  collective guilt and, 158–159
  degrees of culpability and, 171–172
  pedagogy of, 14–15, 169–173
Shotwell, Alexis, 212–213
Simonsen, K., 124–133, 138
slavery, necropower and, 179–180
Social Connection Model of Responsibility, complicity and, 194–197
social control, affective relations and, 46
social identities, right-wing populism distancing from, 41–42
social justice
  anti-complicity pedagogy and, 192–194
  complicity and, 202–203
  critical engagement with, 30
social media
  counterpolitical response and resource and, 49–50
  post-truth and, 54–56
  Trump's mobilization of support through, 42–43
social sciences
  affirmative critique in, 95–97

collective guilt in, 163
complicity scholarship and, 192
social-transformative practices, post-truth pedagogy and, 69
sociopolitical affect
  complicity and, 198–199
  emotions and, 149
  migrant crisis and, 176–187
  post-truth and, 59–61
  shame and, 31–35
sociopolitical context, affect and, 8–10
solidarity
  collective affect and, 64–65
  promotion of, 65–66
Spinoza, affect theory and, 117–118
Staunæs, D.
  on affect and self-management, 62–63
  on affirmative critique, 51–52, 96–97
Stephens, Closs, 131
Steyaert, C., 137
Stoler, A., 184
Straker, G., 33–34
Strangers in Their Own Land (Hoschild), 42–43, 59–61
strategic criticism and critical praxis, anti-complicity pedagogy and, 205
strategic empathy, backfire effect and, 67–69
Strick, S., 181, 183–184
structural racism, minimization of, 19–22
subjectivity
  affect and, 62–63
  Butler on critique and, 101
  complicity and, 198–199
  microfascism and, 73
  unmaking of, in microfascism, 84–88
suffering
  Arendt on emotions of, 145–147
  guilt in education on, 158–160
  necropower and, 179–180
  pedagogy on, 170–172
Sullivan, C., 92–93
Sullivan, S., 30
sympathy fatigue, post-truth pedagogy and, 67–69

Tarnopolsky, C., 28
Tea Party movement, 42–43
  post-truth and, 59–61, 105–106
technologies of death, necropower and, 179–180
Tesich, Steve, 54n.4
third way politics, 116
A Thousand Plateaus (Deleuze & Guattari), 12, 71–73, 77–80
Thrift, N., 64–65, 137, 200–203
Tinning, R., 80–82

Todd, S., 158–163, 170–172
Tomkins, Silvan, 24–28
Tooze, A., 213–214
totalitarianism, Arendt on emotion and, 144–145
transpersonal affect, 61–63
Trump, Donald
  affective rhetoric of, 24, 35–36
  politics of shame and rise of, 19–22
  post-truth in claims by, 57
  racist rhetoric of, 10–11
Trump Pedagogy, 11
  affective ideology of, 45–48
  affect theory and, 37–38
  affirmative critique of, 51–52
  cruel optimism in, 50
  democratic education as response to, 48
  micropolitics and, 49–50
truthiness, affective grounding of, 56–61
truth-telling practices
  context and, 69
  pedagogical promotion of, 66
  post-truth in relation to, 57–58
Tryggvason, A., 41, 48, 119, 138
Twitter, affect analysis of Trump's responses on, 24

unwieldy knowledge, response-able pedagogy and, 106
'Us-the-Good-People vs. Them-the-Evil' people division, Trump pedagogy and, 45–48

virtue, critique and, 100–103
Vlieghe, J., 94, 101–104, 106
Vogelmann, F., 106–107
von Scheve, C., 1–2, 41–42

Wächter, C., 192
Wahl-Jorgensen, K., 42–43
Washington Post, Fact Checker website of, 57
Watkins, Megan, 24

Weheliye, A., 180–181
welfare chauvinism, populism and, 39–40
Wetherell, M., 136
"What is Critique?" (Foucault), 92–93
"What is Critique? An Essay on Foucault's Virtue" (Butler), 92–93, 100–103
white complicity, denial of, 194–197
white fragility, 24
white guilt
  anti-racist education and, 162
  shared responsibility and, 170
white multiculturalism, shame and, 31–32
whiteness, critical engagement with, 30
white privilege
  critical engagement with, 30
  shame and, 31–35
white shame, 19–22
  Trump's politics and, 29
white supremacy
  affective ideology and, 46–48
  critical engagement with, 30
  historicization of, 32–33
  shame and, 19–22
  Trump's politics and, 29
Whitt, M., 196–197
working-class and poor whites
  pedagogies of shame about, 33–34
  politics of shame and, 19–22
  post-truth and, 59–61
  shame felt by, 31–35
  Trump's influence on, 27–28
wrongdoing, complicity and, 192

xenophobia
  populism and, 39–40
  post-truth as symptom of, 63–64

Young, Iris Marion, 166–169, 194–197
  on shared responsibility, 14–15, 169–170

Zamojski, P., 94, 103–104, 106

CPSIA information can be obtained
at www.ICGtesting.com
Printed in the USA
LVHW080920030821
694401LV00004B/293